# The Politics of Voice in Education

**Pedagogies: Deleuze and Education Research**
Series Editors: Elizabeth de Freitas, Sam Sellar and Greg Thompson

This series takes up Deleuze's project of putting philosophy to work in practical fields by applying his concepts in education research. Books in the series will develop, adapt and apply Deleuzian concepts to a range of contemporary educational issues. The series responds to a widespread interest across education research for Deleuze's work and addresses the need for new innovative interventions as the field takes up new technics, including the proliferation of 'datafication', global reform movements, new modes of corporate and managerial governance, pharmaceutical and neurological interventions and machine learning software.

**Editorial Advisory Board**
Ian Buchanan, Claire Colebrook, Anna Hickey-Moody, Hillevi Lenz-Taguchi, Andrew Murphie, Inna Semetsky, Bettie St. Pierre, Nathan Widder

Books available
Eve Mayes, *The Politics of Voice in Education: Reforming Schools after Deleuze and Guattari*

# THE POLITICS OF VOICE IN EDUCATION

Reforming Schools after
Deleuze and Guattari

*Eve Mayes*

EDINBURGH
University Press

Edinburgh University Press is one of the leading university presses in the UK. We publish academic books and journals in our selected subject areas across the humanities and social sciences, combining cutting-edge scholarship with high editorial and production values to produce academic works of lasting importance. For more information visit our website: edinburghuniversitypress.com

© Eve Mayes, 2023, 2024

Grateful acknowledgement is made to the sources listed in the List of Illustrations for permission to reproduce material previously published elsewhere. Every effort has been made to trace the copyright holders, but if any have been inadvertently overlooked, the publisher will be pleased to make the necessary arrangements at the first opportunity.

Edinburgh University Press Ltd
13 Infirmary Street
Edinburgh EH1 1LT

First published in hardback by Edinburgh University Press 2023

Typeset in 11/13 Sabon LT Pro
by Cheshire Typesetting Ltd, Cuddington, Cheshire

A CIP record for this book is available from the British Library

ISBN 978 1 4744 5120 8 (hardback)
ISBN 978 1 4744 5121 5 (paperback)
ISBN 978 1 4744 5122 2 (webready PDF)
ISBN 978 1 4744 5123 9 (epub)

The right of Eve Mayes to be identified as the author of this work has been asserted in accordance with the Copyright, Designs and Patents Act 1988, and the Copyright and Related Rights Regulations 2003 (SI No. 2498).

This work was supported by Deakin University's Alfred Deakin Postdoctoral Research Fellowship (2020–2021) and the Australian Research Council (Discovery Early Career Research Award, grant number: DE220100103, 2022–2025).

*For the Steering Committee and Yolanda*

# Contents

| | |
|---|---|
| List of Figures | viii |
| Breathing, Speaking, Writing Voices | 1 |
| 1 Troubling Student Voice in School Reform | 8 |
| 2 Mis/using Voices and Theories in Research with Children and Young People | 46 |
| 3 Ordering Voices and Bodies in the History of Schooling | 71 |
| 4 Representing Difference in School Governance | 97 |
| 5 Understanding the Atmos-fear of the Dialogical Encounter | 120 |
| 6 Evaluating the Perplexing Outcomes of School Reform | 148 |
| 7 Conspiring with the Trees | 174 |
| Bibliography | 204 |
| Index | 245 |

# List of Figures

1.1 A real estate agent sign standing on the border of a primary school: 'Junior Council of the Year'. Photo credit: Rachel Finneran.   24
2.1 A screenshot from a video of a puppet scenario, created by a group of students. Four puppets (sheep, chicken, boy and marionette) are positioned around a table, starting a lesson.   47
2.2 A marionette mis/used in student research focus groups. My hand is in the marionette's glove, above the marionette's head. The marionette sits, head angled downward.   60
3.1 A Year 8 student-marionette rises to their feet to ask a question.   71
3.2 A teacher-puppet negates the student-marionette's question.   71
3.3 A Year 11 student-marionette sits and asks a question.   83
3.4 A teacher-puppet answers the student-marionette's question.   83
4.1 A school council meeting arrangement in stickers.   110
5.1 The teacher-puppet is starting a lesson.   127
5.2 The chicken-puppet says 'bok'.   127
5.3 The chicken-puppet collapses forward on the table, beak down.   127
5.4 The puppets move closer together to talk.   128
5.5 The chicken-puppet taps their beady eyes on the table twice.   128
6.1 A RESP token.   150
6.2 A photograph of part of the 'Hiromi Hotel: Moon Jellies' exhibition, commissioned by Hazelhurst Regional Gallery and Arts Centre. The exhibition was a performance installation involving local community participation, including students from this school,

## List of Figures

    brought together by artist Hiromi Tango. Photo credit:
    Greg Piper.   164
- 7.1 A young person holds a cardboard sign: 'I SPEAK FOR THE TREES (They say DO BETTER SCOMO)', 21 May 2020, Sydney School Strike 4 Climate rally. Creative Commons 2.0 by School Strike 4 Climate. Original image cropped.   182
- 7.2 A young person holds a cardboard sign: 'I speak for the trees because they can't (they don't have any tongues)', 21 May 2020, Sydney School Strike 4 Climate rally. Creative Commons 2.0 by School Strike 4 Climate. Original image cropped.   186
- 7.3 A young person holds a cardboard sign: 'I Speak FOR The Trees And The Trees Say FUCK YOU!!!)", 21 May 2020, Sydney School Strike 4 Climate rally. Creative Commons 2.0 by School Strike 4 Climate. Original image cropped.   196

# Breathing, Speaking, Writing Voices

I start in the middle of a recurring dream. There is a viscous substance stuck on my tongue and the roof of my mouth. Perhaps it is the soft mixture of stone, sand and water that hardens into concrete. Perhaps it is the sticky contents of two chewed packets of chewing gum. I am trying to grasp and grab and pull the viscous substance out. Sometimes, it is unmoveable. Other times, it loosens and surges and doesn't stop – like some endless handkerchief pulled from a magician's coat sleeve. When this happens, it feels like my intestines are evacuating through my open mouth.

To speak – to 'give voice' – involves muscles and guts of the speaker: air flowing through larynx, vocal cords shaping and tensing, vibration, cartilage, stomach muscles, tongue, lips. Voices are physical and material, issuing from bodies and felt by bodies. Lines of breath rendered resonant by the vibrations of vocal cords become speech in material and social configurations. To speak implies (though not always) a listener – a living, breathing interlocutor – whose facial expressions, raised eyebrow, encouraging nod, whisper, laugh, groan can spur the speaker on or somehow move the speaker to close their mouth. Voices respond and intermingle with their sonic and social environments: pitch levels of speakers may align when the speakers are in agreement, or escalate in volume in situations of conflict, or mimic the contours of other voices when power relations are asymmetrical. Sometimes, in the moment of speech, something else surges forth, breaking the boundaries of bodies and skin and guts: a blush springs to the surface, tears spill out, rage burns up, laughter escapes. The spoken voice is also inextricably bound up with silence – not the opposite of speech but entangled with it. The physicality of a voice can alter the material environment – the force of a cry can enliven an object to vibrate, or combine with other proximate frequencies to compose a soundscape.

The term 'voice' is also used for the written, authorial voice – the *I* that writes what they have thought-felt and are thinking-feeling. Crafting an authorial voice is fraught, particularly when the authorial *I* is preoccupied with the problem of how to think-feel-relate-act with the voices-bodies of (human and more-than-human) others that are inextricable from themselves. An authorial voice is meant to have authority and to inscribe itself with textual tactics, and to decide how to carve out lines demarcating their voice from the voices of others. The authorial voice is privileged in position; the *I* is hewn in a different temporality to the physical, spoken voice who spoke to them in an interview or focus group. The spoken voice is 'dangerous because it is immediate and cannot be taken back,' but in writing, the author can 'censure and delete our blunders, our self-sufficiencies (or our insufficiencies), our errors, our complacencies, sometimes even our breakdowns' (Barthes 1974: 4). The authorial voice can strategically quote from some great white man like Roland Barthes to grant themselves some authority – and to be sardonic, since Barthes also declared the author to be dead (1977/1984).

Maybe you are rolling your eyes at this authorial excess; I am imagining that you are. Because I am more and more wary of such types of writing, and wary of writing it. Having trouble speaking and breathing is not a joke. Racialised respiratory violences teach us that – Dylan Voller shackled to a restraining chair by his wrists, ankles and head and in a spit-hood at Don Dale Detention Centre; George Floyd with Derek Chauvin's knee on his neck, gasping, 'I can't breathe'. Protesters accosted with chemical weapons in the form of tear gas or pepper spray demonstrate that – whether at Black Lives Matter protests in the USA, pro-democracy demonstrations in Hong Kong, or protecting water at Standing Rock. Countless people without access to ventilators at the height of the COVID-19 pandemic compel attention to breath. As I explore in Chapter 7, these are times where different con-spiracies (Choy 2016, 2020, 2021) are needed – not the life-denying conspiracies of those who would gather together to affirm their 'rights' as 'sovereign citizens'. Such conspiracy theories-actions exemplify what this book argues against – the atomised human subject who 'has a voice' and affirms their right to not be concerned with others.

I write from the lands and waters now known as Australia, where the legal fiction of *terra nullius* – empty land – continues to be, as Wakka Wakka Gooreng Gooreng woman and educator[1] Jay Phillips (2021) writes, 'an invisible, but powerful regulator of contemporary thought' (9). *Terra nullius* exemplifies the White[2] settler colonial gaze of deficit – not able to see (or wilfully not seeing) how multiple sovereign nations care for Country – encompassing land, water, sentient and non-sentient beings (Bawaka Country et al. 2020: 2) – and instead seeing Country as ready for the possessing (Moreton-Robinson 2015). In Australia, this settler colonial founding habit of thought and action has also come to shape settler colonial institutions – including schooling – which frequently fail to apprehend and affirm the strength and wisdom of Indigenous ways of knowing, being, relating and acting. As a teacher and teacher educator, I have noticed the habits (which have threaded through my thinking too) of interpreting what students (across multiple identity markers and positionings) say and do through pre-established grids of intelligibility, according to what they *lack*, and have wondered how to collectively interrupt these processes and affirm multiplicity, strength and capacity (Tuck 2009). I acknowledge the traditional custodians of the lands on which I have taught, researched, written and lived while the work contributing to this book was undertaken, and pay respect to the Elders past and present, and emerging leaders on these lands: the Gadigal and Darug peoples, the Dabee peoples, the Wadawurrung, Bunurong Boon Wurrung and Wurundjeri Woi Wurrung peoples.

This book took a very long time to write, and I am grateful to those who patiently breathed with me in the process. I am thankful for the opportunities to work with various school communities in New South Wales and Victoria as a teacher and a researcher, and for opportunities to work with the VicSRC, a non-governmental organisation (NGO) representing school-aged students in Victoria. In particular, I acknowledge the school where I taught from 2007 and where my doctoral research was undertaken. I thank the senior leadership of this school for trusting me, and for their support, care and responsiveness. I thank the teachers, staff and students at this school for their willingness to explore with me the contradictory conditions of contemporary schooling and the relationalities that are still possible. I thank the students from this school for what they shared, and what they did not share because it was too important.

The cover image for this book, as well as Figure 6.2, are photographs of parts of a performance installation brought together by artist Hiromi Tango at Hazelhurst Art Gallery in 2013. Students from the school where my doctoral research was undertaken were part of the creation of this performance installation, alongside multiple other community groups, through a project organised by the art teacher in the school's support unit for students with a diagnosis of autism.

This art project involved the literal enfolding of fabric, threads, balls, hoops and strips of paper in processes modelled by Hiromi Tango in the video *Art Magic with Hiromi Tango* (Hazelhurst Regional Gallery and Arts Centre 2013a); works of art created in class were later combined and conjoined with work created by other students, teachers and community members in this performance installation. During this art project, in class time, students took photographs using the iPad application Photo Booth (with students selecting their own filters and selecting what they wanted to photograph). In my engagements with students, teachers and the works of art during this art project I was fascinated by the project's literal blurring of pedagogical boundaries (as students and teachers worked alongside each other), subject disciplinary boundaries (as the project spilled across the timetable into other designated subject times and spaces), and boundaries between speech, writing and art creation. The photographs of these objects worked upon me, iridescent with their own intensities, seeming to gesture towards something that I was attempting to think, feel and write. I acknowledge and thank these students, their art teacher and support educators for their work, and Hiromi Tango and Greg Piper for permission to use photographs from the exhibition in this book.

I am deeply grateful for the research mentorship of Deb Hayes, Susan Groundwater-Smith, Wayne Sawyer, Marie Brennan, Lew Zipin and Julian Sefton-Green. I am thankful to forerunners, leaders and colleagues in the field of student voice whose pedagogical kindness I experienced from my earlier years of creative experimentation with student voice and critical pedagogies – in particular, to Susan Groundwater-Smith, Michael Fielding, Alison Cook-Sather, Dana Mitra, Sara Bragg, Barbara Comber, Roger Holdsworth, Emily Nelson, Jennifer Charteris and Roseanna Bourke; it is my hope that this book thickens your rich work. EJ Renold, Deborah Youdell and Anna Hickey-Moody were generous examiners of the doctoral thesis which some of the chapters of this book extend upon. Thank you to Eileen Honan for sharing her PowerPoint from the 2013 Australian Association for Research in Education conference symposium 'A Key to All Mythologies: Deleuze and Education' which she chaired, with Ian Buchanan and P. Taylor Webb as featured speakers (Australian Association for Research in Education 2014). I acknowledge that Eileen's table on the datafication of Deleuze in education informed and inspired the brief overview of the uptake of their work in education in Chapter 1.

Past and present colleagues have been interlocutors to much of this work, and I have learnt a great deal from these conversations: Kadek Arya-Pinatyh, Sonya Honey, Deb Talbot, Meghan Stacey, Ulrika Bergmark, Catrine Kostenius, Teija Löytönen, Riikka Hohti, Monique Dagleish, Be Parnell, Stewart Riddle, Stephanie Springgay, Kim Powell, Sarah Truman, Sophie Rudolph, Kim Davies, Amanda Keddie, Lucinda McKnight, Emma Rowe, Jacqui Righetti, Robin Bellingham, Lucinda McKnight, Peta White, Joe Ferguson, Monica Green, Bronwyn Sutton, Blanche Verlie, Alicia Flynn, Michele Lobo and Laura Bedford. The chapters of this book were strengthened, in their preparation, by close readings from Sarah Truman, Rosalyn Black, Shiva Zarabadi, Blanche Verlie, Steven Lewis, Nicole Mockler, Remy Low, Emily Nelson, Rachel Finneran and Christopher Mayes. I am thankful for research work on various projects discussed in this book: by Pinchy Breheny, Rachel Finneran, Yasmin Mobayad, Michael Hartup and Evan Center. Thank you to Nina Laitala and Krista Seddon for facilitating opportunities to co-research with VicSRC student Executive and Ambassadors. I am thankful for the opportunities to collaborate with Dana Mitra and Stephanie Serriere, Remy Low and Nicole Mockler, Rosalyn Black and Rachel Finneran, and Melissa Wolfe and Leanne Higham. It is unlikely that this book would have been completed without the institutional support of Julianne Moss, Julian Sefton-Green and Andrea Witcomb and research time afforded by Deakin University (Alfred Deakin Postdoctoral Research Fellowship) and the Australian Research Council (Discovery Early Career Research Award, grant number: DE220100103).

I am deeply appreciative of Helen Nixon for her expertise and work in preparing this manuscript for publication. Gratitude to Melissa Wolfe for her expertise with converting video footage to high-resolution images, Elisabeth Devereux and Emma Rowe for help with other low-resolution files, Yasmin Mobayad for re-scanning data for higher-resolution images, and Marzieh Asgari for skilled Endnote support.

Thank you to the series editors Greg Thompson, Sam Sellar and Elizabeth de Freitas for the invitation to submit to this series, and for support throughout the process. Thank you to Carol MacDonald, Sarah Foyle and Judith Mackenzie at Edinburgh University Press for your advice and work throughout the publication process, and to Caroline Richards for copyediting work.

Sections of this book draw upon and rework material that was originally published, in earlier forms, in the following publications:

Mayes, Eve (2016), 'Shifting research methods with a becoming-child ontology: Co-theorising puppet production with high school students', *Childhood*, 23(1): 105–22. [Sage]

Mayes, Eve (2017), 'Reconceptualizing the presence of students on school governance councils: The a/effects of spatial positioning', *Policy Futures in Education*, 17(4): 503–19. [Sage]

Mayes, Eve (2019), 'Student voice, desire and power with Deleuze and Guattari', in M. A. Peters (ed.), *Springer Encyclopedia of Teacher Education – A Living Reference Work*, Dordrecht: Springer, pp. 1–6. [Springer]

Mayes, Eve (2019), 'The mis/uses of 'voice' in (post)qualitative research with children and young people: Histories, politics and ethics', *International Journal of Qualitative Studies in Education*, 32(10): 1191–209. [Taylor & Francis]

Mayes, Eve (2020), 'Student voice in an age of "security"?', *Critical Studies in Education*, 61(3): 380–97. [Taylor & Francis]

Mayes, Eve (2021), 'Politics of solidarity in educational partnerships', in M. A. Peters (ed.), *Encyclopedia of Teacher Education*, Singapore: Springer Singapore, pp. 1–5. [Springer]

Permission was granted from Taylor & Francis to reuse a three-page extract from the following publication in Chapter 6:

Mayes, Eve (2020), 'Student voice in school reform? Desiring simultaneous critique and affirmation', *Discourse: Studies in the Cultural Politics of Education*, 41(3): 454–70. [Taylor & Francis]

Finally, thank you to Chris and Yolanda, for helping me to respair (see Chapter 7).

March 2022

## Notes

1. The positionality of cited authors in this book is named where the author foregrounds their nation, affiliation and relations, and where the author(s)' standpoint knowledge shapes their onto-epistemic authority to speak. Yet, as Métis scholar Max Leboiron (2021) notes, white settlers and white scholars 'almost always remain unmarked', and that this unmarking 'is one act among many that re-centres settlers and whiteness as an unexceptional norm, while deviations have to be marked and named' (3, n.10). Goenpul scholar Aileen Moreton-Robinson (2000/2020) has thoroughly accounted for how white middle-class feminists 'write about their gendered oppression, but whiteness remains

invisible, unnamed and unmarked in their work' (42). Whiteness, 'as race, as privilege and as social construction', thus 'remains the invisible omnipresent norm' and the 'standard by which certain "differences" are measured, centred and normalised' (Moreton-Robinson 2000/2020: xviii, xix). The politics of naming and remaining silent about positionality in citational practices have significant consequences for notions of 'voice' in knowledge production.

2. Throughout this book, White is capitalised when referring to Whiteness as a socially constructed political position tied to social status, or a political ideology (as in White supremacy). Black is capitalised when referring to specific movements and disciplines (for example, Black Lives Matter and Black Studies). Quoted authors' choices about the capitalisation of white/White and black/Black are retained.

# 1

# Troubling Student Voice in School Reform

Over the past thirty years, student voice has become a popular educational reform strategy, particularly across education systems in Western liberal democracies. The term 'student voice' is frequently used to describe a range of initiatives where students contribute to decision making about matters affecting them, including on classroom- or school-wide practices, curricula and pedagogies, educational governance and policy and educational research. Student voice is argued to play a pivotal role in crafting relations of respect, understanding, empowerment and trust in educational institutions.

Proponents of student voice draw on international rights to advocate for the active participation of students in school decision making. Article 12 of the United Nations Convention on the Rights of the Child (UNCRC; United Nations 1989) declared the 'right' for children and young people to 'express' their views 'in all matters affecting them'. The UNCRC became 'the most ratified human rights treaty in history' (UNICEF 2021), though it is still not ratified by the USA. Following the UNCRC, the term 'voice' has been used to describe 'the enactment of the child's participatory rights to express an opinion, remain silent, access information and be included in the decision-making processes on matters affecting them' (Gillett-Swan and Sargeant 2019: 400). In multi-medial worlds, voice also takes many more-than-linguistic and more-than verbal forms – including gaze, facial expressions, silence, stance, gestures, touch, adornment, body art, clothes, drawings, emojis and digital/arts creation in spatial-material arrangements of power (Mannion 2007; McGregor 2004; Thomson 2011: 23). An expansive definition of voice is 'any expression of any student, anywhere, anytime about anything related to learning, schools or education' (SoundOut 2021: para. 1).

Student voice can take myriad forms, with multiple political trajectories and consequences. From the early years of student voice research, Michael Fielding (1999a) has advocated for 'radical collegiality' between students and teachers as a 'rupture of the ordinary' in schools (Fielding 2004: 296). Yet, as Fielding maps, there are many ways in which students can be positioned in student voice endeavours – from 'data sources', 'active respondents', 'co-inquirers', 'knowledge creators', 'joint authors', to being part of collective processes of 'intergenerational learning as lived democracy' (Fielding 2011: 12). Voice initiatives can have various explicit and implicit, overlapping and diverging purposes: to critique the educational status quo, to rebuild student and educator relationships, to honour the rights of the child, to support student well-being, to improve student outcomes, to market the school (Bragg and Manchester 2012; Charteris and Smardon 2019a; Hadfield and Haw 2001). Voice can be used to describe brief and tokenistic consultations with students by teachers, student Attitude to School surveys, student representation on governance councils, students as researchers endeavours, as well as student-led activism within and beyond schools (for example, the School Strike for Climate movement). Voice may have (or may not have) practical consequences for the structures, processes and practices of schools – indeed, many advocates have stressed that '"voice" is not enough' (Lundy 2007): that students' 'presence and power' (Cook-Sather 2006) need to be acknowledged and that institutional response and action must follow student voice (Bourke and Loveridge 2018).

Voice has its own history and geographies, connecting with a constellation of contemporary local, transnational and global social, economic and political concepts. I undertook the work and writing for this book in times when the concept of voice was yet again moving, metamorphosing and mutating in economic, political and social contexts beyond educational institutions, zigzagging across planes, combining with other concepts, solving and creating problems. Populist neo-fascist groups were invoking notions of the 'voice of the people'; loosely allied conspiracy and libertarian groups were publicly gathering in groups and chanting, 'my body, my choice' in protest against COVID-19 face masks, vaccinations and lockdowns; citizen-customers were encouraged to give digitised evaluations (star ratings and comments) of everything from their Uber driver to their Amazon purchase to their educator's teaching; reality TV viewers were tasked to be part of the judgement of which housemate/singer/potential spouse to eject from the show. The digitisation of everyday life blurred boundaries between the human and more-than-human voice – from Siri and Alexa's feminised voices on smart phones to the normalisation of voice recognition software for identification.

Overlapping with these frequently perverse invocations of and invitations to voice, there have also been profound calls in Australia from

Aboriginal and Torres Strait Islander peoples, in the Uluru Statement from the Heart, for a First Nations Voice to Parliament: that is, 'a representative body giving Aboriginal and Torres Strait Islanders a say in law and policy affecting them' (The Uluru Statement 2021). At the 2019 Garma Festival (an annual four-day celebration of the cultural, artistic and ceremonial traditions of the Yolngu people of northeast Arnhem Land in Australia), sixty-five Indigenous and non-Indigenous students from years 6 to 12 gathered for a Youth Forum and wrote their 'Imagination Declaration' as their own follow-up to the Uluru Statement from the Heart:

> With 60,000 years of genius and imagination in our hearts and minds, we can be one of the groups of people that transform the future of life on Earth, for the good of us all.
>
> We can design the solutions that lift islands up in the face of rising seas, we can work on creative agricultural solutions that are in sync with our natural habitat, we can re-engineer schooling, we can invent new jobs and technologies, and we can unite around kindness. [. . .]
>
> To our Prime Minister & Education Ministers, we call on you to meet with us and to work on an imagination plan for our country's education system, for all of us.
>
> We are not the problem, we are the solution. (Youth Forum at Garma 2019)

In recent years, there have also been creative and critical forms of voice in social movements initiated and organised by young people: from the transnational School Strike for Climate movement, to the student-led gun control advocacy following the mass school shooting in Parkland, Florida in the USA, to student-led movements for racial justice and anti-racist curriculum and instruction, to the Teach Us Consent movement in Australia (see Chapter 7; Welton and Harris 2022). Katherine Schulten writes, in her introduction to a 2020 anthology of persuasive essays by school-aged students in the USA, that '"student voice" is having a bit of a moment' (xii).

This book undertakes an analysis of the concept of voice in education, considering the ontology, ethics and politics of voice in education. I am interested in how the concept of voice metamorphoses across contexts as it becomes an educational reform policy priority – as simultaneously transformational and problematic. As explained later in this chapter, the work of philosopher Gilles Deleuze and psychoanalyst and philosopher-activist Félix Guattari has prompted me to explore the question: *What can voice(s) do?* – that is, what voice can do in its embodied, physical manifestation, what voice can do as a concept in schools, and what voice can do as a provocation for methodology and for writing. This book is for those perplexed by how the concept of voice moves as it is enacted in education and the felt ambivalences of voice – whether students, teachers, school leaders, policy makers, advocates, activists and/or researchers. The term 'enactment' draws on Stephen Ball, Meg Maguire and Annette Braun's (2012) analysis of policy enactment – that is, the creative interpretations, adaptations and mutations of a concept as a process (rather than policy 'implementation'). I have written this book to contribute to different conceptions and practices of voice beyond Western liberal humanist individualism in a world ravaged by the legacies and continuities of colonialism and capitalist extractivism. In this book I aspire to contribute to collective pedagogical attunement to radical interdependencies across differences, and to the possibility of re/generating the world, in common.

## *Situating the Authorial Voice*

Over the last ten years, I have been an educator,[1] researcher, evaluator and advocate for student voice in primary, secondary and tertiary education contexts. I am thoroughly committed to radical[2] democratic educational practices and relations, even as this book considers the political ontology of student voice and accounts for its simultaneous potentialities and dangers. As a cisgender female, white,[3] middle-class,[4] able-bodied secondary and tertiary educator and researcher, my embodied experiences, advocacy and mistakes with voice shape this work, just as these intersecting positionalities have shaped what could and could not be said and heard in conversations with students and teachers (see also McDermott 2020a). The politics of this book are situated with feminist (that is, pursuing equity and non-binary thinking across diverse sexes, genders and sexualities), anti-racist and anti-colonial politics. Having been enfolded within various institutional attempts to 'give' students a voice in their education, I have felt at times inspired, disappointed, incensed and optimistic, and often all these feelings at once, across various configurations of bodies, words and things. I have been committed to and complicit in the work of voice as an educational reform strategy, simultaneously championing and cynical about the potential of the concept of voice for institutional transformation. This book seeks to 'stay with the trouble' (Haraway 2016) – specifically, 'the trouble of (or with) voice' (Mazzei and Jackson 2009: 3; cf. Bragg 2021: 42) and the trouble with school (Youdell 2011).

This book draws upon materials from a number of research projects in and beyond educational settings that I have been enfolded within, where students and educators engaged in student voice initiatives. I 'think with' (Jackson and Mazzei 2012) memories of spoken voices and the written transcribed voices of school students, teachers and school leaders, with policy documents, with photographs from research encounters, and with past and contemporary research and theory. Later chapters begin with a particular concept frequently used in student voice – representing (Chapter 4), understanding (Chapter 5), evaluating (Chapter 6) – and move from the perplexities that I have felt in specific research sites and studies that resonate with perplexities from other settings and studies. Chapters 3, 5 and 6 draw upon my doctoral research, which took place in the comprehensive, co-educational government high school in southwest Sydney where I previously worked as an English and English as an Additional Language teacher. This school had received a significant amount of federal government funding over a four-year period for the purposes of reform, as an identified 'low socio-economic school'.[5] One of the reforms hastily organised due to government funding timelines was a students as researchers (SaRs), or student voice, initiative; this group was called the Steering Committee by the students, and SaRs by senior executive staff (see Chapter 6). I suggested this reform initiative and was its facilitator in 2010 and 2011 as a teacher. Each year between 2010 and 2013, a group of approximately twenty students in Year 9 were apprenticed as co-researchers to devise, design and conduct their own research inquiries, working with a teacher-facilitator and an academic partner. Students became familiar with qualitative and participatory research methods including interviews, focus groups and participant observation, the development and analysis of surveys, visual and embodied methods, and participatory data analysis. General research topics guided the students' inquiries each year: The School I'd Like (2010), The Teachers I'd Like (2011), The Learner I'd Like to Be (2012) and What I'd Like to Learn (2013). My doctoral research (2012–16) explored, with students, educators and parents, how people had made meaning of these experiences of student voice as a school reform strategy, in the fourth year of the reform funding (see Chapters 5 and 6).

In subsequent years, I have engaged in research concerned with questions of voice in other educational settings, including a contracted study of students' and principals' views and experiences of student representation on school governance councils (2016; see Chapter 4), a study of critical education in the context of Countering Violent Extremism interventions into schools (2016; see Chapter 5), and a media analysis and interview study of school-aged students' climate justice activism (2020–1, see Chapter 7). Other studies that are not explicitly discussed, but which also inform the work of this book, include a participatory action research study with students conducting their own research in the city of Geelong (2017–20; see Mayes and Kelly 2022), a contracted three-year evaluation of a student voice programme called Teach the Teacher (2017–20; see Black and Mayes 2020; Finneran et al. 2021; Mayes et al. 2019, 2021), and a study of tertiary educators' perspectives on student evaluations of teaching in a university (2016; see Mayes 2018).

It is important to note that these studies were all located in Australian educational settings (primary, secondary and tertiary), and that compulsory schooling is where the majority of this work has been conducted. This means that there is a specificity to the focus of this book: Australian education. However, I have also been part of international student voice initiatives, communities, conferences, publications and collaborations – including the international University of Cambridge Student Voice seminars convened by Alison Cook-Sather between 2011 and 2015 (see Morgan 2021), and a case study of a democratic elementary school with Dana Mitra and Stephanie Serriere in the USA (Mayes et al. 2016b). Since student voice is a popularised globalised educational reform strategy across all levels of education (including tertiary education), and since issues of difference, governance and desire are not specific to education alone, I hope that the problematics and perplexities of this book will resonate, even if in different keys, across a diverse range of geographical and institutional settings. While some of my previous publications have been co-authored with students (for example, Mayes et al. 2013, 2016a, 2017), this book operates more as a philosophical deliberation on the ontological, ethical and political questions surrounding this work. I hope that it will catalyse dissonant dialogue between differentially positioned bodies in education towards more affirmative ways of thinking-feeling-relating-conspiring in and beyond formal schooling.

In this opening chapter, I introduce the history of philosophical and political movements that have informed the popular concept of voice in education. Working with a photograph of a sign outside a school, I introduce the possibilities and ambivalences of appropriating the thought and work of Gilles Deleuze and Félix Guattari for analysing the movements of the concept of voice within and beyond education, and the key concepts that will be mobilised across this book. I outline some of my doubts about the limits of Deleuze and Guattari's work, introduce the other currents of thought that also inform the work of this book, and summarise the chapters that follow.

## *Historical Rationales for Voice*

Student voice has been argued to be under-theorised and praxis-oriented (Taylor and Robinson 2009: 161). At the same time, various histories have been chosen and traced for it – histories that sometimes overlap and sometimes diverge. Student voice can be advocated on the basis of a standpoint epistemological rationale that seeks out students' lived knowledge, a liberal humanist rationale that celebrates dialogue in schools, a critical pedagogic rationale that calls for student empowerment, and a school improvement rationale that argues that encouraging and listening to student voice will improve institutional outcomes. These rationales were hewn in specific historical and geographical contexts; when these lines of thought are translated and transported to other locations, certain nuances of thought may remain, and others may be lost or morphed in translation. In this section, I introduce these rationales to foreground some of the ontological assumptions that may creep into student voice practice: in particular, liberal humanist assumptions about the autonomous subject, the rationality of communication, and the onward progress of individuals, institutions and society.

STUDENTS' KNOWLEDGE: THE STANDPOINT EPISTEMOLOGICAL
RATIONALE

Educators and researchers advocating student voice have argued that students' embodied and situated knowledge and experiences make them 'expert witnesses' to schooling (Rudduck 1999). This epistemological rationale is that students 'experience a reality relatively unknown to the adults who govern their school experience' (Silva and Rubin 2003: 1) and that students should be positioned and respected as agents, actors, resources and producers of knowledge (Bragg and Fielding 2005; Cook-Sather 2020; Fielding 2001).

This epistemological rationale – that students know things that adults in schools don't know and that this knowledge should be valued as a resource – is indebted to early formulations of feminist standpoint theories in the 1970s and 1980s. Feminist standpoint theorists from the 1970s foregrounded: (1) the social situatedness of knowledge – that is, that embodied experiences are a way of knowing; (2) that those situated at the margins of established relations of power know more and know differently, since they know that their knowledge is not valued; and (3) that research should begin with this marginalised knowledge, positioning those previously marginalised as agents, critics, and creators of knowledge rather than as objects of knowledge (Harding 1987, 2004; Hartsock 1983/2016).[6] In a resonant way to how Nancy Hartsock (1983/2016) drew parallels between the knowledge of the oppressed proletariat worker (in relation to capitalism) and women (in relation to patriarchy) in the 1980s, scholars working in the New Sociology of Childhood in the 1990s argued for the reconceptualisation of children and young people as active social agents, critics and creators of standpoint knowledge about their worlds (Alanen and Mayall 2001). These scholars argued for the status of children as *beings*, critiquing deficit developmental psychological constructions of children and young people as in the process of *becoming*-adults (for example, James and Prout 1990; see Chapter 2). In the student voice research and practice community, it was argued that children and young people are increasingly responsible, competent and involved in complex relationships outside of school, but that schools' structures and patterns of relationships have remained locked in hierarchical modes of relating that justify the exclusion of students from classroom and school decision making (Bron and Veugelers 2014; Rudduck and Flutter 2004).

The argument for repositioning students as knowers, agents and actors in schools was made from quite a different position to other standpoint epistemologies: by adults on behalf of children and young people. There is a risk, as I explore in later chapters, of repeating the issues associated with early standpoint theories – in particular, the problem of 'speaking for' others and the elision of difference. In 1991, Linda Alcoff warned in 'The Problem of Speaking for Others' that, in describing and representing the situation of others, one may be 'speaking in place of them, that is, speaking for them', representing 'the other's needs, goals, situation, and in fact, who they are' (9; see also Fielding 2004). Indeed, earlier formulations of feminist standpoint research were criticised for essentialising the identity of groups and erasing differences between groups of women (for example, Fuss 1990), and for appropriating the voice of the Other and remaking Other women into white women's image (for example, hooks 1990). In advocacy for student voice, adult researchers and advocates spoke for children and young people's ontological status – as *beings*, not *becomings* – as an altruistic strategic reconceptualisation to promote students' agentic capacity in schools. Yet, this ontological claim had other potential consequences: if children and young people are 'given' a voice on the basis that they are competent, responsible and agentic, but do not perform (in the research or school setting) in alignment with this claim, their 'right' and capacity to 'have a voice' at school might also be questioned or dismissed by those with institutional power (see Chapter 6). As Sara Bragg (2021) powerfully writes: 'If we simply claim for the child the qualities of autonomy, agency, reason and knowledge that others see as properly only adult, we leave the categories and binaries themselves untouched' (44). There are ontological questions about the constitution of institutional power, pedagogical relations and communicative conditions that need to be further interrogated in the institutional enactment of student voice. In turn, within and between students, there are myriad differences and intersecting fluctuations of power and oppression across shifting configurations; some students may also come to 'speak for' other students, even when all are ostensibly 'given' an institutional voice. In Chapters 4 and 5, I further analyse what happens when students are asked to 'represent' their peers and to speak for them, and when students are compelled to give an account of their standpoint knowledge and feelings in schooled spaces.

## STUDENTS' AND EDUCATORS' DIALOGICAL UNDERSTANDING: THE LIBERAL HUMANIST RATIONALE

Student voice has been also rationalised as facilitating dialogue: fostering new understanding across differences between students and educators. The metaphor of the bridge is frequently used to describe dialogical engagements where students and educators reach an understanding between students and educators, and home and school (for example, Groundwater-Smith et al. 2014; Mitra 2006). Destabilising student and educator roles in voice encounters is argued to engender 'restless encounters' and 'restless dialogue' (Fielding and Moss 2011: 79, 152) that enable students and educators to 're-see' each other as 'persons, not just as role occupants' (Fielding 2011: 13). Dialogical encounters are argued to enable educators to see from students' perspectives (Rudduck and Flutter 2000), 'gain a deeper understanding of [. . .] teaching and learning processes' (Flutter 2007: 343) and disrupt teachers' '"default" style of teaching' through viewing 'their teaching practice from multiple (often contradictory) perspectives' (Kane and Chimwayange 2013: 60). In enabling 'different kinds of conversations than [students and educators] would normally have had in the classroom' (Cox and Robinson-Pant 2008: 462), student voice is said to support students to move beyond experiences of schooling as 'unwelcoming, inflexible and indifferent' (Robinson and Smyth 2016: 223). These arguments for the value of student voice stress the positive feelings, new understandings and solidarity built through student voice. Student voice is framed as a form of speaking *with* students: adults and young people speaking together. This rationale foregrounds human rationality and the possibility of understanding across difference (Robinson and Taylor 2007: 8).

Jürgen Habermas's (1984) ideal speech situation and assumptions about communication underpin this rationale for dialogue in education (Mockler and Groundwater-Smith 2015; Robinson and Taylor 2007). In brief (see Honneth and Joas 1991; McCarthy 1978; Porter and Porter 2003), Habermas defines social interaction as an 'exchange of communicative acts', where language use is 'orientated towards reaching an *understanding*' (1984: 44, my emphasis). Habermas (1984) theorises language as social and rational, premised on reasoned argument and cooperation (86), and towards 'achieving, sustaining and reviewing consensus' that rests on 'the intersubjective recognition of criticisable validity claims' (17). While the ideal speech situation has been stressed to be an 'aspiration' rather than a reality (Mockler and Groundwater-Smith 2015: 15), this book is interested in the consequences of these aspirations for the student voice encounter in schools.

This second rationale for student voice – that it builds bridges to mutual understandings between students and educators – has also been troubled by postcolonial (Said 1989) and psychoanalytic (Phelan 1993) work. As Chapter 5 explores, critiques of dialogue have interrogated how theorisations of the dialogical encounter are frequently staged in a sanitised, abstracted space, distanced from messy sites where power, knowledge and desire are struggled over (Porter and Porter 2003). Neutralising power relations in hierarchical institutions through dialogue may, as Fielding (2007) warns, 'presume too much' (307). Dialogue, far from a neutral zone of encounter, is a 'political struggle' (Alcoff 1991: 15), deeply entwined with assumptions about communicative norms and rationality that privilege those from particular classed, gendered and racialised positions and invalidate the speech of others (Arnot and Reay 2007). As Argentine feminist philosopher Maria Lugones powerfully puts it in a dialogue with 'white/Anglo' feminist philosopher Elizabeth Spelman:

> We and you do not talk the same language. When we talk to you, we use your language: the language of your experience and of your theories. We try to use it to communicate our world of experience. [. . .] But since your language and your theories are inadequate in expressing our experiences, we only succeed in communicating our experience of exclusion. We cannot talk to you in our language because you do not understand it. (Lugones and Spelman 1983/2000: 575)

Chapter 5 takes up these assumptions about the possibilities of understanding across difference, building on these critiques of dialogue. Exploring movements of power and desire in concrete, immanent experiences of dialogical encounters, I think with Edward Said's (1989) critique of the colonial dialogical encounter, Édouard Glissant's call (1990/1997) for the 'right to opacity', and Kara Keeling's (2019) further exploration of the politics and possibilities of refusing to make oneself understandable.

STUDENTS' EMPOWERMENT: THE CRITICAL PEDAGOGIC RATIONALE

'Empowerment' is a third rationale for student voice, a concept that has shifted and moved across time and territories. Youth Participatory Action Research (YPAR), student voice, students as researchers and youth–adult partnerships have been argued to empower and liberate young people to engage in social and institutional change, through interrogating and challenging inequalities and injustices in their own lives and schools (Cammarota and Fine 2008; Fielding and Moss 2011; Rubin et al. 2017). Students are repositioned from being 'silent witnesses' of their schooling (Smyth and McInerney 2012: 3) to being 'empowered' to interrogate power relations and structures and to take collective action to 'make a difference' in their communities and world (Giroux 1983; Shor 1980). Students and educators form a 'radical collegiality' (Fielding 1999a) where democracy is lived in the here and now in pedagogical and research relations and praxis (Fine et al. 2007; Holdsworth 2000).

This critical, transformative praxis confronting historical and present institutional injustices can be traced to the critical pedagogical work of Paolo Freire in Brazil. The concept of praxis – acts which shape and change the world – is rooted in Karl Marx's imperative to 'change' the world rather than only 'interpret' it (Marx 1978: 145). Paolo Freire's critical pedagogy, developed in the context of political and social injustices in Brazil in the 1960s, aimed to foster adult workers' capacity to read the 'word' in order to read and change 'the world' (Freire and Macedo 1987). Freire (1970) sought to counter a 'banking mode' of education, where the educator 'deposits' knowledge in the student's mind without listening to the student. In this mode of education, knowledge is lifeless and sterile, and the student's revolutionary consciousness is not awakened; the student will see the world as unmoveable and themselves as needing to assimilate to the status quo. Freire formed, instead, a 'problem-posing' mode of education, where the educator repositions the student as active agent able to shape and transform the world, as they gain consciousness of their class interests and collective revolutionary potential. In turn, the educator is changed; both student and educator are transformed in the relation (Freire 1970). Since Freire, the legal binding of the right for children and young people's knowledge to be recognised within and beyond the school, in the United Nations Convention on the Rights of the Child (United Nations 1989), strengthened the case for children and young people's participation in institutional decision making and research about issues that affect their lives (Lundy 2007).

Freire's ideas, forged in and with adult workers in Brazil, has been transported to schooling in the Global North as critical pedagogy, and reworked in various forms of Participatory Action Research – including Youth Participatory Action Research, student voice, students as researchers and youth–adult partnerships. This process of conceptual translation sometimes maintains its politically transformative edge, as evidenced, for example, in the work of the Warrior-Researchers (students and educators) of Kia Aroha College in Otara, in South Auckland, Aotearoa New Zealand – a school that draws on critical pedagogic theories within a decolonising, culturally responsive 'learning environment where Māori and Pasifika cultural identities, customs, languages and knowledges, and the philosophy and practice of whānau (extended family), are the norm' (Milne 2020: 87). In 2018, Warrior-Researchers chose to conduct research on 'racism, as we and our families [and] community experience it' (Warrior-Researchers, cited in Milne 2020: 88), and to 'actively speak back' to colonising processes through a range of community and academic forums.

Critical pedagogic concepts and practices have also been 'translated' (Rubin et al. 2017), or 'schoolified' (Keddie 2021), in widely different school settings, with widely different impacts and embodied experiences. The risk is that, while students may be 'quite willing to get political and trouble power hierarchies', those in 'positional power in schools often choose a politically neutral stance' (Welton et al. 2022: 6). When students are 'empowered', there may be controversy, reprimand and backlash (Fine and Torre 2004). In one elite private school in the USA, a group of junior girls' YPAR project about 'micro-aggressions' perpetrated 'by the majority white population towards minority students' was met with 'strong backlash' from 'some of the white males who were "offended" and "strongly disagreed" that they were perpetrating micro-aggressions' (Keddie 2021: 384–5). In another YPAR project where student researchers found that 'Black students consistently reported their school to be a more negative environment than their Latinx peers', students were convinced of the importance of 'uplifting the voices of Black students and naming anti-Black racism' in their school (Clay and Turner 2021: 410, 413). However, the facilitating teacher directly intervened to remove references to students' racialised identities, telling the students: '"But we can't just make it about Black students. The teachers won't hear it. Trust me, as soon as you mention race, they will shut down"' (410). Adult concerns with teachers' racial sensitivities and fragilities 'changed the nature of their project' from an 'explicit focus on Blackness' to 'how *all* students felt' about the school, deracialising 'what the students felt was an explicitly racialised experience' (411, 412, original emphasis). What students say may directly contradict or stand in tension with the established grammar of schooling (Mayes 2020a; Rubin et al. 2017: 176) and their tone, words and research findings may be steered, co-opted, silenced or shut down by others (Biddle and Hufnagel 2019; Bragg 2007; Clay and Turner 2021). Students may experience paternalistic adult 'surprise' at their research capacities, professionalism and motivation (Bertrand 2016), 'managerialist subterfuge' that muffles the political potential of students' research findings into interlocking inequalities (Clay and Turner 2021), and minimal policy changes in response to even the most persuasive and well-researched student research efforts (Berryman and Eley 2018). Students' attempts to 'make a difference' may entrench difference (Black 2012; Mayes et al.

2016b). In 1989, Elizabeth Ellsworth asked a question that continues to be asked in the enactment of student voice work: 'Why doesn't this feel empowering?' (Ellsworth 1989). This question is tied up with broader questions about paternalism and power in participatory endeavours – particularly when a privileged party with institutional power claims to 'empower' another (Cook-Sather 2007; Cooke and Kothari 2001). In Chapters 5 and 6, I take up these questions of the uneven experiences of 'empowerment' in schools.

SCHOOL IMPROVEMENT: THE INSTITUTIONAL REFORM RATIONALE

Finally, student voice is advocated as an essential element in school reform. The above rationales (standpoint knowledge, dialogue and empowerment) are entwined in the affirmation that student voice can improve schools. These rationales frequently quote from the work of philosopher John Dewey, particularly in North American contexts. An oft-cited quotation from Dewey, across these rationales, is that 'all those who are affected by social institutions must have a share in producing and managing them' and a 'voice in shaping them' (Dewey 1937: 218). Listening to students' voices is argued to improve leadership practices and democratise school governance processes (Brasof and Mansfield 2018) and to be 'an important catalyst for change' (Flutter 2007: 344) for students' engagement and learning, educators' professional learning, and schools' cultures.

Advocates argue that student voice strengthens student wellbeing, engagement, motivation, confidence and communication skills (Graham et al. 2016, 2022; Mitra 2004), sense of belonging and attachment to school (Allan and Duckworth 2018; Baroutsis et al. 2016; Quinn and Owen 2016), metacognition and the acquisition of new language to describe learning processes (Rodgers 2018; Wall 2012), appreciation for the challenge and complexities of educators' work (Keddie 2015; Mayes et al. 2013), leadership and citizenship skills (Brasof and Spector 2016; Holdsworth 2000) and academic outcomes (Kahne et al. 2022). Advocates stress the learning that occurs for both students and educators in student voice encounters: educators learn from students about effective pedagogy in their specific classroom contexts (Charteris 2016; McIntyre et al. 2005; Nelson 2015). Student voice experiences may radically reorient educators' professional subjectivities and understanding of pedagogical relationality (Groundwater-Smith and Mockler 2019; Messiou 2019).

Student voice advocates also argue that involving students in school decision making is an important contributor to fostering a positive school 'climate' (Aldridge et al. 2015), 'ethos' (Graham 2012) or 'atmosphere' (Sebba and Robinson 2010: 19). Messiou (2019) argues that student voice can bring about a 'cultural change', becoming 'a catalyst for inclusive development', provided that students' 'views are heard and acted upon' (768). Mager and Nowak (2012) describe improvements to school 'ethos' to include 'student engagement', student attendance, climate, atmosphere, discipline, 'a democratic school ethos', and better 'acceptance of discipline or compliance with rules' (47). Other researchers associate student voice with generating positive school cultures characterised by mutual trust, care, connection, and respect (Aldridge et al. 2015; Anderson and Graham 2016; Bergmark and Kostenius 2009; Johnston et al. 2021). More tangibly, student voice activities can lead to material and political shifts in schools, including '[c]hanges to or improvements in facilities and influence on rules, policies and procedures' (that is, the physical environment, toilet facilities, playground equipment, food, school uniforms) (Mager and Nowak 2012: 47). Such positive school cultures and improvements in the material conditions of schooling in turn are connected with school effectiveness and improvement (MacNeil et al. 2009), particularly for schools in disadvantaged communities (Muijs et al. 2004). School effectiveness and school improvement rhetoric has enfolded this language of student voice into calls for schools' continuous improvement in consultation with key stakeholders (Quaglia et al. 2020).

But, as I consider further in the following section and the chapters that follow, what are the politics of student voice in school improvement efforts? Who decides who or what needs to reform or be improved? Over what period of time does improvement need to be demonstrated, and according to what criteria? As promising as improving schools through listening to students sounds, what happens as the concept of student voice, with its various concepts, histories and geographies, moves through schools? How do these rationales – sometimes written in universalising terms from high-income, Western national contexts – shift and morph as they are enacted across diverse settings? To begin to consider some of the politics surrounding voice in education, I turn to a photograph of a sign taken outside a primary school in a major Australian city (Figure 1.1), and a narrated memory. This sign has prompted me to ask what has happened in the educational systems within which I have worked over the past fifteen years.

## What Happened?

*A few years ago, I arrived at a primary school in suburban Melbourne, ready to conduct focus groups with students and teachers about student voice at their school.*[7] *My colleague, Rachel Finneran, had arrived just before me, and stood on the corner of two streets bordering the school. As I crossed the road, she gestured towards a sign (see Figure 1.1) strategically located near the corner of two streets, opposite a line of local shops on the other side of the road.*

*Three logos are emblazoned across the sign: at the top right, the logo of the local real estate agent; just below this, the logo and name of the primary school; near the bottom of the sign, the logo for a non-governmental organisation supporting schools to enact student voice. In the photograph, the state Minister for Education (at the time) stands next to three well-groomed primary school-aged students. Two students hold a certificate each, and another student holds a glass trophy. The students look like the ideal student leader – the kind of student who a parent desires their young child to aspire to be and to become.*

The reader might question the relationship between the historical rationales for student voice and the cardboard sign photographed in Figure 1.1. Did these students posing for the camera feel like agentic knowers, speaking from their situated standpoints about their experiences of school? Had they engaged in dialogue with their educators and come to a mutual understanding across their differences? Did they risk 'speaking for' other students as student representatives? Were they encouraged and 'empowered' by the experience of expressing their voices? Were they frustrated by the necessity to speak in terms that their educators and school would understand? Did they experience an awakening to critical consciousness, or did they come to desire their own self-censorship, to please their educators? Did 'having a voice' transform their school? What were their doubts and joys, ambivalences and certainties, before and amidst the declaration that their school had been recognised as 'Junior School Council of the Year'? What happened, such that a school would erect a sign, presumably paid for by a local real estate agent, to publicise this award? What work does this sign do – as it faces the local shops where parents, community members, and children and young people stop for a coffee or a milkshake?

# THE POLITICS OF VOICE IN EDUCATION

*Figure 1.1* A real estate agent sign standing on the border of a primary school: 'Junior School Council of the Year'. Photo credit: Rachel Finneran.

Reading this narrated memory, some readers may object that this school's practices do not necessarily constitute 'real', 'authentic' or 'transformative' student voice, and that this sign, rather, is suggestive of the instrumentalisation, consumerisation and depoliticisation of student voice. I agree. Student voice, a movement seeking to build democratic relationships in schools, has become interwoven, perhaps paradoxically, with the accountability pressures, competition and individualism that bolster hierarchical relations between schools, educators and students (Charteris and Smardon 2019b; Fielding 1999b, 2004; Nelson and Charteris 2020). The sign is indeed suggestive of how student voice has become a form of branding to present a pleasant public face and boost the institution's market appeal (Bragg and Manchester 2012).

Indeed, across the educational jurisdictions where I have taught and researched, student voice has become the object of state educational policy enthusiasm and emblazoned as a school priority on individual schools' websites – a marketable feature of a school community's life together. Voice – and concepts that accompany it on various ladders of participation and empowerment (for example, 'agency' and 'leadership') – has become a priority in schools' strategic planning across many state and national jurisdictions. School principals now seek out and pay consultants and external organisations for support to help them with 'innovative' methods to 'give' their students a voice, or for the licence to use particular student voice survey instruments (Finefter-Rosenbluh et al. 2021). Policy imperatives (in some jurisdictions) to value student voice can catalyse welcome shifts in schooling relationships; to mandate a practice can lead to its production and proliferation. However, prioritising student voice in official documents does not necessarily change pedagogical practices and relations and the lived experiences of students. There may be dissonances between how school leadership and teachers perceive and enact the concept of student voice (Skerritt et al. 2021). Policy prioritising of student voice, in the context of contemporary culture wars, can also provoke neoconservative backlash, in 'a suffocating refusal to encounter difference' (Bragg 2021: 48). Blockages to voice, notwithstanding its official policy prioritisation, are particularly pronounced for students and communities that are minoritised – those, as Māori scholar Russell Bishop (2011) has put it, that are 'not necessarily in the numerical minority' but 'treated as if one's position and perspective are of less worth' (110; see Chapter 5).

Student voice practices, while ostensibly liberatory, are entwined with established practices of educational governance. Student voice data (for example, student feedback on educators' lessons) have become a way to evaluate educators: voice data can now be taken up by entrepreneurial educators for their self-curated performance review responses and promotion applications; voice data can also become a weapon against educators – a new form of educator surveillance (Nelson and Charteris 2020; Page and Charteris 2021). But the educator who questions or resists student voice practices may be dismissed; their ambivalence about student voice may be interpreted as evidence that they do not value students' voices and are 'old-fashioned' in their pedagogies (Black and Mayes 2020). Student voice, in a consumeristic evaluative mode, has also moved beyond institutionally sanctioned evaluations, onto public websites like Rate My Professors and Rate My Teachers, as well as closed social media pages of student cohorts (Mayes 2018). At the same time, while students may publicly name and praise or shame particular educators in and beyond schools, educators have been concomitantly positioned as needing to monitor the words, actions and behaviour of students in national security discourses imported into schools (see Chapter 5). Voice has become both a means for students and teachers to express their feelings and desires, and also a technology to monitor the feelings and desires of both students and educators.

When student voice practices are taken up by schools, encounters between students and educators may not always meet the expectations of valuing multiple standpoints, mutual understanding, empowerment and school improvement. There may be uncertainties, anxieties and more perplexing feelings at work, alongside and entwined with feelings of connection, pleasure, respect, trust and enthusiasm. But is this an issue of inconsistency or contradiction between ideals and institutional enactment? Are there 'two narratives' of student voice, that exist in binary relation: 'student voice as democratic and transformational' and 'student voice as "policy" and strategic initiative' (Hall 2017: 181); how do these varying animations of voice overlap and interweave? How else might these perplexing twists and turns of voice – as a concept moving in and through, and forming and re-forming educational institutions – be analysed?

## Thinking Differently

Over the last ten years I have been trying to make sense of these movements of the concept of voice – and, specifically, what are often described as its inconsistencies and contradictions. It is a Marxist axiom that society is defined by its contradictions, and this is true at a macropolitical scale. The reader might think of David Harvey's (2005) analysis of the inconsistent, incoherent, contested and contradictory logics of neoliberalism – liberal freedoms for the individual go hand in hand with the freeing of the market; constant choices and frequent feedback breed anxious anticipation of each day's evaluations. Michel Foucault's analysis of disciplinary societies and governmentality has helped me to understand shifts in governance patterns in educational institutions: historically, disciplinary environments have been divided and structured to mould and produce the 'good' student who is governed through observing them hierarchically; the student is socialised into habits of judgement and examination against prevailing norms for speech, behaviour, the use of time, and the use of the body (Foucault 1991). The individual's speech, behaviour and the use of the body were (and continue to be) made visible in order to regulate them more effectively (Foucault 1991: 139). In his later *Security, Territory, Population* lectures at the Collège de France, Foucault (2007) argued that disciplinary societies' patterns of governance are in the process of being slowly overlaid by governance through mechanisms of choice, regulation through incentives, and self-responsibilising processes. The subject is reframed as '*Homo œconomicus*' – entrepreneur of the self (Foucault 2010: 226).

Thinking with Foucault, feminist poststructuralist scholars have interrogated critical pedagogic rationales for voice, underlining the 'impositional potential' (Cook-Sather 2007) and inadvertent oppressions of 'empowerment', warning that critical pedagogy may reinforce rather than break down relations of domination in the name of the *telos* (goal) of liberation (for example, Ellsworth 1989; Gore 1993; Luke and Gore 1992). These scholars complicated critical pedagogy's modernist assumptions of power/knowledge as a property that a person has or does not have or a structure that one is positioned within, in favour of a Foucauldian view of power as relational, dynamic and productive (Foucault 1976/1990: 92–4). Following Foucault, these scholars argued that 'everything is dangerous' (Foucault 1983: 231), that critical pedagogues are 'always implicated in the very structures they are trying to change' (Ellsworth 1989: 310), that '"liberatory" and "emancipatory" discourses have no guaranteed effects', and that the educator must 'constantly question the "truth" of one's thought and oneself' (Gore 1993: xv, 11). Later critiques of student voice, also drawing on Foucault, have analysed how voice has become an 'ethico-political strategy': 'a new form of internal policing' (Bragg 2007: 352), positioning students as self-governing and responsible for their own speech, bodies, behaviour and learning. Following Foucault, voice in education has been critiqued as an instrumental technology of power to better govern students and educators, notwithstanding the possibilities for resistance (Bragg 2007; Raby 2014; Robinson and Taylor 2013).

I have found these critiques of critical pedagogy and student voice to be compelling and to frequently ring true. I have continued to wonder at the troubling feelings that circulate as student voice is enacted as an educational reform, and how and why such educational reforms frequently redirect schools back to the status quo. But at times these critiques have seemed to compel me to side-skirt students' and educators' more affirmative accounts of their voice work as indicators of false consciousness, deception or naivety, leaving me with a sense of inevitable governance. Other affects exceeded and eluded these accounts and needed to be cut out from analysis – the only option seemed to be noting moments of students' and educators' oppositional resistance (Mayes 2020c). At times, I felt soaked in the 'hermeneutics of suspicion' that Eve Sedgwick (2003) describes as a 'mandatory injunction rather than a possibility among other possibilities' (125). I continued to wonder about how desire intersects with governance. Do students want to be governed through student voice? What other dynamic movements of formation, re-formation and de-formation of subjectivity are at work? I sought ways to make sense of the dynamic movements and multivalent politics of voice as it moves through and beyond schools. I pursued ways to map simultaneous co-options and liberations, resistances and acceptances of voice, particularly as they intersect with students' and educators' subjectivities and reform imperatives. I looked for ways to rethink the boundaries between celebration and critique, theory and praxis, student and teacher, and voices, feelings, bodies, texts and worlds (see also Pearce and Wood 2019; Robinson and Taylor 2007; Zembylas 2007a). This required 'a different way of feeling: another sensibility' (Deleuze 1962/1983: 198).

## *Troubling an Educational Reform after Deleuze and Guattari*

The voices of the philosopher Gilles Deleuze and psychoanalyst and activist Félix Guattari have become interlocutors – along with students, educators and other researchers and theorists – in my attempts to think-speak-feel-listen-relate differently to voice and the politics of education. Deleuze and Guattari's engagements in simultaneous theory and practice offer resources that can be appropriated for re-thinking and re-working the concept of voice in schools. In the following sections, I introduce transversality, affect, agencements, desire, and Deleuze and Guattari's critique of reform and rights.

### TRANSVERSALITY

Deleuze and Guattari's work enables examination of how commonsense understandings, relations, institutions and the social order are constituted, as well as creative experimentation with what other modes of existence might be possible. Their philosophical exploration and creative experiments in transversality are relevant to considerations of voice and pedagogical relationality (cf. Cole and Bradley 2018a).[8] Guattari developed his writing on transversality in working alongside psychiatrist Jean Oury at the La Borde clinic in France, a clinic that actively experimented with transversalising relations among 'boarders' (patients), staff and doctors, with the 'boarders' taking an active part in running the facility (see Dosse 2007/2010; Genosko 2009). According to Guattari:

> Transversality is a dimension that tries to overcome both the impasse of pure verticality and that of mere horizontality: it tends to be achieved when there is maximum communication among different levels and, above all, in different meanings. (Guattari 2015: 13)

For example, in experiments like a boarder becoming 'cook for a day', traditional patient and clinician hierarchies were interrupted, refashioned, but also 'productively inhabit[ed]' (Ringrose 2015: 399; Walkerdine 2013). Experiments with transversality, and group analyses of these processes, enact Guattari's rethinking of the psychoanalytic conception of desire and of institutional power relations (Guattari 2015). La Borde's transversal practices were modelled on the open schoolrooms and non-hierarchical pedagogies of Celestin Freinet and Fernand Oury, as well as on the clinical practices of the 'mental hospital' run by François Tosquelles (Genosko 2009: 34–7; Wallin 2013). Fernand Oury's pedagogical practices included the production of a collective correspondence within and between schools and cooperative councils led by students, upending 'the institutionally alienated individual and the asymmetrical teacher student dyad' (Wallin 2012: 160, n.10). Parallels can be drawn here with previous descriptions of student voice – for example, Michael Fielding (2001) a key figure in the student voice movement, has similarly described student voice as a 'transformative "transversal" approach' that reconfigures student/teacher relationships (124).[9] Indeed, Guattari's reworking of Marxist notions of praxis offers post-Marxist and post-psychoanalytic possibilities for augmenting forms of education that seek to be anti-capitalist and to promote more liberatory modes of life. 'Praxis', for Guattari, is experimental rather than teleological in orientation (Guattari 2000: 23), involving experiments in arranging new relations of ideas, affects, bodies, texts, spaces and time as configurations of people 'interpret their own positions' as 'group-subjects' (Guattari 2015: 71). It is at this point that Guattari (and Deleuze, by association), may be closest to Paolo Freire.[10]

There remains a slipperiness, though, to notions of transversality, that make it a generative concept for analysing the movements and mutations of voice in and through school. While Guattari's transversality was modelled on and inspired by leftist movements, in his later work he notes how transversality might be used in political struggles, but also be co-opted in the service of state warfare (Guattari 2011). Google, Apple, Microsoft and Amazon also appear 'to act according to an understanding of transversality; their core competencies are dispersed and embedded, [...] they do business in a zone of potentiality rather than reliance on norms', for profit (Ryder 2018: vi). Student voice rhetoric has also taken on the logics of market-driven consumer satisfaction surveys – such surveys might scramble traditional pedagogical relations of power, but also create new modes of tyranny and aggression (Mendes and Hammett 2020; Page and Charteris 2021). There is an inherent ambivalence in transversality – transversality might provoke micropolitical revolution or become a new technology for control (Watson 2018: 22). As Janell Watson (2018) has paraphrased Deleuze and Guattari: 'It would be a mistake to think that transversality alone can save us' (21). Their cautious approach to claims of emancipation also offers tools for nuanced analyses of student voice work.

AFFECT

A central question of this book is: *What can voice(s) do?* This question is concerned with the capacity of voice to affect and to be affected: physically, conceptually, methodologically and textually. This question is a modification of another question asked by Deleuze and Guattari, which appropriates a question asked by the seventeenth-century philosopher Baruch Spinoza: 'What can a body do?' (Deleuze and Guattari 1980/1987: 256). The word 'body' encompasses human and non-human entities: living beings, emotional intensities, thought, voice and matter (Deleuze 1992a: 256). Human bodies do not have a monopoly on voice; this book explores how human voices are formed in relation to historical, material, textual and affective elements beyond human subjects. Deleuze and Guattari's question can be understood in relation to another question that they ask: 'Of what affects is a body capable?' (Deleuze and Guattari 1980/1987: 257). I replace their word 'body' with 'voice' to foreground my interests in the relations between voice and affect, and the conditions that enable the capacity of a body to speak and to act:

> We know nothing about a [voice] until we know what it can do, in other words, what its affects are, how they can or cannot enter into

composition with other affects, with the affects of another [voice], either to destroy that [voice] or to be destroyed by it, either to exchange actions and passions with it or to join with it in composing a more powerful [voice]. (Deleuze and Guattari, 1980/1987: 257)

Chapter 3 considers what the felt force of voice can do – that is, the pragmatic consequences of the physical voice: what words do to bodies, relations and subjectivities, and how words participate in ordering the world. Voice is felt before it is cognitively processed, affecting the body before the body articulates how they feel and who they are. Investigating the generative and destructive felt force of voice is important because of the profound educational consequences of feeling in schools for present subjectivities and lived futures. Sociologists of education have closely analysed the consequences of power relations and emotional intensities in schools: from the 'hidden injuries' (Furlong 1991: 296) connected to students' rejection of schooling, to the 'high affective' (Munns and Sawyer 2013: 24) relations and pedagogies that contribute to student engagement. In exploring what the felt force of voice does, this book contributes to discussions of the constitution of schooled subjectivities and the arrangements and blockages of pedagogical desire in schools. Exploring this question involves listening to and beyond the verbal and linguistic voice: attending to affect.

Affect is important to the work of this book, though my use of it is not always consistent with Deleuze and Guattari's account of it. Affect is the capacity of (human and/or more-than-human) bodies to affect or to be affected (Deleuze 1988). As a noun, affects can destroy or be destroyed, exchanged or conjoined (Deleuze and Guattari 1980/1987: 257); affect is an action and an ongoing process (Wolfe 2021: 40). Affect is simultaneously pre-personal, intimately personal and more-than-individual. Affect is autonomous – before and beyond human perception (Massumi 2002), even as it may sometimes be sensed as prehension – the 'almost felt' that is non-linguistic and somatic (Manning 2013; Renold and Ivinson 2019). *Affectus*, in Spinoza's terms, is felt as transitions, variations or passages from one state to another in encounter with another body (Deleuze 1988: 49). Affect may also linger as a fleeting feeling or a lasting impression – as *affectio* – becoming part of the formation of embodied emotional habits and dispositions (Watkins 2010). Affects are to be distinguished from 'emotions', which are the labelling of these sensations in language (Massumi 2002). Emotional articulations narrate affect;

emotions are generally named within the political boundaries of what is considered to be acceptable and unacceptable to be said (Ahmed 2004; Manning 2007). As Chapters 5 and 6 explore, emotions in schools (articulated accounts of somatic sensations) are intensely political – there are inconsistent norms and rules for the expression of emotion that may render Other bodies who are morose, frustrated, anxious or emotionally ambivalent: bodies that correlate with racialised, classed, queer and non-neurotypical bodies (Ahmed 2010; Mayes et al. 2020). Notwithstanding the politics of naming and describing the ambivalent movements of affect in and through schools, various concepts and instruments have been developed to attempt to measure a school's 'climate', 'ethos' or culture' – schools' elusive 'affective atmospheres' (Anderson 2009). In education, affect is 'ordinary' and elusive (Stewart 2007) and yet of weighty consequences for individual lives: a felt sense of 'affirmative relationality' is vital for students' flourishing in schools (Wolfe 2021: 42). Analysing how voice is intimately entangled with these politics of affect and emotion is a central concern of this book (see Chapters 3, 5 and 6).

AGENCEMENTS (ASSEMBLAGES)

The spoken voice is threaded through with affects, speaking from collective assemblages before, beyond and between human bodies. Deleuze and Guattari do not understand voice as 'expressed' by the rational Cartesian human subject via a self-contained, transparent, interior consciousness who thinks in language. Discussing Foucault's 'radical critique' of the phenomenological presumption of the interiority of the subject (Deleuze 1999/1986: 80), Deleuze and Guattari undo the assumption of a distinction between the inside and outside of subjectivity and relations, subjectivity and the world, and between the world (as reality) and texts written about the world (as representation) (1980/1987: 23). Rather than separate bodies (human and/or non-human) from the world and from representation, there are only collective *agencements* (the French word most frequently translated as 'assemblage') constantly arranging and rearranging desire and power. Agencements are 'ongoing process[es]' (Buchanan 2021: 21) whereby heterogeneous human and non-human elements – bodies, voices, texts and matter – constitute and reconstitute individuals, groups and societies; this use of the word 'agencements' foregrounds the dispersed agencies at work in any encounter (displacing the centrality of the human in notions of agency). In *Schizoanalytic Cartographies*

(1989/2013), Guattari uses the word *voix/voie* for voice/pathway – with the French allowing a 'homophonic link between path and enunciation' (3). This link between path and enunciation productively entwines the subjective and material (which were never separate) and conjoins the utterance with the path(s) of its formation – that is, the specific situation when and where the utterance is articulated. As the methodological work of Alicia Youngblood Jackson and Lisa Mazzei has persuasively demonstrated, thinking with Deleuze and Guattari (for example, Jackson and Mazzei 2013; Mazzei 2016; Mazzei and Jackson 2017), voice is what is spoken from collective agencements of enunciation – bodies, affects, discourses, environments, matter, objects, histories, memories, visions – rather than the 'expression' of an individual human subject (Deleuze and Guattari 1980/1987: 80–5). This reconceptualisation of voice matters because it focuses greater attention on differential material institutional conditions of voice – that is, how and why some voices are 'heard', while others are not.

Attention to agencements enables analyses of how subjectivities form in and through the entanglements of words and things in institutional life. In Guattari's essay 'Institutional Schizo-analysis', he 'reclaim[s] what was most important in Freud and Marx':

> ... that subjective formations don't, could not and should not coincide with an individual 'profile'. Subjectivity establishes itself, at a minimum, in a complex relation to the other, mother, father, family, caste relations, class struggles, in short all levels of social interaction. (Guattari 1985/1996: 269)

One's 'experience' is never one's own, nor separable from all zones in and beyond formal institutions where subjectifications are effected in dynamic intersectional movements. Experience and existence, voice and expression, for Deleuze and Guattari, are processual, non-foundational, and constituted in creative experimentation in material configurations (see also Bignall 2014; Semetsky 2003). The *I* that communicates and is addressed, then, is an *event* existing each moment at the intersection of a range of processes (Guattari 1995): agencements of enunciation composed of lines. Agencements of individuals, groups and institutions form, de-form and re-form in 'a multiplicity of dimensions, of lines and directions' (Deleuze and Parnet 2006/1977: 100). There are three types of lines that make up agencements of individuals or groups: the line of rigid segmentarity, the molecular line and the line of flight (see Deleuze and Guattari

1980/1987: 208–31; Deleuze and Parnet 2006/1977: 93–111). The line of rigid segmentarity is binary, linear, classificatory and hierarchical, dividing from all directions: adult/child, teacher/student, voice/silence. The second type of line – the molecular – traces subtle modifications and detours, slightly diverging from the line of rigid segmentarity through new linkages and configurations (Guattari 1989/2013: 52). A configuration where a student interviews a teacher, perhaps, might slightly differ from the traditional teacher/student relation, but remain close in relationship to the student–teacher pedagogical dyad (see Chapter 5). Lines of flight are the third type of line, where a rupture breaks with the segmentary or molecular line – in moments of immanent experimentation where things suddenly shift. These lines of flight may be productive or destructive and must be analysed for what they do in specific configurations. While distinct, these three lines overlap and are tangled, 'caught up in one another' (Deleuze and Parnet 2006/1977: 94). In Chapter 3 I explore the work of language (including words spoken) in effecting subjectifications in educational institutional life – that is, how words come to order and effect transformations to bodies in schools. Examining processes of communication and the 'lived surfaces' of everyday life in schools (Stewart 2007: 4), this book aims to contribute to broader conversations about the words, relations, educational configurations and environments that compound positive affects between bodies, augmenting the capacities of bodies to act and the mutual learning that is possible.

DESIRE

Deleuze and Guattari's attention to what flees and escapes from institutional capture – desire – is particularly potent for analysing the multivalent politics of education operating in and through student voice as an educational reform strategy. Departing from Freudian and Lacanian understandings of desire as individualised *lack* (wanting what one does not yet have), desire for Deleuze and Guattari is affirmative and productive. Desire is force and capacity seeking connection in mundane everyday processes that are inextricable from social and economic relations (Deleuze and Guattari 1980/1987: 229); Deleuze and Guattari re-engineer and entwine psychoanalytic libidinal economies of desire with Marxist theories of political economy, history and society (Buchanan 2013; Ringrose 2015). Desire 'is always assembled' (Deleuze and Guattari 1980/1987: 229) – that is, always in the process of moving and changing, never existing in a free and unbounded state. Desire forms the institution itself rather than being separate from, or an additional feature to, institutional relations (Deleuze and Guattari 1983: 63), moving in and through the dialectic of structure and agency, macroanalyses of schools and systems and microanalyses of power and resistance (Ringrose and Renold 2011). While at times imperceptible, desire is revolutionary: 'capable of calling into question the established order of society' (Deleuze and Guattari 1983: 116), and to form different relations between heterogeneous terms. Desire enables nuanced analysis of how voice moves and what it does in desiring-agencements.

Deleuze and Guattari's understanding of desire is interwoven with power as *puissance*: force, capacity or intensity (Surin 2011). Power is 'an affection of desire' (Deleuze 1994) and a component in complex perpetual reconfigurations of desire. Desire creates relations that enable the operations of power (Colebrook 2012: 215). Deleuze and Guattari's understanding of desire and power draws on seventeenth-century philosopher Baruch Spinoza's *potentia*: formed in immanent (here-and-now) relations, becoming perceptible in flashes, where a body's capacity to act increases (Deleuze 1988). *Potentia* is concerned with the capacity to move from relations of *potestas*: power in its forceful, formal, institutionalised mode – as in the fixed formation of student and teacher subject positions (see also Braidotti 2019; Deleuze 1988: 128–9). There can be no analysis of politics and power without analysis of desire, since it is these 'affects or drives' that 'form part of the infrastructure [here, a school] itself' (Deleuze and Guattari 1983: 63). It is these micropolitical workings of power and desire that this book considers – particularly as connected to the concept of voice.

Thinking with desire enables apprehension of moments of abundance and potentiality, rather than operating from a logic of deficit (for example, assuming a pre-existing lack in students and educators) in student voice encounters. I have questioned: what relations compound the capacity of a body (including but exceeding a student or educator) to speak, feel, listen, and act powerfully? But analyses of configurations of desire are also concerned with how desire becomes blocked and recoded as lack – for example, assuming that students have pre-existing deficits in their communication, that a student's negative evaluation of teaching exposes pre-existing deficits in the educator's instructional methods, and that the educator must satisfy the desire of the Oedipal student subject who lacks pedagogical satisfaction (Mayes 2018). Desire can be made to desire its own repression in social relations that become internalised in psychic repressions – to shut one's mouth and to love it (Deleuze and Guattari 1983). Studying movements of desire and self-censorship is significant in a time when young people are framed, at times, as politically apathetic, or alternatively as holding onto cultural, religious, ecological and/or political attachments that are considered over-emotional, risky or extreme (see Chapters 5 and 7), and at a time when pre-service and in-service educators are encouraged to form and develop their teacher subjectivities according to predetermined professional teaching standards (Mayes 2019b: 4). Attending to desire as productive also enables analysis of the popularity of student voice in a marketised schooling system, where schools seek to distinguish themselves from other schools in processes of perpetual promotion. Analysing desire has taught me to understand how, with the commodification of education, social democratic ideals of voice, equity and justice are intertwined with market-driven competition and choice. Desire is produced for the school that listens to its consumers.

REFORM AND RIGHTS

It is important to acknowledge, from the outset, that Deleuze was certainly not a philosopher of democracy in its liberal democratic form, and railed against notions of reform, rights and opinion. In his scathing 1992 account of what he described as the emerging 'societies of control', Deleuze writes, '[t]he administrations in charge never cease announcing supposedly necessary reforms' of 'environments of enclosure – prison, hospital, factory, school, family': 'to reform schools, to reform industries, hospitals, armed forces, prisons' (Deleuze 1992b: 4, 3). For Deleuze, these reforms are 'stupid and hypocritical' not only because they are made by 'people who claim to be representative' and not those directly affected (Deleuze, in Deleuze and Foucault 1977: 208–9), but also because those making the reforms fail to apprehend that 'these institutions are finished' (Deleuze 1992b: 4). This book brings these critiques into relation with a movement that has, in many ways, celebrated notions of rights and opinion for the purposes of institutional reform – wondering what happens after these rights are given.

For Deleuze, the autonomous liberal humanist subject who possesses 'rights' is a 'pure abstraction' (Deleuze, in Boutang 1996) removed from the messiness of what happens in institutional life. Deleuze declared human rights to be matters of jurisprudence – the human 'invention of rights, invention of the law' – rather than universal (Deleuze, in Boutang 1996; Deleuze 1995). The declaration that rights are a matter of jurisprudence is not a denigration of rights, but instead gestures to their historical and cultural contingency, and draws attention to the political question of what attributing rights to a group *does* – that is, the 'immanent modes of existence of people provided with rights' (see Deleuze and Guattari 1994/2009: 107; Perry-Hazan 2021). Deleuze and Guattari were also highly critical of notions of public 'opinion' as perpetuating common-sense modes of thought; in *What is Philosophy?* they critique opinions as the recognition and articulation of what has already been understood (Deleuze 1994/2009). For them, opinions are used by people to shield themselves from chaos. They invoke D. H. Lawrence: 'people are constantly putting up an umbrella that shelters them and on the underside of which they draw a firmament and write their conventions and opinions' (Deleuze and Guattari 1994/2009: 203). They write that, in contradistinction to the writing of opinions on the underside of the umbrella, poets and artists 'make a slit in the umbrella, they tear open the firmament itself, to let in a bit of free and windy chaos' (203). Yet, Deleuze and Guattari do not valorise a sudden creative leap from established conventions and relations – as in (mis)readings that the 'line of flight' is necessarily creative and liberatory. They warn that lines of flight 'always risk abandoning their creative potentialities and turning into a line of death, being turned into a line of destruction pure and simple (fascism)' (Deleuze and Guattari 1980/1987: 506). If voice is the expression of opinions by the autonomous individual possessing 'rights', Deleuze and Guattari are not interested in it. Yet, their philosophical resources enable dynamic analyses of what happens in schools when slits are made in the institution's umbrella of common-sense modes of thought.

In using the work of Deleuze and Guattari, I acknowledge the contested relationship between their work and the desire for democracy. Indeed, there have been 'many mediators and interpreters' of their work in political theory (Conio 2015a: 26). There have been debates in Deleuze and Guattari studies surrounding Deleuze and Guattari's relationship with Marxism (Thoburn 2003) and anarchism (May 1989), the political efficacy of the politics of the 'minor' that Deleuze and Guattari articulate (Mengue 2005), the political implications of their conceptions of 'becoming-democratic' and 'becoming-revolutionary' in *What is Philosophy?* (1994/2009; Patton 2008), and whether the 'new earth and a people that does not yet exist' (Deleuze and Guattari 1994/2009: 108) is politically possible (Baugh 2016). Deleuze and Guattari's politics have been extended and appropriated using the language of 'democracy', including Hardt and Negri's post-Marxist trilogy (Hardt and Negri 2000, 2004, 2009) and the anti-globalisation movement (for example, Conio 2015b). This book does not attempt to conduct an exegesis of Deleuze's views on democracy in relation to these debates. In short, I agree with Paul Patton and Simone Bignall that Deleuze rejects 'actually existing democracies', but that this does not negate the 'prospect that other actualizations of the concept of democracy might be possible' (Bignall 2014: 105). Patton (2000) describes Deleuze and Guattari as not envisaging 'global revolutionary change' but rather engaging in philosophical and creative experimentation 'played out in between economic and political institutions and the sub-institutional movements of desire and affect' (7). Their work offers 'a political ontology' for analysing and accounting for creative and potentially transformative forces and movements in education (Patton 2000: 9).

## *Thinking With and After Deleuze and Guattari*

The work undertaken in this book is indebted to previous scholarship that has engaged in 'thinking with' (Jackson and Mazzei 2012) Deleuze and Guattari for education across a range of conceptual and geographical territories over the past twenty years at least. Tracing an ancestral tree for the movement of Deleuze and Guattarian concepts into the field of education is counter to their thinking (Deleuze and Guattari 1980/1987). Speaking only for my own reading of where their thought has moved in education, Elizabeth St. Pierre (1997) and Donna Alvermann (2000) could be positioned as early adopters of Deleuze and Guattari's thought in education. In the 2000s, various concepts were taken up and moved across educational territories – from the rhizome (for example, Gough 2004; Honan 2007; Knight 2009), to nomadic inquiry (Roy 2003; Semetsky 2008), to affect (Albrecht-Crane and Slack 2007; Hickey-Moody 2007a), to desire (Zembylas 2007b). Work in the 2000s took up their concepts to think differently about early childhood (Leafgren 2009; Olsson 2009), literacy (Masny and Cole 2009), art and embodiment (Springgay 2008), teachers' work (Webb 2009), dis/ability (Goodley 2007; Hickey-Moody 2007b), resistance (Renold and Ringrose 2008), Whiteness (Mazzei 2008), educational methodology (Jackson 2003;

Jackson and Mazzei 2009) and pedagogical encounters (Davies and Gannon 2009).

I took up the thought of Deleuze and Guattari in the early 2010s – a decade of proliferation in educational research using Deleuze and Guattari (Carlin and Wallin 2014; Coleman and Ringrose 2013; Semetsky and Masny 2013). Educational scholars were using Deleuze and Guattari to further rethink classroom and playground configurations (de Freitas 2012; Knight 2016; Mulcahy 2012), student well-being (Lenz Taguchi and Palmer 2014), educational governance through data (Sellar 2014; Thompson and Cook 2012a), difference (Bright 2020), Blackness and the politics of race (Ibrahim 2014, 2015), matter in schools (Cole 2019), teacher education and teachers' work (Strom and Martin 2017; Webb 2009), and student feminist-queer desire and activism (Renold 2018; Ringrose and Renold 2014), amongst myriad other conceptual and pedagogical experiments. As Chapter 2 further explores, Deleuze and Guattari's thought has been brought into relation with other theorists and resonant movements associated with the ontological turn – including feminist 'new' materialisms, posthumanism and intradisciplinary turns to affect and research creation.

My thinking in this book is connected and indebted not only to the work of, and work stirred by, Deleuze and Guattari, but also to critiques and extensions of their work; the subtitle of this book includes the preposition 'after' to honour the processual emergence of thought across temporalities.[11] This book was written after their lives – in some ways 'takes after' (is inspired by) their collective style of writing and working – and was written 'after' a period of intense work with their concepts. Chapter 2 situates the work of this book in relation to critiques of the ontological turn as ahistorical and apolitical. I engage with Unangax̂ scholar Eve Tuck's (2010) account of her break-up with Deleuze and extensions of Deleuze and Guattari's work by queer, Black and First Nations scholars including Jasbir Puar, Alexander Wehilye, Kara Keeling, Daryle Rigney and Steve Hemmings. I think with Deleuze and Guattari in troubling the ideal liberal humanist 'Man' that informs student voice in Chapters 3 and 4, and also with Jamaican writer and cultural theorist Sylvia Wynter's critique of 'the West's liberal monohumanist' Man (Wynter and McKittrick 2015: 23). Chapter 4 works with critiques of Deleuze and Guattari from the time of their writing – including Gayatri Chakravorty Spivak's (1987) critique of Deleuze and Foucault in 'Can the Subaltern Speak?' In unsettling notions of dialogue in student voice in Chapter 5, I think with Deleuze and Guattari, as well as with poet, novelist and theorist Édouard Glissant and queer studies scholar Kara Keeling. In addressing how to think-feel-speak-listen-relate differently in a warming world, Chapter 7 discusses the Ngarrindjeri concept of *Yannarumi*, 'speaking as Country' – as articulated by Ngarrindjeri scholar Daryle Rigney, Ngarrindjeri scholar Steve Hemming and settler scholars Simone Bignall and Katie Maher. I explain in Chapter 2 how my thinking is informed by those positioned as 'participants' in student voice practice and research in vernacular forms of theorising. I seek to think with but also 'after' Deleuze and Guattari, partly because I am committed to attempting to commitment to enacting research that intervenes in and beyond institutional political life – to make a political difference with (human) others. As Jessica Ringrose (in Ringrose and Zarabadi 2018) has put it: 'We [researchers] do not have the luxury of sitting around and playing with theory' (214). As Bessie Dernikos, Daniel Ferguson and Marjorie Siegel put it, in the face of escalating eco-social-viral-injustices, we (researchers) must '*act,* not only think, with theory' (Dernikos et al. 2019: 434, original emphasis).

## *Overview of Chapters*

This book stages a dissonant dialogue about the concept of voice between the students and educators with whom I have been privileged to speak, Deleuze and Guattari's thought, other theorists, the theories (standpoint theories, dialogue and critical pedagogy) that have previously offered foundations for student voice, and examples of the movements of voice in educational institutions. For Deleuze, a 'dialogue' is deliberately fraught with perplexity and misunderstanding. Deleuze and Claire Parnet, in *Dialogues II* (2006/1977), disparage the logics of the conventional interview or dialogue. Their account of the limits of dialogue is helpful for thinking about the limits of the encounter between Deleuze and Guattari's thought and voice in education. In a dialogue, according to Deleuze and Parnet, the participants are 'never in the same rhythm', 'always out of step'; what happens is not 'grasped' 'at all in the same way' (Deleuze and Parnet 2006/1977: 13). Bringing the work of Deleuze and Guattari, and those who extend and critique their work, into relation with examples of what is done in the name of student voice generates productive, if perplexing, encounters. Deleuze and Guattari's work, in dialogue with others, troubles some of the liberal humanist ontological assumptions of these formative influences and generates other possibilities that I explore in the chapters that follow.

Throughout this book I include transcribed renderings of spoken utterances and photographs of objects – 'data' from my previous research – from particular moments where students and I played with puppets, drew pictures and moved objects. The research context of each photograph is noted in the captions. When I quote transcribed utterances from students speaking with puppets, I do not understand these transcribed words as 'representing' the views of the 'research participants' who created them (see Chapter 2). Each photograph memorialises affects from particular conjunctions of bodies and materials. Each photograph simultaneously has a continuing life of its own – affective intensities, speeds and slownesses – that unfold and move when brought into relation with the words of this book. I encourage the reader to not (only) consider what the photographs might represent, but also to note what they provoke, for you, in combination with the words of this book and the dynamic configuration(s) of your reading (including your memories of research, teaching and learning, the environments where you read this book, and so on). Working with transcripts and photographs from puppet scenarios is an attempt to repeatedly remind the reader that these 'data' are (literally) dramatic productions (rather than 'authentic' representations of the experiences of others), taken up and reanimated to generate new connections and thought.

Chapter 2 is concerned with the mis/uses that have been made of the voice of the child and young person in research – as an extractible resource (for 'science'), as liberatory tool (with a problematic theory of change), and as loaded concept to move beyond and/or to creatively experiment with. This chapter reviews the mis/uses made of and with voice in work associated with the ontological turn (including postqualitative inquiry, feminist 'new' materialisms, PhEMaterialisms, posthumanism, affective methodologies and research-creation) and how Deleuze and Guattari's work has been mobilised in these mis/uses. I give an account of, and then reread, a specific research practice from my research (the use of material puppets) with and through these critiques – from queer feminist, First Nations, Black Studies and Marxist theoretical vantage points – particularly critiques that the ontological turn is dehumanising and depoliticising. I consider three possible responses to critiques of the ontological turn: defensiveness, walking away, and extension and expansion. This chapter considers the potential of attuning to microfascisms in 'staying with the trouble' (Haraway 2016) of the history, ethics and politics of voice in education.

Chapter 3 considers the ordering of voices and bodies in the history of education: what happens when words are spoken, and what spoken words do to bodies. I explore histories of common sense surrounding what a student's voice is supposed to sound like and what a student is meant to say; this common sense conditions how students, educators and schools respond to calls to 'give' their students a voice in the present. I draw upon Deleuze and Guattari's pragmatic linguistics to give an account of the politics and materiality of voice in schools – the felt force of sounds issued forth from human bodies, viscerally apprehended by bodies. This chapter considers the historical and sociological murmurs that intersect with the concept of voice – in particular, the order words of age, ability and emotionality, alongside institutional imperatives for schools and educators to construct data that order complex subjectivities and events. I am interested in this institutional common sense because it operates as a felt force in student voice practices, compelling the universalised 'student', 'child' and 'young person' to speak and act in accordance with this order.

Chapters 4, 5 and 6 each consider a particular concept associated with student voice, as they move in and through specific research studies: representing (Chapter 4), understanding (Chapter 5) and evaluating (Chapter 6). In Chapter 4 I work with data from a commissioned study of school students' and principals' views on student representation on school governance councils in the state of Victoria, Australia. This study contributed to a policy change in the state of Victoria in 2018 that made it mandatory for schools to have student representatives on school governance councils. This chapter interrogates the logics of representation that undergird advocacy for student representation on school governance councils (and other governance boards), thinking with Deleuze's philosophy of difference, Sylvia Wynter's critique of liberal monohumanist Man, and Gayatri Chakravorty Spivak's critique of Deleuze and Foucault's conception of difference speaking for itself.

Chapter 5 explores the politics and ambivalences of attempts to support students and educators in schools to 'express' themselves and come to 'understand' each other through dialogue. I draw attention, via a perplexing conversation staged as a puppet scenario, to the limits of dialogue in voice endeavours, and the intractability of understanding. The chapter pivots from trying to 'understand' the student (as a site of deficit and risk) to the politics of seeing, listening and attuning in schools – with particular attention to contemporary atmos-fears. Questions are raised about whose understandings are privileged in classroom and school life, the affective sensorium surrounding classroom events, and the subjectifications effected in the dialogical encounter. Thinking beyond classroom and school 'climate', I consider the targeting (and creation) of the student (so-called) at risk of radicalisation to violent extremism via schools – through the preventative logic of listening to students. Thinking with Édouard Glissant and Kara Keeling, I argue for the value of opacity and the right not to be compelled to be understandable.

Chapter 6 is concerned with this logic of evaluation in and of schools, particularly evaluations of and with student voice. Thinking with what happened during one school's evaluation of two reform interventions, I consider the majoritarian logics of change in contemporary educational reform that looks for growth according to predetermined targets. Thinking with Deleuze and Guattari's analysis of desire as productive, as well as with the concept of minoritarian evaluations, I turn from the majoritarian evaluation typed on A4 pieces of paper to a smaller piece of paper: a RESP token (a behavioural token). Working with this RESP token, I explore an immanent, minoritarian mode of evaluation that notes moments of joy when bodies' capacity to act compound (Deleuze 1988; Deleuze and Guattari 1980/1987). Minoritarian evaluations, I suggest, are evaluations that exceed or escape from the targets or criteria for success set by a dominant party (for example, a school or educational system). The chapter concludes with doubts about the notion of school reform.

Chapter 7 considers the political potency of contemporary student activisms. I think through the possibilities and ambivalences of school-aged students' climate justice activism which, like student voice in schools, is a tangled moving mesh of many politics and many lines. I take up three photographs of cardboard signs from student strikes that invoke Dr. Seuss's (1972/2012) *The Lorax* and the phrase, 'I speak for the trees' to explore the politics and perplexities of student activism. I examine how media representations and academic analyses 'spoke for' the school strikers, as well as the politics of the school strikers' speech. I consider how schools steered and at times attempted to co-opt students' activism, and what exceeds and escapes institutional capture. The book concludes with the concept of con-spiracies (Choy 2016, 2020, 2021) – breathing with others: never an individual or human affair, not always harmonious, not always easy, but vital for compounding the capacities of all to breath-speak-listen-relate-act-live together in a troubled world.

## Notes

1. Across this book, the term 'educator' is used as a broad term that encompasses those working in early childhood, primary or tertiary education. The term 'teacher' is used when specifically referring to school-based educators.
2. 'Radical', like 'voice', is a concept that moves and morphs in meaning across political life and the history and sociology of education (see Fielding and Moss 2011: 40–4; Mayes 2019a: 157–9; Williams 1983). To pursue 'radical' politics (Latin *radix*, 'roots') can be to struggle for fundamental change at the roots of society (whether from the political left or right) and (sometimes) to return to past practices (sometimes 'traditional' and sometimes 'progressive'). Radical left political movements are multiple in goals, forms and strategies – from seeking communist revolution to socialist democracy to anarchist dismantlement of the state. As Deborah Youdell summarises, these left political movements 'identify relations of domination, oppression and exploitation, understood in a range of ways, as the necessary locus of radical change; change that would no doubt shift fundamentally the shape and nature of society and the political system that is a part of it' (Youdell 2011: 18). Education is central to radical politics – as a site where educators and students can 'imagine and enact a future which rests on very different assumptions and values to those which define the basis and the boundaries of the current system' (Fielding and Moss 2011: 40). This book's use of the term 'radical' in relation to education is indebted to and entangled with Michael Fielding's account and practice of 'radical democratic education' and 'radical collegiality' (Fielding 1999a; Fielding and Moss 2011: 40–57), and to Deborah Youdell's account of education as 'a site for counter-political action' (2011: 17). Yet, as Chapter 5 explores, to be identified as 'radical'/'radicalised' in educational spaces can lead to intensified monitoring and surveillance as a 'risky' subject (see Youdell 2011: 19–22).
3. My mother is Russian and emigrated to Australia as a child from Shanghai, and experienced the racist taunts associated with migrant difference in 1950s Australia; my father is British. While my mother and her extended family speak Russian, I cannot speak Russian. I was born and spent the first twelve years of life in Hong Kong under British colonial lease. I have benefited from the colonial racial privileges of whiteness both in Hong Kong and Australia.
4. Class is a complex and contested concept in Australia. This book

uses the term 'middle class', after Aileen Moreton-Robinson, 'in the Weberian sense to refer to one's social status and prestige based on capital, occupation, skill and education' (2000/2020: xvii), with the acknowledgement of the dynamic entanglements of class with settler colonialism and Whiteness (see Threadgold and Gerrard 2022).

5. To describe a school as low socio-economic homogenises a community and strips and de-politicises the historical, socio-economic and political circumstances, policies and practices through which certain communities experience disadvantage more acutely, while other settings and groups enjoy privilege and sustain and enhance their children's advantages. See Chapter 3 for a further discussion of the force of language in schooling.

6. A narrow genealogy is deliberately traced here – indeed, there are myriad versions of standpoint theories that have critiqued and rearticulated standpoint theories – including Patricia Hill Collins's and Kimberlé Crenshaw's Black feminist standpoint and intersectional theories (Collins 2000; Collins and Bilge 2016; Crenshaw 1991), Indigenous standpoint theories and Indigenist research (Nakata 2007; Rigney 1999), and Donna Haraway's situated knowledges (Haraway 1988). In tracing this narrow genealogy here, I am drawing attention to the reconceptualisation of the school student as an agentic *being* to foreground some of the potential issues that may accompany such a reconceptualisation.

7. This photograph was taken during a school visit as part of a three-year research evaluation of the VicSRC's Teach the Teacher programme (for further details, see Black and Mayes 2020; Finneran et al. 2021; Mayes et al. 2019, 2021).

8. While Deleuze developed the concept of transversality in his analysis of the sensory dynamism of signs in Marcel Proust's work (Deleuze 1964/2008), here I focus on Guattari's clinical practice and theorisation of transversality.

9. Fielding has analysed historical examples of radically democratic, intergenerational pedagogical relations in and beyond schools, based in participatory rather than representative traditions of democracy (see, for example, Fielding 2005; Fielding and Moss 2011).

10. However, there is more to say about Guattari, Deleuze and Freire's different relationships to the work of Hegel (see also Buchanan 2014; Cole and Bradley 2018b).

11. See Peter Kraftl (2020: 2–7) for a thorough discussion of the possibilities and limitations of 'after' when used as a preposition in relation to childhood.

## 2

# Mis/using Voices and Theories in Research with Children and Young People

Ten years ago, I regularly sat at a small table in a meeting room in a school library with small groups of secondary students who had been part of student voice initiatives at their school, for formalised research focus groups. Students and I sat with seven puppets and one marionette (borrowed from my university's library), as well as sheets of paper, coloured markers, postcards, an iPad and my university laptop. After a conversation about how they defined 'student voice' and their recollections of being a researcher as part of the school's student voice group, I invited students to speak, draw or compose a scenario relating to student voice, using any of the materials in the room. I told students that the scenarios could build on their personal experiences, or that they could compose a fictionalised story or explore an issue that they felt to be important surrounding student voice. Scenarios could be composed in written, visual or audio-visual form (e.g., write a narrative, draw a picture, video a puppet scenario, record a radio interview). Many groups elected to use the puppets and marionette for their scenario-creation, performing scenes that seemed to parody teachers' responses to students' speech in classrooms. During one conversation when I asked students whether the puppet scenarios were a form of data, one student said that they 'show what happens daily in our school' (see Figure 2.1).

Before, during and after these conversations, I questioned the ethics and politics of writing about what students said and produced in such research encounters. There are many uses that have been made of the voice of the child, and many theories to account for what voice *does* in and through research. I did not want to treat students' words as extractible resources, objectified and abstracted from the specific material circumstances of their embodied formation. As I explain further below, I hoped to position students as theorists of their own lives and experiences; later that year, students viewed and analysed each other's scenarios (see below). Yet, I also was wary of making claims that positioning students as theorists of their own lives was necessarily liberating, or that co-theorising would necessarily

*Voices and Theories in Research with Young People*

*Figure 2.1* A screenshot from a video of a puppet scenario, created by a group of students. Four puppets (sheep, chicken, boy and marionette) are positioned around a table, starting a lesson.

change their school (Mayes 2016b). I found scholarship that reconceptualised voice – thinking with Deleuze and Guattari and Karen Barad, amongst others – helped me work with the simultaneous possibilities and perplexities of voice. Voice, reconceptualised after the ontological turn, emerges from relations among objects, spaces, affects, bodies, discourses, texts and theory, in dynamically shifting arrangements and rearrangements. The ontological turn is, of course, not a single turn but a multiplicity of turns, re-turns and detours; the ontological turn is a broad term for diverse interdisciplinary bodies of work that privilege questions of being, relationality and intraconnectedness, beyond the atomised liberal humanist subject and beyond binaries of male/female, body/mind, nature/culture, civilised/uncivilised, normal/abnormal, human/machine, human/environment, researcher/researched, entangling matter–meaning, words–affect, language–matter, human–more-than-human.[1] Yet, to turn attention to ontology raises its own ethical and political questions.

In this chapter, I re-turn to research conducted with students and puppets in 2013 – more than ten years ago – and read this work again through critiques of the ontological turn from queer feminist, First Nations, Black Studies and Marxist theoretical vantage points. I use Karen Barad's word 're-turning' – which is not to reflect or go back to the past as separate, but rather: 're-turning as in turning it over and over again' – like earthworms turning the soil, 'ingesting and excreting it, tunnelling through it, burrowing, all means of aerating the soil, allowing oxygen in, opening it up and breathing new life into it' (Barad 2014: 168). Elsewhere, Barad describes re-turning as 'a troubling matter, a matter of troubling' (2018: 81). I re-turn to material remnants of my past research – animated in particular configurations of space-times-matter – and think with the 'troubled histories' that re-turn in and through 'voice' research practices (McDermott 2020b: 350), and the tensions felt in mis/using concepts from the ontological turn. I deploy a forward slash in the term mis/uses to evoke the ambivalent cutting together and apart (Barad 2014) of 'uses' and 'misuses' – any methodological 'use' of voice may simultaneously be an injustice, appropriation or evisceration, and must be analysed for its consequences. This chapter accounts for but also troubles my mis/uses of voice in research. I give an account of my mis/uses of puppets and the transcribed spoken voices of students animating these puppets, since photographs of these puppets and transcribed words spoken by young people appear in this chapter and later chapters of this book. I consider the risk of microfascism in ostensibly 'new' thought and methodological practices, thinking with Deleuze and Guattari's discussion of the danger of thinking that one has undone the binary, molar line. Perhaps this chapter is less about methodology (explaining to you what I did and why), and more a 'reckoning with my intellectual inheritances' (Truman 2021, personal communication).[2] In doing so, this chapter grapples with the politics and ethical response-abilities of thinking with dead white male philosophers in troubling times.

In what follows, I review and question the mis/uses that have been made of the voice of the child and young person in research – as an extractible resource (for 'science'), as liberatory tool (with a problematic theory of change), and as loaded concept to move beyond and/or to creatively experiment with. I then further introduce the ontological turn and my mis/uses of voice in one study. I reread a specific research practice from my research (voice and puppets) with and through critical and creative engagements with the ontological turn and clarify my stance in this book towards the history, ethics and politics of voice in education. I conclude with a discussion of attending to microfascisms in grappling with the consequences of mis/uses of voice in research.

*Voices and Theories in Research with Young People*

## *Historicising voice in research with children and young people*

### EXTRACTIBLE RESOURCE

Sounds escape from mouths as vocal cords – folds of tissue in the throat – vibrate with the movement of breath. These sounds that issue forth from human flesh have been extractible resources for research, particularly in attempts to order bodies. In studies of normative patterns of cognitive (Piaget 1977), psychosexual (Freud 1925/1968) and linguistic (Chomsky 1965) development, voice has been detached from the body of the child. Voice moves from its embodied manifestation – sound escaping from flesh – to become a research object extracted, objectified and analysed by the allegedly distanced researcher. Such detachments of the voice from the body for analysis have aimed to establish the origins of adult behaviour and the stages of natural processes of development, through observation and scientific experimentation (see Chapter 3).

These (so-called) objective studies of the child's voice were critiqued by those in the New Sociology of Childhood as delimiting and defining young people's cognition, sexuality, speech and bodies, in order to render them comprehensible and manageable (see Malone et al. 2020, ch. 2, for a synthesis of the New Sociology of Childhood). Such representations were argued to ossify and judge the child's capacities from the adult researcher's standpoint, who speaks and writes about the child. These representations were argued to dismiss children's everyday realities and ways of knowing that exceed established normative understandings. To use Deleuze and Guattari's term from their critique of Freud's mode of analysis, such extractions and representations of the child's voice are examples of *interpretosis*: interpretations that capture and attempt to stabilise the subject's pathology, identity, or the meaning of what they say or do in time according to a particular interpretive framework (Deleuze and Guattari 1980/1987). In the case of Freud's interpretation of Little Hans, a Viennese child with a fear of horses, Little Hans's utterances are 'reduced to a prefabricated and predetermined grid of interpretation' that the child 'cannot escape' (Deleuze 2007: 89): the 'family-territory', so that everything is interpreted as representative of the mother, father and Oedipus (90). One line of escape from these extractivist modes of research on children and young people's voices was/is to attempt to reclaim and return voice back to the speaking subject.

### LIBERATORY TOOL FOR CHANGE

'Liberating' the voice of the child has been connected, by its advocates, to feminist standpoint theories and notions of women's voice, as well as civil rights, First Nations sovereignty and rights, LGBTQI+ (lesbian, gay, bisexual, transgender, queer and intersex) rights, and disability rights movements. When applied to research with children and young people, the voice of the child is reconceptualised as a useful tool for the child and young person, who is repositioned as a *being* (not developmental *becoming*) with agency (see Chapter 1). There is a theory of change here; as Unangax̂ scholar Eve Tuck and K. Wayne Yang have put it: 'a belief or perspective about how a situation can be adjusted, corrected, or improved' (Tuck 2009; Tuck and Yang 2014a: 13). There is a theory of change (sometimes explicit and sometimes implicit) in research that is reconceptualised as conducted 'with' the voices of children and young people. This theory is that the adult researcher can liberate hitherto subjugated voices; now empowered, these voices can speak forth their experience and knowledge to the researcher, and the researcher can publish these voices in the service of political transformation. As Tuck and Yang write of this theory of change, '[r]eporting on that pain with detailed qualitative data and in people's "real voices" is supposed to yield needed material or political resources' – particularly when they are stories of 'pain and humiliation' (Tuck and Yang 2014b: 812). For example, according to this theory of change, if school leaders or policy makers could only just 'hear the voices' of students about their negative experiences of schooling (via a student voice researcher, or via student-led research reporting back to school leaders and policy makers), school leaders and policy makers would be emotionally moved to act and make changes that respond and act on students' concerns. Yet, 'serving up pain stories on a silver platter for the settler colonial academy' may better serve the researcher (and school leader and policy maker) than those researched, with these shared stories becoming commodified plunder (Tuck and Yang 2014b: 812). Presenting pain stories to teachers, school leaders and policy makers may momentarily move individuals, but may leave intact entrenched institutional habits of being, knowing, speaking, listening and relating. As Kakali Bhattacharya (2021) puts it, 'it is painfully apparent to many of us who reside on multiple margins that no amount of transparency or rich, thick description has really changed the status quo for us' (181). The researcher can misinterpret and essentialise who the speaker is and what they are trying to say, coming to speak for them (Alcoff 1991). The researcher purports to centre the young person's voices and their problems – but simultaneously is the one privileged to make the selections and interpretations of these voices (Mazzei and Jackson 2012).

## *Reconceptualising Voice with the Ontological Turn*

Theories of change at work when 'liberating' the voice of the child were being troubled at the same time as other ontological reconceptualisations of voice were emerging; voice and spoken language were becoming concepts for methodological experimentation. In the early 2000s, in her landmark article 'Rhizovocality', Alicia Youngblood Jackson (2003) conceptually mapped the emerging sense, amongst feminist poststructural researchers, of the ethical limits and political insufficiencies of the concept of voice in qualitative inquiry, tracing the influence of, for example, critiques of emancipatory feminist research by feminists of colour (for example, hooks 1990), postcolonial feminists (for example, Spivak 1987), Derrida's critique of being-as-presence (1967/1973), and feminist deconstruction of phenomenological 'experience' (for example, Scott 1992). From this entangled map of the movement of voice, Jackson coined the term 'rhizovocality', bringing together Deleuze and Guattari's rhizome (1980/1987) with vocality: the signifier rhizovocality 'offers a vision of performative utterances that consist of unfolding and irrupting threads' (Jackson 2003: 707). In 2009, Alicia Jackson and Lisa Mazzei edited a collection of essays from the USA, UK, Canada and Australia, describing contributing authors as not giving in 'to a paralysis that can occur by the seemingly limitless interpretations and inadequacies of voice, but in a Deleuzian fashion, [. . .] exploit[ing] what is produced by the trouble of (or with) voice' (Mazzei and Jackson 2009: 3). In recent years, Deleuze and Guattari and Karen Barad's work, amongst the work of others, has inspired radical rethinking and revisioning of questions of ontology, epistemology and ethics.[3]

After these reconceptualisations, spoken utterances can be theorised as spoken from collective assemblages of enunciation, with the utterance inextricable from its assemblages.[4] With this reconceptualising of voice comes the suspension of the assumption that there is a prior rational, self-knowing, autonomous and human agent to recognise, and the affirmation of a different conception of agency and ethical responsibility from humanist research (Strom et al. 2019). The child as subject is decentred and entangled relationality is foregrounded (Spyrou 2017). More 'measured' and 'modest' claims about going '"beyond"' voice and agency are called for (Kraftl 2013: 14). Agency is reconceptualised not as the possession of speaking subjects, but as materially distributed, assembled and networked (see chapter 5 of Spyrou 2018), 'de-reified, contingent and uncertain' (Malone et al. 2020: 91). A radical relationality is affirmed, embracing not only human bodies and voices, but also the intertwining of matter, affects and signs in research intra-actions (Kuntz and Presnall 2012). Ethics are not able to be predetermined or externalised, but are predicated in entanglement; researchers become 'responsible to entanglements of which we [researchers] are a part' (Barad, in Dolphijn and van der Tuin 2012: 52). Shifting the focus from human subjects (in isolation) and from their spoken accounts of their experiences (their voices) has been argued to shift 'thinking about education into more insecure territories' (Pedersen and Pini 2017: 1051), even as it offers the possibilities of reconceptualising 'learners as emergent in relational fields in which non-human materials are inevitably at play' (Gough and Gough 2017: 1119).

As a consequence of these reconceptualisations, voice and spoken language have become concepts for experimentation: for example, as without a subject (Mazzei 2016), as wild, sensory events (Hackett et al. 2021), and as thoroughly material (de Freitas and Curinga 2015). Analysing voice only becomes possible 'in the middle of things, in the threshold, as theoretical concepts and data constitute one another in our analytical practice of thinking with theory' (Mazzei 2020: 198). Ethics, too, become a matter of immanent response-ability, arising in situated attentiveness and receptiveness to what happens. It becomes an ethical imperative, according to John Weaver and Nathan Snaza (2017), to let *the world speak* in order to 'face the *political* task of seeking just, sustainable, democratic relations among all actors – human and not – abiding by the earth', attuning to the precarious exposures and entanglements of humans and the more-than-human (1063, original emphasis). Yet, in recent years, both scholars who identify with the ontological turn, and those who do not, have questioned the ethical and political ambivalences of this work, as I explore later in this chapter. But first, I further contextualise my mis/uses of voice in one study.

## Mis/uses of Voice in One Study

In my doctoral research, I experimented with the concept of voice as arranged and extended with material puppets in research encounters in one secondary school that I introduced in Chapter 1 (Mayes 2016a, 2016b). This study explored students', teachers' and parents' accounts of a four-year student voice initiative at their school – that is, a particular institutional programme where students were encouraged to 'have a voice' in teaching and learning processes at their school, and where some students were apprenticed as co-researchers to devise, design and conduct their own research inquiries. Formal research methods included sixty-eight interviews and focus groups with over 100 participants. Beyond spoken human voices, I considered the co-constitution of spoken voices with matter, discourse, affect and space, across temporalities. These focus groups and interviews did not *elicit* voices (which presumes an interior voice waiting to be released); rather, I understood these methods to be events where concepts and scenarios were *created* in entanglement with the human and the more-than-human.

Towards the end of the year of fieldwork, students who had been part of these focus group discussions and I met together for a whole-day collaborative analysis workshop. In the first two hours of the collaborative analysis day, students worked in analytical groups, viewing and responding to the scenarios of other groups. Students wrote, on A3 pieces of paper, their responses to the following prompts:

- Initial reactions/emotions: Does it remind us of any of our own experiences?
- Big ideas in this scenario.
- Questions for discussion that this scenario makes us think of.
- Connections between this scenario and other scenarios (for example, similar ideas/words/characters) and differences.

This analysis was less about having students 'code' the scenarios, which would reduce the singularity of each scenario (Honan 2007); rather, students and I mapped the connections between the scenarios, between the scenarios and their own experiences, and how a particular variable might change what could happen. When the larger group reconvened, each analytical group shared their analysis with the broader group. Diverging responses were encouraged rather than attempting to come to a definitive interpretation of the scenarios. One student from each group shared their group's responses to the prompts, and another student from the group wrote key points on the whiteboard, drawing connections between different scenarios.

During the second half of both collaborative analysis days, I shared with students how my theorising had been shaped through their words and our research. I hoped to position students as theorists, but also to discuss particular philosophical concepts and see if they seemed to resonate with them. This practice was a legitimacy test, or perhaps a test of the concepts' 'catalytic validity' (Lather 1986: 67) – that is, a curious exploration of whether and how these concepts might be of interest and use for them, positioning students as 'theoretical provocateurs' (Liddiard et al. 2019). For example, at one stage of the collaborative analysis day, I offered Judith Butler's discussion of interpellation in *Giving an Account of Oneself* (2005), in discussing a particular puppet scenario where a teacher called out to a student across the playground, telling them to pick up their rubbish. 'Thinking with' (Jackson and Mazzei 2012) the concept of interpellation, we discussed the pragmatic implications of a student turning and answering the term of address when a teacher addresses them as a particular 'type' of student ('naughty', 'smart', and so on). These discussions dynamically repositioned students as theorists and their puppet scenarios as art-prompting-thought, intertwining these with academically recognised 'philosophy' (cf. Murris 2016). While I hoped that the knowledge, concepts, skills and affects generated in these discussions could be useful, enhancing students' capacity to act – perhaps – there were other tensions. Looking back, the theories I offered were reified theories of white philosophers. What might have been different if the students and I more explicitly discussed, for example, Freire's banking model of education and institutional racism (cf. Clay and Turner 2021), white privilege, white guilt and colour-blindness (cf. Welton et al. 2017), heterosexism and heteronormativity (cf. Coll et al. 2019), and/or ableism and posthumanism (cf. Hickey-Moody et al. 2021; Liddiard et al. 2019)? The theories that a researcher offers, the researcher's embodied positionality, as well as the ever-shifting material-affective-discursive conditions of the conversation, are part of shaping what is possible and what is not possible to be said, thought and done in such co-theorising events.

As a way for students to be able to identify their contributions to my research, towards the end of these collaborative analysis days, I invited students to choose their own pseudonyms, and to write on a sticky note how they would prefer me to describe them. Since I asked students to describe themselves (rather than, for example, giving them a demographic survey to fill in), I do not summarise participating students' demographic data. Students who participated in this study were from a range of backgrounds, with countries of their parents' origins including Lebanon, Samoa, Pakistan, India, Vietnam, Greece, Jordan, Denmark, the UK and Australia. In choosing pseudonyms, students most frequently chose Anglicised names, with a few exceptions. Some of the students wrote names of sports celebrities or characters from television shows or computer games. Some students wrote a pseudonym but did not write a self-description. Sometimes students' self-descriptions were earnest and 'truthful' (with the description recognisable to me as who I knew this student to be), while at other times they seemed to be exaggerations, fantastical, humorous or ironic. In the fold (of a sticky note), the self is 'created on each occasion' in relation to the 'the present-time stratum that serves as a limit: what can I see and what can I say today?' (Deleuze 1999/1986: 87, 98). In the chapters that follow, I include the students' self-selected pseudonyms and self-descriptions where I have included their spoken words. At times, I quote from students who participated in the study but did not attend the collaborative analysis days, and so did not write their own pseudonym – in these instances, I have given pseudonyms to these students, but I have not written a description for them.

I later formed transcripts from the words spoken and action performed in these puppet scenarios and collaborative analysis events, understanding these transcripts not to represent past interactions but to reconfigure reality – a re-presentation (Nordstrom 2015: 395). I brought these words into arrangement with educational sociological theory and the concepts of Deleuze and Guattari in a doctoral research thesis and other publications. In one article, writing between quotations from students and quotations from Deleuze, I argued that '[d]ifferent forms of knowing were constituted through direct material engagement with the puppets' (Mayes 2016b: 112), enabling students to perform their embodied knowledge of the order of schooling and dramatise the mundane, everyday ways in which students' voices are apprehended, understood and ordered in schools. In the puppet scenarios, voices had been loosened from the subject of enunciation; the material puppets 'disembod[ied] and transferr[ed] the [verbal] voice, so that the puppets "spoke" through the hand that moved them, the lips under the table and in intra-action with the jostlings of other puppets moved by another hand and set of lips' (Mayes 2016b: 111). In my account, the puppets enabled students to anonymously 'ventriloquise teachers' (Mayes 2016b: 112). '[T]he material supplement of the puppet offered an extension to what students could say and do' (Mayes 2016b: 112), as they escaped and exceeded dominant identity categories and segmentary relations. I quoted from one Year 11 student, Monique,[5] who said:

> You got to express yourself and the previous situations through puppets, so you didn't really care how you looked or how you sounded, because you couldn't really see your face. [...] It could be coming from the student that never gets in trouble or a student that always gets in trouble. You wouldn't know. (Group discussion, collaborative analysis day)

I theorised, with Deleuze and Parnet, that as students wrote down 'big ideas' on A3 paper, they were identifying the 'dominant utterances' that signal the established order of schooling (2006/1977: 97) – habitual, common-sense phrases and modes of speaking that the puppets mimicked, parodied and stuttered (Mayes 2016b: 112). I wrote about how, in discussing the scenarios, the micropolitics and micro-intensities of everyday schooling practices were disclosed; students amplified these utterances, noting taken-for-granted modes of speaking-listening-teaching-learning-feeling in operation, and, perhaps, momentarily interrupted them (Mayes 2016b).

This use of puppets, to be clear, retains its human entanglements and still attends to what (in conventional qualitative research) is described as the voice of human participants. In this way, it differs from Deleuze and Guattari's discussion of puppets, which draw on Heinrich Von Kleist's (1972) 'On the Marionette Theatre'. In *A Thousand Plateaus*, Deleuze and Guattari describe puppet strings as a 'rhizome or multiplicity', *not* as tied to the will of the puppeteer, but tied 'to a multiplicity of nerve fibers, which form another puppet in other dimensions connected to the first' (Deleuze and Guattari 1980/1987: 8, original emphasis). According to Aline Wiame, the marionette, in Deleuze's *The Logic of Sense* (1969/2013), is 'stuck in the state of the present', but this is 'not a trap, it is an occasion of freedom' (Wiame 2016: 66). After Kleist and Deleuze and Guattari, puppets, marionettes, mechanical dolls and automata are approached not 'according to their resemblance to human figures', but rather 'by following the lines they draw in space' (Wiame 2016: 65). My invitation to students to create scenarios with puppets still connects 'the supposed will of an artist or puppeteer' (Deleuze and Guattari 1980/1987: 8) as they moved puppet limbs and marionette strings to form lines in space (see also MacLure et al. 2010). In using puppets with students, I was and still am interested in the students-as-puppeteer's 'will' – and in how the students and I could, together (but not unproblematically), expand and create theories about voice and schooling – in particular, about how the voice of the young person can become interpreted to be too 'willful'. For Sara Ahmed (2014), 'the willful child' 'has a story to tell', fails to comply 'with those whose authority is given' and is diagnosed as 'a problem' (1, 3). Yet, of course, to invoke the notion of will may be judged as incommensurable with the problematising of human consciousness and agency associated with the ontological turn.

To be upfront, my use of puppets in this study (and this chapter) was/is not particularly or consistently Deleuzian (cf. Strom 2018b). The puppets worked with and across (imposed) demarcations between 'conventional' qualitative and what is called post-qualitative research, representationalism and non-representationalism. This particular research practice that I mis/used in my doctoral fieldwork – thinking voice with puppets – simultaneously works with and beyond conventional qualitative conceptions of voice. This simultaneity makes this research practice useful for thinking with and through critiques of the ontological turn and the ethics and politics of voice in research.

## Critical and Creative Engagements with(in) the Ontological Turn

### THE VIOLENCE OF THE NEW

The ontological turn has been critiqued as reinscribing Eurocentric epistemologies, ontologies and temporalities, reifying the term that preceded the 'post' and discarding what came before. This critique of the 'new' materialisms is not new: in 2008, Sara Ahmed critiqued feminist new materialism for its 'forgetful feminism', arguing for the need to engage with feminism(s)' historical engagements with materiality, and with how 'matter matters in different ways, for different feminisms, over time' (2008: 32, 36). Posthumanist and 'new' materialist scholarship that has drawn on Deleuze and Guattari has been critiqued as 'new' forms of philosophical colonialism: eliding or appropriating the force of First Nations knowledge systems, omitting non-Western and non-dualist epistemic traditions that have long critiqued Western anthropocentrism and recognised the vitality of matter (Bignall and Rigney 2019; Sundberg 2014). As I elaborate below, Eve Tuck (2010) narrates how her early delight in Deleuze's notions of 'rhizomatic interconnectedness' were complicated by her Indigeneity, since 'interconnectedness has been the mainstay in many Indigenous frameworks [...] It's an issue of false inventions and giving credit where credit is due' (646). Citizen of the Chickasaw Nation of Oklahoma Jodi Byrd (2011) critiques Deleuze and Guattari's use of 'becoming-Indian' as 'ventriloquising the speaking Indian', 'transforming the becoming- into *replacing* Indian' (16, their emphasis). In Byrd's account of Deleuze and Guattari, First Nations people become 'the transit, the field through which presignifying polyvocality' is figured (19). As Tiffany Lethabo King (2017) summarises Byrd's analysis: Deleuze and Guattari's 'ethos of experimental and rhizomatic lines of flight' is 'only possible as a form of white self-actualizing posthumanism due to the death of Indigenous peoples and their excision from the Earth/land' (171–2). Zoe Todd (2016), Red River Métis, Otipemisiwak feminist scholar, critiques the lack of credit given by scholars associated with the ontological turn to 'Indigenous thinkers for their millennia of engagement with sentient environments, with cosmologies that enmesh people into complex relationships between themselves and *all* relations, and with climates and atmospheres as important points of organization and action' (6–7). Kakali Bhattacharya (2021) describes feeling 'dizzy' in reading of the many ontological turns, 'especially when for so many communities around the world, the knowledge gained from Western academics' ontological turns were a given' (182). Feminist geographer Juanita Sundberg (2014) argues that vital materialisms and posthumanism remain within the orbit of Eurocentric epistemologies and ontologies – for example, in references to 'dualisms as if they are universal foundations of thought, which only serves to perpetuate their presumed universality' (35). According to these critical engagements, in rejecting anthropocentrism and decentring the human, posthumanists risk obscuring how colonialism and imperialism have denied humanity to some humans according to racialised categorisations in both the past and the present. Calls to decentre the human are critiqued as eliding questions of how some humans are more centred than others, and how moving past humanism can have further dehumanising consequences.

In the educational research community, there have been a number of extensions to these critiques of the mis/use of history in the ontological turn as manifested in educational research. Jessica Gerrard, Sophie Rudolph and Arathi Sriprakash read the post-qualitative literature 'from a postcolonial lens', arguing that the invocation of the 'new' and the 'search for a "break" from the old' may 'reiterate a modernist-colonial impulse in which progress is positioned along a development trajectory of linear time' (2016: 388). Citing Tuck and Yang (2014b: 813), Gerrard, Rudolph and Sriprakash (2016) question whether post-qualitative research may, in seeking the 'new', 'echo the "poetics of Empire: to discover, to chart new terrain, to seek new frontiers, to explore"' (388). Jintin Wu and colleagues also argue that, when Continental philosophers are privileged in what is taught, studied and cited in educational and social science research, the White supremacy of the academy is reinforced (Wu et al. 2018). Sarah Truman (2022) notes that there is a 'concept-economy' in the academy that drives this 'ongoing push for the new' – the drive to 'come up with the "new" and market/circulate it constantly' in accordance with the logics of 'citational indexes, productivity measurements, guilt at not working constantly, the push to publish and produce' (142).

Reading my work through these critiques and creative reworkings of the ontological turn as historically problematic compels a further engagement with the historical mis/use of puppetry and ventriloquism in anthropology. I think of the histories of Western anthropologists fascinated with the 'folklore' of Other cultures, including the vocal transformations and ventriloquising supernatural practices of shamans, mediums and priests (Davis 1998). The ventriloquist has been a fascinating 'Other' to study, interpret and represent to the West. More than thirty years ago, Appadurai described a 'curious double ventriloquism' in anthropological fieldwork:

> While one part of our traditions dictates that we [anthropologists] be the transparent medium for the voices of those we encounter in the field, that we speak for the native [sic] point of view, it is equally true that we find in what we hear some of what we have been taught to expect by our own training, reading, and cultural backgrounds. Thus our informants are often made to speak for us. (Appadurai 1988: 16–17)

The first ventriloquism, according to Appadurai (1988), is the expectation that the ethnographer becomes the puppet – the 'transparent medium' through which the 'voices [they] encounter in the field' speak (16–17). The conceit of this first ventriloquism was dismantled by postcolonial and poststructural critiques of voice; the researcher can never unproblematically 'speak for others' (Alcoff 1991) nor 'let the subaltern speak' (Spivak 1987). (Even so, this first mode of ventriloquism continues in arts-based therapeutic approaches

*Figure 2.2* A marionette mis/used in student research focus groups. My hand is in the marionette's glove, above the marionette's head. The marionette sits, head angled downward.

to research that offer children puppets to 'help' them 'free' their 'authentic' voices. Figure 2.1 could be interpreted as such a mis/use of puppets.) The second ventriloquism, according to Appadurai, is when the voices heard by the ethnographer come to 'speak for' the ethnographer – to speak what the ethnographer expects to hear from their 'training, reading, and cultural backgrounds' (perhaps the reader may think of training and reading in the ontological turn, thinking about voices as more-than-human). When I bring a cloth puppet to a school, the puppet carries the weight of these material (literal puppets)-discursive (metaphorical) histories (see Figure 2.2). When I invite students to create accounts of past experiences with puppets, and when I offer them other theories to think with, these histories of 'freeing' voices through puppetry, fascination with spectral Other voices, and past appropriations and ventriloquisms of voices hover and thread through the immanent research encounter (see Figure 2.1).

## WHAT DOES THE NEW DO?

Critics have also questioned what 'new' ontologies achieve politically. While work in the ontological turn writes of shocks to thought, ruptures and metamorphoses, little seems to materially change – fascisms, racisms, patriarchy, heteronormativity, and ableism persist and proliferate (King 2017; Weheliye 2014). Political theorists Bonnie Washick and Elizabeth Wingrove query the political consequences of understanding phenomena to not exist prior to their intra-action (or assembling), wondering whether such 'giddy indeterminancy' makes it 'difficult to name and so hold in view the continuities, durabilities and often monotonous predictabilities' of 'systems of power asymmetry (such as capitalism, patriarchy, racism)' (in Washick et al. 2015: 66). From a Marxist position, if 'humans are simply another node in the relational net of lively matter then how exactly can we be seen to act in and on the world, in particular, in the pursuit of human projects of emancipation?' (Cudworth and Hobden 2015: 135). Desire to flatten ontologies may be more akin to a 'liberal fantasy' of equality that eclipses the materiality of difference and unevenly experienced relations of power (Kuntz 2021: 12). Scholars in Black Studies have critiqued calls to move 'beyond' the human as presuming that 'all subjects have been granted equal access to western humanity and that this is, indeed, what we all want to overcome' (Weheliye 2014: 10). Zakiyyah Iman Jackson (2015) incisively asks, '*whose* conception of humanity are we moving beyond?' (215, original emphasis). Tiffany Lethabo King (2017) analyses 'how perverse and reprehensible it is to ask Indigenous and Black people who cannot seem to escape death to move beyond the human or the desire to be human' (167). For King, such white and whimsical posthumanist and Deleuzian self-abnegation and self-critique are not only politically insufficient but also violent (2017: 164). Washick and Wingrove (in Washick et al. 2015) question whether such approaches leave researchers with 'little but the self to work on: our only choice appears to be to opt out of assemblages we find ethically problematic and, even then, only imperfectly and incompletely' (66); for them, this is a 'remarkably individualistic vision of political action oriented toward change' (75).

Critics of educational research aligned with the ontological turn have similarly interrogated its individualistic political consequences. Bhattacharya interrogates the positionality of 'powerful, white academic[s]' 'questioning the authenticity of voices, when so many voices are always already erased from the history of the world' (2021:

181). Gerrard, Rudolph and Sriprakash (2016) note that human subjects are frequently still part of such research, but that researchers seem preoccupied with their 'research products and practices – data, fieldwork, interview transcripts – and not the women, men, and children who are the basis of these research products' (390). For them, such preoccupations dishonour 'the people who gave their time' and allowed the researcher to 'witness, participate and be involved in their lives' (390). The danger, as they put it, is that 'these accounts may easily slip [. . .] into colonizing acts: they marginalize, trivialize, romanticize, and exoticize' through a focus on 'problematics related to the researcher-self' and her 'affective and visceral reactions' (Gerrard et al. 2016: 390). In turn, data may become anthropomorphised in the attribution of human-like agency. Eva Bendix Petersen questions whether 'all the non-human actors cartographed and sensed in much new materialist work [. . .] even *want* the agency and privilege now bestowed so well-meaningly on them' (2018: 11, original emphasis). She argues that this scholarship might 'come to speak on behalf of' non-human actors and 'come to colonise [them]' (2018: 12). While Petersen's tongue-in-cheek questions about 'speaking for' objects arguably transfer the logics of autonomy and selfhood to the object, rather than engaging with the ontological shift at work towards dynamic intra-relationalities, these critical engagements prompt a further engagement with the ethics and politics of voice in work inspired by the ontological turn.

As I read these critical engagements, ethical and political concerns about the conduct of research in the ontological turn materialise, and I re-turn to Tuck and Yang's (2014b) critique of the 'inquiry as invasion' practices of the settler colonialist academy that thieve and commodify sacred objects, and report on the pain of others 'in people's "real voices"' (811, 812). Yet, the issue is not only about the appropriative presentation of 'pain stories on a silver platter for the settler colonial academy' (or educational leaders and policy actors) to consume (812). If, after the ontological turn, voices are no longer the property of speaking subjects, but rather shift and change with the assemblage, does that make utterances free game for the resourceful researcher – to pick up, 'plug in', explore with, generate new ideas with, and profit from (see Figure 2.2)? Reading Gerrard, Rudolph and Sriprakash (2016), such practices could be described as an example of 'persisting colonial knowledge practices in research' (388) where the researcher appropriates utterances, transmutes them into a research text, and is the one to benefit from the resulting research product. The utterance becomes taken up into the researcher's authorial voice – reassembled to consider questions that those entangled in the research intra-action may have had little interest in exploring. Reading these critical engagements, I have wondered whether my 'participants' would find my 'densely theoretically led approach bewildering' (Gerrard et al. 2016: 386) – or, at least, to find what I have done with their spoken utterances to be confusing (see Figures 2.1 and 2.2). Thinking with these critiques, there are risks of doing violence to children and young people when stories, dreams, hopes and fears that research participants articulate to researchers are taken up into onto-epistemological speculations and experiments. The risk is that human voices may become tools for play and appropriation in these 'new' research assemblages, creating new (if inadvertent) oppressions: microfascisms.

## *Mis/using Deleuze and Guattari*

What are the implications of these critiques for those working with theory from the ontological turn? There are a number of possible responses to these critiques of the ontological turn, and to the uptake of Deleuze and Guattari in particular: defensiveness, walking away, and extension and expansion. First, there is a tendency for Deleuze and Guattari scholars to, as King puts it, 'work through and repair or do damage control for Deleuze and Guattari' (2017: 174). This approach often seeks to contextualise what Deleuze and Guattari meant in their political context, or to refute the objections of their detractors.[6] I find this practice of defensively reterritorialising on particular concepts (for example, 'nomadology' and 'schizo') to be rather out of step with Deleuze and Guattari's practice of changing their language when a concept no longer served them, when a concept had become something else in other people's hands, and/or when their thinking had shifted (for example, their shift from the language of 'desiring-machines' in *Anti-Oedipus* to 'agencements' in *A Thousand Plateaus*). To refuse to double down on Deleuze and Guattari entails being willing to let go of concepts that no longer are of use. It is for this reason – refusing to do damage control – that I choose not to use reified terms from Deleuze and Guattari that perpetuate problematic colonialist and neurotypical stereotypes – for example, words like 'nomad', 'primitive' and 'schizo'.

A second possible response to apprehending the limits of Deleuze, Guattari and the broader ontological turn is to walk away. Eve Tuck

(2010) gives an account of her early delight in reading Deleuze and Guattari. She narrates how she wanted them to say that desire is 'purposeful, intentional, agentic; that it can teach itself, craft itself, inform itself' (2010: 645) – to claim a notion of desire drawn from Indigenous knowledge systems that is wise, sovereign, accrues over generations, and is 'integral to our humanness' (2010: 644). Tuck narrates reaching an 'impasse' (647) where her desire for a desire that serves Indigenous self-determination, sovereignty and resurgence are negated by Deleuze's notions of desire as impersonal, and where Indigenous cultures are the example for philosophical appropriation. She ultimately 'breaks up' with Deleuze, while continuing to 'value' the 'incommensurable' in this move. Philosopher Claire Colebrook has praised Eve Tuck's account of the limits of Deleuze and Guattari' (2020: 337). For Colebrook, Tuck 'offers the most profound path to reading their work in an age of extinction'; Tuck demonstrates the ultimate foolishness and futility of thinking that any philosopher (whether Deleuze or another) can 'save us' (Colebrook 2020: 339).

A third response to the limits and violences of the ontological turn – and Deleuze and Guattari in particular – is to extend, expand and connect their work to other modes and directions for thought. Examples of such extensions, expansions and connections emerge in specific bodily and territorial milieus – as Black Studies scholar Alexander Weheliye puts it, 'beyond the snowy masculinist precincts of European philosophy' (2014: 47). It is in these milieus where the limits of these Continental concepts become clear, and where there emerges a necessity to 'productively rearticulate and reframe Deleuze and Guattari's thoughts' and 'produc[e] new concepts and assemblages' (Weheliye 2014: 47). For example, Jasbir Puar reads Deleuze-inspired assemblage theory with intersectionality in the context of what she calls 'homonationalism' in the War on Terror (Puar 2007). Puar (2012) describes reading of assemblage theory with intersectionality as not seeking to render them 'analogous', nor 'reconcilable', nor 'oppositional'; rather, Puar's approach is to read assemblage theory with intersectionality as 'frictional' (50). In a resonant way, Alexander Weheliye refuses to engage in reparative readings of Deleuze and Guattari (that would, for example, disprove critiques of Deleuze and Guattari's relationship to colonialised peoples and feminism), but instead finds it 'necessary to create a conversation between' Deleuze and Guattari's assemblage, Stuart Hall's articulation, and the work of Sylvia Wynter and Hortense Spillers (2014: 48). Citizen of the Ngarrindjeri Nation and scholar Daryle

Rigney, writing with philosopher Simone Bignall, accounts for the need to refuse and/or betray certain 'conceptual assemblages originating in the (imperial) West' (Bignall and Rigney 2019: 176); they refuse the concept of deterritorialisation, as one example of '"joyful acts of disobedience and gentle but resolute betrayal"' (Braidotti, cited in Bignall and Rigney 2019: 176). Kara Keeling (2019), in turn, takes up Deleuze and Guattari's work where it advances the study of queer temporality and refusal in upending capitalistic time and Western humanism (see Chapter 5). These scholars exemplify a stance that refuses what has become fascistic – that is, what reinstates us-and-them tendencies of thought – in Deleuze and Guattarian concepts – whilst still affirming what sparks thought for their own work and political projects.

## *Attuning to Microfascisms*

> 'How does one keep from being fascist, even (especially) when one believes oneself to be a '[Deleuzian/ posthumanist/more-than-human/and and . . . researcher]'?
> Michel Foucault, preface to *Anti-Oedipus*

In this chapter, I have attempted to engage questions of history, politics and ethics in the mis/uses of voice in research with children and young people – particularly work associated with the ontological turn. I outlined how voice has previously been mis/used as an extractible resource, a liberatory tool for change, before being reconceptualised again with the ontological turn. I re-turned to my mis/uses of voice in one study, situating this mis/use in the history of mis/uses of voice in research with children and young people. While situating my mis/uses of voice in relation to recent reconceptualisations of voice, I have also reviewed critiques of the ontological turn more generally, particularly those that speak to the dehumanising and depoliticising potential of this turn. These 'new' forms of inquiry risk reifying binaries by presuming they are foundational, appropriating Indigenous ontologies, acquiescing to the concept economy's thirst for the 'new', and concocting abstractions that undermine the utterances of the humans involved in research. I considered three possible responses to these critiques: defensiveness, walking away, and extension and expansion. I have found myself vacillating between these possible responses – perhaps this ambivalent vacillation can be sensed across the chapters of this book. I have situated this chapter early on in this book to foreground the importance of these critical engagements for what follows. Reading other scholars' questions and accounts of disenchantment with Deleuze and Guattari and, more broadly, with the ontological turn has compelled me to address other questions (King 2017: 172). I find the work of Deleuze and Guattari to be 'simultaneously generative and unsatisfying', as Eve Tuck articulates her response to Deleuze's desire (2010: 635).

At the risk of seeming to be reterritorialising on Deleuze and Guattarian concepts, I contend that attuning to microfascisms can be potentially ethically generative in dwelling with and responding to these critiques. Attentiveness to potential microfascisms extends conversations of the limits and insufficiencies, not only of voice, but of the ontological turn in education. In the face of the contemporary ascendance across many liberal democracies of right-wing populism, ethno-nationalism, White supremacism, anti-black, anti-immigrant and anti-refugee violence, misogyny, homophobia, transphobia, biphobia, and religious fundamentalisms, a number of educational philosophers and researchers have taken up the concept of microfascism and considered its pedagogical and methodological implications (for example, Kuntz 2021; Peters 2020; Strom 2018a; Zembylas 2021). While the moniker of fascism, in its political theoretical definition, is frequently associated with its specific political forms between 1919 and 1945 in Germany, Spain and Italy, Deleuze and Guattari's attention is on its psychosociality, both in their period of work and beyond it. They draw upon the work of Freudo-Marxist Viennese psychiatrist Wilhelm Reich's exploration of why Germans embraced fascism rather than communism between 1928 and 1933; how and why people turn towards authoritarian regimes and seek their own repression when it is against their self- and class interests. Reich theorised the root of fascism in the body and sexual desire (Reich 1946/1933). Deleuze and Guattari extend Reich's consideration of desire to an expanded conception of desire as productive, arranged and proliferative (see Chapters 1 and 6). They distinguish fascism from totalitarianism by its everyday workings: where totalitarian regimes are forced '*upon* the general population', fascism 'operates *through* the masses' (Kuntz 2021: 4, orignal emphasis) – and thus is potentially discernible in our everyday behaviour (Evans 2013).

Foucault (1977), in his preface to Deleuze and Guattari's *Anti-Oedipus*, argues that the book's central question is: 'How does one keep from being fascist, even (especially) when one believes oneself to be a revolutionary militant?' (viii). This is the question I am interested in – the seeds of fascism in ostensibly radical politics and practices

– when any 'us and them' style of thought begins to sprout. I am interested in the risks of microfascism in student voice practices, as well as in inquiry practices that purport to move 'beyond' humanism and, in doing so, may generate their own micro-violences. Deleuze and Guattari, in *A Thousand Plateaus*, elaborate on the danger of 'be[ing] antifascist on the molar level, and not even see the fascist inside you, the fascist you yourself sustain and nourish and cherish with molecules both personal and collective' (Deleuze and Guattari 1980/1987: 215). Foucault writes in his preface:

> [N]ot only historical fascism, the fascism of Hitler and Mussolini – which was able to mobilize and use the desire of the masses so effectively – but also the fascism in us all, in our heads, and in our everyday behaviour, the fascism that causes us to love power, to desire the very thing that dominates and exploits us. (Foucault 1977: xiii)

Fascism, in this molecular formulation, reproduces 'in miniature the affections, the affectations, of the rigid [line]'; 'microfascisms lay down the law' (Deleuze and Guattari 1980/1987: 228). Microfascisms bring assurance, innocence and a sense of ethical immunity – perhaps, paradoxically, though declaring oneself to be uncertain, complicit and always-already ethically compromised. At the risk of succumbing to the contemporary trend of calling almost everything and everyone a fascist (Kuntz 2021), in this chapter I have re-turned to and critiqued my own work (rather than critiquing others); it is easy to critique fascism in national political life, but much harder to note where it begins and how it moves. I value Kuntz's (2021) observation that 'our inquiry practices, no matter how critically intended, are certainly not exempt from the force of fascism' (2). Indeed, for Deleuze and Guattari, it is in what they call the 'avant-garde' (and we might think of any claims to be 'new' in thought or claims to have eviscerated methodology) that microfascisms seed.

Microfascism is the danger of the molecular line: that is, the line that slightly diverges from binary, segmentary lines – where there is a troubling of gendered, classed, racialised, sexualised, ableist and ageist lines of demarcation between bodies, and of the lines between the human and more-than-human. On the molecular line, believing oneself to have undone binary lines: 'Everything has the clarity of the microscope. We think we have understood everything, and draw conclusions. We are the new knights; we even have a mission' (Deleuze and Guattari 1980/1987: 228). Perhaps it seems ludicrous to describe work in the ontological turn – whether post-qualitative, posthuman, PhEMaterialist, feminist new materialist, research creation – as having microfascistic potential. Of course, the ontological turn is far from a mass movement, no one scholar is a fascist leader, and the politics of scholars associated with the ontological turn generally align with leftist politics. Yet, Deleuze and Guattari's political concern is before and beyond the formation of macropolitical totalitarian states:

> Fascism is inseparable from a proliferation of molecular focuses in interaction, which skip from point to point, *before* beginning to resonate together in the National Socialist State. Rural fascism and city or neighbourhood fascism, youth fascism and war veteran's fascism, fascism of the Left and fascism of the Right, [fascism of the humanist, fascism of the posthumanist, fascism of the qualitative, fascism of the post qualitative, fascism of the 'old' materialist, fascism of the 'new' materialist], fascism of the couple, family, school and office. (Deleuze and Guattari 1980/1987: 214, original emphasis and my additions in brackets)

In a conversation reproduced in *Molecular Revolution in Brazil*, Guattari describes how there may be 'a dimension of social resistance by a group against exploitation, against alienation, any kind of oppression, while as the same time, within the problems of the group, there may be micro-fascist processes on the molecular level' (Guattari and Rolnik 1982/2008: 185). As an example, the 'militant feminist' may find that she embodies a 'disalienating attitude in the man–women relation, but suddenly discover that she has an incompatible and even micro-fascist behavior in relation to her child or in relation to herself' (Guattari and Rolnik 1982/2008: 188). As another example, a scholar may make great speeches about undoing binaries, response-ability, more-than-human agencies, and at the same time 'have an investment of paranoid power impelling' them to 'take over the auditorium and establish a relation of phallocentric seduction, racist seduction, or whatever' (Guattari and Rolnik 1982/2008: 186). It is easy to criticise the binary thinking of institutions and not see the everyday microfascistic behaviours, anxieties and love of power in one's own life and work. To be alert to one's fascistic tendencies is not about perpetuating a 'confessional culture' (Dean and Zamora 2021: para. 4) but is part of collective processes of attuning to 'everything that blocks the processes of transformation of the social field' (Guattari and Rolnik 1982/2008: 190).

The question becomes, then: how do researchers – particularly those who identify with the terms that open this concluding section's mis/quotation of Foucault ('Deleuzian/posthumanist/more-than-human/and and and . . . researcher-/activist') – apprehend, encounter, and then refuse, such microfascisms as they emerge? This question is relevant too for anyone seeking to be part of collective transformations of the social field – for example, those positioned as educators, school leaders or students in educational institutions. In the chapters that follow, I deliberately work with the ambivalences, not only of the liberal humanist assumptions of student voice, but also of the potential microfascisms of thinking that one is moving 'beyond' the human. In Chapter 7, I revisit the possibilities of encountering and refusing microfascisms, thinking with the work of student climate justice activists. In the chapters that follow, when I bring words and screenshots from the puppet scenarios into arrangement with other quotations, texts and concepts, I am attempting to perform these inescapable ambivalences of working with voice. The puppet form materialises the dangers of voyeuristic appropriation of students' voices in research that generates and problematises the voices of human subjects. The following chapter works with one puppet scenario, created by a group of Year 11 students, to consider how it came to be that the voice of the child became so entwined with the ordering of schooling. The chapter explores the material and political force of spoken language in classrooms – how the felt force of voice is viscerally apprehended, and how these cumulative forces have come to order what is taken for granted about how the institution of school is supposed to run.

## Notes

1. A wealth of theories and theorists are associated with unravelling the binary lines that maintain the privilege and domination of white heterosexual man (Haraway 1991), drawing attention to the porousness and open-endedness of boundaries, the contingency of categories and the potentiality of virtual futures. Various strands of theory and methodology are associated with the ontological turn, including posthumanism (Braidotti 2013, 2019), feminist new materialisms (Alaimo and Hekman 2008; Coole and Frost 2010), affect theories (Clough and Halley 2010; Gregg and Seigworth 2010) and actor network theories (Latour 2005). Over the past twenty years in the educational research community, there has a burgeoning body of research that 'thinks with' (Jackson and Mazzei 2012) these theories and methodologies, sometimes described as post-qualitative inquiry (St. Pierre 2011), feminist 'new' materialisms (Snaza et al. 2016; Taylor and Ivinson 2013), PhEMaterialisms (Renold

and Ringrose 2019; Strom et al. 2019), posthumanism (Niccolini et al. 2018; Ringrose et al. 2018; Snaza and Weaver 2015; Ulmer 2017), affective methodologies (Dernikos et al. 2020) and research-creation (Springgay and Rotas 2015; Truman 2022). There are various origin stories and trajectories that can be traced for these methodologies and research communities in education. As one example, Elizabeth St. Pierre (2018: 3) narrates her 'invention' of the idea of post-qualitative inquiry in her chapter for the fourth edition of the *SAGE Handbook of Qualitative Research* (2011). In the USA, it was a battle with what St. Pierre calls the 'scientifically based, evidence-based police' that generated the invention of qualitative inquiry to spur on thinking and experimentation about what comes after humanist qualitative research (2019: 3). It is beyond the scope of this chapter to narrate the emergence of other terms across other countries and research networks. My focus here is on how the concept of voice has been variously troubled and reconceptualised by scholars aligned with the ontological turn, how this 'new' work has been critiqued, and implications for research with and after 'voice'.
2. Acknowledgements and thanks to Sarah Truman for reading an earlier version of this chapter and for this astute comment.
3. Hein (2016) has asserted that the work of Deleuze and Guattari and Barad is 'incommensurable', arguing that 'Deleuze's is a philosophy of immanence and difference, whereas Barad's is a philosophy of transcendence and identity' (137). My purpose here is to map how Deleuze and Guattari and Barad's work have been taken up in work associated with the ontological turn in education rather than debate Hein's conclusion about the incommensurability of Deleuze and Guattari and Barad. I agree with de Freitas (2017) that Deleuze and Guattari and Barad share a commitment to rethinking difference, with each seeking 'to develop new ways of commingling the continuous and the discrete' (748, n.5). Thiele (2016), in bringing together Deleuze's event with Barad's diffraction, argues that Deleuze's work may be productively 'thickened' by Barad's diffractive work on difference, notwithstanding 'theoretical tensions' (para. 9).
4. This section accounts for the concept of assemblages as it is taken up in research associated with the ontological turn. These usages of the concept of assemblage, however, have been critiqued as a departure from Deleuze and Guattari (see, for example, Buchanan 2021).
5. Monique chose her own pseudonym but did not write a self-description.
6. For example, see Alexander Weheliye's (2014) discussion of reparative readings of Deleuze and Guattari and Foucault (47–52).

# 3
# Ordering Voices and Bodies in the History of Schooling

Pythagoras[1] (narrator): In the Year 8 Maths classroom, a student has a question.
Samantha (teacher-puppet): Good morning class. Now, you should all know who Pythagoras is. We will be learning about him today and how he –
Johnathan (student-marionette): *(Rises to feet)* Miss, how does this even help us in life?
Samantha (teacher-puppet): Shh! *(Nods head vigorously)* You're being disruptive! Please, there's no time for your questions!
Johnathan (student-marionette): *(Jumps)* But it's a good question, Miss.
Samantha (Teacher-puppet): No, it's not. I'll decide if it's a good question or not. *(Student-marionette sits back down again, then lies back on table.)*

*Figure 3.1* A Year 8 student-marionette rises to their feet to ask a question.

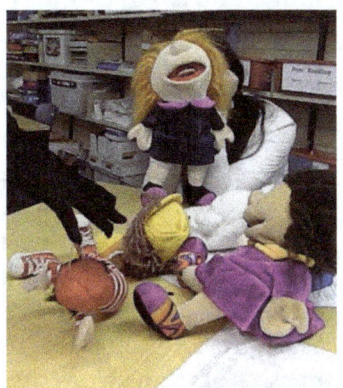

*Figure 3.2* A teacher-puppet negates the student-marionette's question.

When students speak in classrooms, why is this speech sometimes interpreted as 'disruptive', as in the puppet scenario that opens this chapter? The scene played out in this puppet scenario is familiar to me and was familiar to the students who analysed this puppet scenario: some bodies, no matter what they say, are habitually apprehended and interpreted as too 'disruptive'. In 2010, during a student voice research day run by a group of Year 9 students in the public secondary school where I worked, a Year 9 boy wrote on a black and white photo of the school's office area: 'This school is shit'. This student used to be in the 'students as co-researchers group' – the Steering Committee – that was facilitating a student voice morning with all of Year 9. The Steering Committee had designed five arts-based research stations for students to rotate through during class time, facilitated by the student researchers; teachers of these classes were there to supervise the morning. One of these stations was a graffiti station – students were invited to tag black and white photos of various areas of the school in terms of how they felt about their 'learning environment'. At this station, a supervising teacher observed this student writing the words 'this school is shit'. The teacher sent him to a deputy principal. He was stood down from classes and later had a parent interview. While this student wrote 'this school is shit' during a so-called 'student voice' activity, this 'expression' of voice in this place and time was interpreted as a behaviour issue by supervising adults. There are some voices that educators 'don't want to hear' – bodies habitually known to be 'incomprehensible [or] recalcitrant' (Bragg 2001: 70) or interpreted to be 'aggressive, rude or obnoxious' (Pearce and Wood 2019: 21).

This chapter considers the ordering of voices and bodies in the history of education: that is, what happens when words are spoken (or written), and what words do to bodies. To invoke Paolo Freire's (1996) pedagogical entanglement of 'reading the world' and 'reading the word', this chapter explores the relationship between 'speaking the word' and 'speaking the world' in and through schooling. The chapter begins an exploration of the politics and materiality of voice in schools – the felt force of sounds issued forth from human bodies, viscerally apprehended by bodies. Throughout the chapter, sometimes quotations from the above puppet scenario interrupt – in italics – the conceptual discussion of Deleuze and Guattari's pragmatics of language and the ordering words of schooling; at other times I quote from the puppet scenario (and italics are not used). These puppet scenarios were created and collaboratively analysed by various students, in various configurations, over a year-long period of research at one school, in response to the prompt of student voice as a concept (see

Chapter 2). In this chapter and in Chapter 5, I curate and think with these puppet scenarios, reading my teaching and research experiences and conversations with students through these puppet scenarios, as well as through the voices of theory and past research in schools. This chapter works with the above puppet scenario to explore the taken-for-granted, common-sense ways of apprehending voices and bodies that effectuate the conditions of possibility for voices and bodies in schools to be heard (Deleuze and Guattari 1980/1987: 85). I consider the historical and sociological murmurs that intersect with the concept of voice; these murmurs are inextricably entwined with taken-for-granted ways of apprehending, ordering and interpreting students' voices, emotions and actions. That is, there is a history of ways of apprehending and knowing what a student's voice is supposed to sound like and what a student is meant to say that conditions how students, educators and schools respond to calls to 'give' their students a voice in the present.

This chapter engages with Deleuze and Guattari's radical empiricism: that is, a tradition, following David Hume, that emphasises the role of sense perceptions in the formation of knowledge, ideas, philosophical concepts and common sense (Deleuze 1953/1991). By common sense, I refer to dominant taken-for-granted representational ways of knowing that recognise, classify and measure subjects and objects: *this* is a teacher; *this* is a student; *this* is an adult; *this* is a child; *this* is what voice should sound like (Deleuze 1968/1994: 148). In *Difference and Repetition*, Deleuze explains how common sense[2] becomes entrenched. The 'dogmatic image of thought', for Deleuze (1968/1994), categorises and individualises bodies in accordance with common sense and good sense, recognising what has previously been known (148, 266). Recognition reconfirms common-sense ways of thinking and the status quo – one recognises what one has already always known. Stable categories subordinate multiplicity and difference to universality and sameness (Deleuze 1968/1994: 262). Liberal humanist Western common sense is based on recognition of what the 'average' adult-white-heterosexual-able-bodied-male citizen who speaks standard English (Deleuze and Guattari 1980/1987: 105) looks like, speaks like, and does. Jamaican writer and cultural theorist Sylvia Wynter calls this figure 'the West's liberal monohumanist *Man*' (Wynter and McKittrick 2015: 23, original emphasis); this Man was historically produced through the eighteenth-century 'Enlightenment', (social) Darwinism, transatlantic slavery and colonial capitalism (Wynter 2003).[3] It is the stories that are told about Man, and the centring of this image of Man in artistic and institutional practices, that have installed this worldview of the ideal human (Wynter and McKittrick 2015). I am interested in the common sense that recognises and reinforces the supremacy of this Man because it operates as a felt force in schooling and student voice practices in particular: the universalised 'student', 'child' and 'young person' often is expected to speak and act like this Man.

However, to construct an account of the common sense of schooling risks reinscribing the common sense that the author (whether myself, or the authors who I read) has inherited – namely, Western ways of being and knowing that presume to know and understand the world, interpreting the Other in ways that essentialise, exoticise, diminish and dismiss multiplicities of knowing, being and becoming. In this chapter, I take up Deleuze and Guattari's radical empirical thought with the question that Sarah Truman (2022) incisively frames: 'Is my radical empiricism actually radical imperialism?' (25). That is, '[i]n what ways is my thinking unsettling established assumptions and engaging with an anti-racist, de-colonial, and feminist politics?' (25). There is an acute tension when bringing into relation Deleuze and Guattari's 'average' citizen with Sylvia Wynter's liberal monohumanist Man. As Tiffany Lethabo King (2017) has eloquently put it, Sylvia Wynter distrusted:

> the ability of Western theory – specifically its attempt at self-critique and self-correction in the name of justice for humanity – to revise its cognitive orders to work itself out of its current 'closed system,' which reproduces exclusion and structural oppositions based on the negation of the other. (165–6)

Wynter is explicit that the purpose of interrogating the categories from which taken-for-granted notions of ontology, knowledge, causality and temporality are built is to decolonise thought itself (Luiz 2020). Miranda Luiz (2020) has highlighted the resonances between Wynter's project and Deleuze and Guattari's (as well as Michel Foucault and Jacques Derrida) critique of 'the historical and semiotic systems that produce knowledge' (158). For Wynter, what is necessary is 'interrupting thought processes to examine how these thoughts are produced – what epistemic structures engender them, and what social implications these structures carry' (Luiz 2020: 158). In thinking Deleuze and Guattari's radical empiricism alongside and in friction with Wynter's decolonial critiques of Man, I am attempting to consider how these Western sensibilities are imposed, alongside how this imposed order might be evaded and diverted.

In what follows, I give an account of the ordering of voices and bodies in school, drawing on Deleuze and Guattari's pragmatic approach to linguistics in *A Thousand Plateaus* (1980/1987), and narrate an account of the words that order and murmur around the concept of voice in education: age, ability, emotionality and data.[4] These order words are part of the institutional infrastructure that I explore, in concrete places and times, in Chapters 4–7. The latter part of the chapter notes the cracks in the order of schooling and considers further directions for institutional analyses of the politics of voice in schools.

## *Sensing and Ordering Voices*

Habits of communicating and relating and modes of interpreting voices and emotions in schools do not emerge from nowhere, but are formed, patterned, repeated and reinscribed each day through micrological affective intensities. Modes of communication, for Deleuze and Guattari, are built from the capture and ordering of moving streams of desire into codes: the implicit presuppositions or common-sense logics of a group, institution or society. Chaotic, mobile, ambivalent streams of intensities surge through schools and are apprehended by human bodies – movements of arms, legs, pencils, fans, eyelids; speeds and slownesses in the playground, the exam hall, the classroom; sudden surges of bodies when a bell rings; a rush of blood when a student speaks out of turn. Bodies 'receive sudden jolts that beat like arteries' (Deleuze and Guattari 1994/2009: 201). These affective intensities, or atoms of experience, have 'no qualities except vivacity and a certain tendency for resonance', 'like a musical note' (Goodchild 1996: 18). When comparable intensities repeat, they become interrupted, reduced, codified and stratified, into codes. *'You're being disruptive!'* These intensities, associated with similar experiences, and the experience of other proximate bodies, become expected, so that when comparable intensities repeat, habits and communicative conventions become encoded. Codifying these flows 'see[s] to it that no flow exists that is not properly dammed up, channelled, regulated' (Deleuze and Guattari 1983: 33). *'(Student-marionette sits back down again.)'* There become 'implicit presuppositions' and 'social obligations' (Deleuze and Guattari 1980/1987: 79) that shape what is understood as a common culture, linked together 'according to a minimum of constant rules' (Deleuze and Guattari 1994/2009: 201). Codes become abstracted from the multiplicitous intensities felt at the level of the body and the living exchange between bodies. *'Miss, how does this even help us in life?'* The reduction of chaotic multiplicities helps to make sense of the world. These habitual codes are daily repeated and reiterated. In this way, codes become common sense through the senses: senses felt and brought into relation with other senses and discourses to categorise experience.

Deleuze and Guattari, in *A Thousand Plateaus* (1980/1987), articulate an account of the social function of speech in schooling – the relationship between language and the formation of common sense – through a pragmatic approach to language. They were deeply sceptical of a privileging of linguistics and language: the 'idea that we can only think within a language and that language structures our perceptions' (Colebrook 2010: 308). At the same time, they took an 'active part' in the linguistic turn, in elaborating a 'Continental brand of pragmatics' (Lecercle 2002: 28). Pragmatic linguistics troubled the structuralist linguistic introduction of a 'natural order' (Saussure 1959: 9) and the imposed separation of language (*langue*) from speech (*parole*), to instead foreground speech-acts and grammatical markers as markers of power. This view of language is distinguished from representational theories of language (where language represents the world).

For Deleuze and Guattari, words are inseparable from the world, caught in and intervening in the world, enmeshed in the constant arranging and rearranging of relations of desire and power. The concept of agencement (frequently translated as assemblage) displaces the focus from the individual speaking subject and what they say to 'the necessarily social character of enunciation' and the dynamic collective arrangements from which utterances are spoken (Deleuze and Guattari 1980/1987: 79–80, see ch. 1). Agencements combine a 'form of content' (material dimension – the machinic arrangement of bodies) and the 'form of expression' (the attributive dimension – the collective arrangement of enunciation) – though these are 'dimensions of an active, ongoing process, not a static whole' and 'something always escapes' (Buchanan 2021: 33). Statements are spoken from a 'collective [agencements] of enunciation', a fragment extracted from a 'crowd' or constellation of voices in shifting material, affective, spatial, temporal and discursive conditions (Deleuze and Guattari 1980/1987: 3, 84). This conception of enunciation does not give up on words or voices, but rather entangles them in the historical, sociopolitical, material and discursive milieu in which they are situated (Mazzei and Jackson 2017).

When the statement 'having a voice' is used, other associations murmur around the statement (cf. Deleuze and Guattari 1980/1987: 77, 84). The term 'statement' refers to linguistic events not defined by the speaker's intention, nor by content (the information that is said) or materiality (the sounds that are heard) alone, but rather multitudinously related to other statements (Deleuze 1999/1986: 8). Statements refer back to 'an institutional milieu' which produces particular subject positions (for example, students or teachers) (Deleuze 1999/1986: 9). Deleuze and Guattari call the '"first" language, or rather the first determination of language' 'indirect discourse':[5] 'all manner of voices in a voice, murmurings, speaking in tongues' (1980/1987: 76–7, their emphasis). These indirect discourses – murmurs – are not only citations or paraphrases of what I have heard before (for example, replicating the phrases my teachers used when I was a student), but are the expansive echoes of received sayings, clichés, hearsay, wisdom that exceed me and my history (Cole 2013); they are the 'vast echo of other sayings' beyond the individual subject (Grisham 1991: 47–8). When I am teaching, and I use a particular phrase with a student, I am not quite sure whether these words have come from my past, or a textbook, or a television show, or somewhere else. *'Please! There's no time for your questions.'*

Among a statement like 'having a voice', 'there are also whole families or formations of statements, whose catalogue is open-ended and subject to constant change', transformed and transforming 'as in a kaleidoscope' (Deleuze 1999/1986: 17). When an educator hears about students 'having a voice', they may think of the development of speech and language acquisition. They may think of communicative competencies and students' capacities to speak in articulate terms and with a confident tone of voice. They may think of behaviour management – the attempt to keep the volume of voices in a classroom at a suitably subdued level. The murmurs around a concept such as 'voice' vary in each discursive, historical and sociological formation, forming links with other statements, subjects, objects, concepts, events, practices and processes, defined by these 'inherent lines of variation' and 'field of vectors' (Deleuze 1999/1986: 7). As David Cole (2013) has put it, such indirect discourse is 'received, "passed on" or clichéd'; 'it may not be clear who is speaking or where the words have come from' (103). Even before an order word is spoken in a classroom, these indirect discourses are the 'prior orders' (Deleuze and Guattari 1980/1987: 75).

For Deleuze and Guattari, the 'compulsory [Western] education machine does not communicate information', but rather 'imposes upon the child' the 'dual foundations' of the socius (male/female, teacher/student, successful/failing) (1980/1987: 75–6). Wynter, too, notes how foundational categories of thought are conveyed through language: grammar distinguishes nouns from verbs, imposing the separation of things and bodies from each other (Wynter 1984).[6] Speech is used in classrooms not only to convey (curricular) content, but also to effect identity categories and power relations: who is permitted and who is not permitted to speak, to make knowledge claims, and to initiate change. *'I'll decide if it's a good question or not.'* Speech cannot be separated from the field of implicit presuppositions about who can speak, who should be silent, and how the world and the institution operate.

Order words shape what voices say, condition how a student's utterance is heard, and enable and constrain what voices can do. *Mots d'ordre*, usually translated as 'order words', are not necessarily commands, but may be sentences, questions or promises that connect prior orders, implicit presuppositions and social obligations (Deleuze and Guattari 1980/1987: 79), with localised effects. As Massumi explains in his translator's endnote, '[w]ords of order' create, arrange and reinforce political arrangements and classifications of bodies in relation to other bodies, spaces and things (Deleuze and Guattari 1980/1987: 523): students/teachers, male/female, junior/senior, mature/immature, articulate/inarticulate, rational/irrational, successful/failing, obedient/disobedient, 'good'/bad'. *'But it's a good question Miss.'* / *'No it's not.'* Bodies and subjectivities are segmented in a *'binary* fashion' and a *'linear* fashion': 'You're not at home anymore' (Deleuze and Guattari 1980/1987: 209, original emphasis). Spaces, too, are socially segmented in order words: striations demarcated for specific purposes and bodies (1980/1987: 208). *'(In the Year 8 Maths classroom.)'* These order words impose the lines of rigid segmentarity – the first type of line that Deleuze and Guattari describe as composing and re/decomposing arrangements of individuals and groups. The line of rigid segmentarity is binary, linear, classificatory and hierarchical, dividing from all directions (Deleuze and Guattari 1980/1987: 208). Adult/child. Teacher/student. Voice/silence. Language organises bodies in society.

## Ordering Voices and Bodies in the History of Schooling

So what happens to bodies when ordering words are spoken? Each time a student and/or an educator speaks, corporeal and political changes are inaugurated, effected or reinscribed, loosening and reforming lines of subjectification,[7] effecting incorporeal transformations that affect the physical body. An 'incorporeal transformation' is the 'pure instantaneous act' that occurs when a person utters a statement concerning another person's status, engendering a psychical shift (Deleuze and Guattari 1980/1987: 80–1). Deleuze and Guattari use the example of age to explain how order words effect incorporeal transformations:

> Bodies have an age, they mature and grow old; but majority, retirement, any given age category, are incorporeal transformations that are immediately attributed to bodies in particular societies: 'You are no longer a child': this statement concerns an incorporeal transformation, even if it applies to bodies and inserts itself into their actions and passions. (Deleuze and Guattari 1980/1987: 81)

The biological domain of age, statements of age categories and perceptions of maturity are correlated through these incorporeal transformations. The words of the judge announcing the sentence 'Guilty' incorporeally transforms the accused into a prisoner, even before the accused's body has been chained (Deleuze and Guattari 1980/1987: 80–1). The judge's statement accomplishes the act of transforming the accused into a prisoner because it is empowered by and connected to the whole juridical collective agencement of enunciation: texts, acts, spaces and utterances that collectively meet in the form of the judge. The statement does not represent the body; it intervenes in the body.

In the puppet scenario that opens this chapter, the teacher-puppet's response *('No it's not')* to the student-marionette's question and defence of their question effects instantaneous incorporeal and corporeal transformations. The student-marionette sits down, then lies down with the words: *'I'll decide if it's a good question or not.'* The student-marionette is abjected, and its corporeal deportment also shifts – from jumping, to sitting, to lying down – the statement pulses with force. This utterance reinforces the 'code-territory complex (do not approach my territory, it is I who give the orders here . . .)' (Deleuze and Parnet 2006/1977: 96). In this gridded space, the student-puppet who is sent out is unrecognisable as a legitimate or valued speaker, in comparison to the teacher-puppet.

These types of incorporeal transformations are accomplished daily, hourly, moment by moment in classrooms, as students are declared to be, for example, 'mature', 'immature', 'low ability', 'high ability', 'a leader' and/or 'at risk'. The order word articulated by a body directly impacts and intervenes in other bodies and shifts the atmosphere, slows down or speeds up affective transformations, and alters the field of relations. Order words propel bodies to adopt particular postures: ways of thinking-speaking-feeling-acting-moving. A student knows the postures that they should adopt if they are to be recognised as in line with the social order. As one student said when analysing the above puppet scenario, speaking of their own classroom experiences: 'There are times when you don't act mature and then the teacher still treats you as if you are mature, because the teacher actually knows that you are mature' (Shaniqua,[8] Year 10, collaborative analysis). The statement inserts itself into the student's actions and passions – they may choose to 'act' mature now they are treated accordingly or return to acting mature because the teacher 'knows' them to be mature: controlling their bodies, sitting still, picking up a pen and focusing on the paper. The order word effects divisions between teacher and student, young and old which, in turn, transform how the student and teacher understand themselves and hold their faces. A sound or sign 'melds with our physico-affective matrix' (Roy 2003: 167). Bodies are affected by the speech of others – the force of the order word forms and constitutes who bodies think they are and what they can do.

Language, rather than presuming subjectivity, produces subjects; language serves an 'existentialising function' in the processes of subjectification (Guattari 1995: 22). Subjectification – the production of subjectivity – is effected through language: 'You will be a subject, nailed down as one, a subject of the enunciation recoiled into a subject of the statement' (Deleuze and Guattari 1980/1987: 159). Each time a student and/or a teacher speaks, political changes are inaugurated, effected or reinscribed. Certain bodies are recognised as legitimate speakers of order words, while other bodies' voices and articulations are unrecognisable, illegitimate, unspeakable (cf. Butler 1997), dismissed because they are too immature, too unrefined, too emotional. As Fred Moten has said, speaking of the classroom context, 'in order to be recognisable, you have to answer the call to order' – 'to be recognisable within the terms of order' (in Harney and Moten 2013: 125). Deleuze and Guattari (1980/1987) note the contingency of the response to a declaration of war: 'I declare a general mobilisation' (82) – a statement that might be compared to the student-marionette's declaration: 'It's a good question.' If there is not the 'effectuated variable' that gives 'that person the right to make such a statement', such a statement will be regarded as 'an act of puerility or insanity, not an act of enunciation' (Deleuze and Guattari 1980/1987: 82).

There may also be statements made by adults and governing institutions (for example, policy statements that students can now 'have a voice' in school decision-making processes) that also do *not* have the effects that they desire. Indeed, various order words and their accompanying incorporeal transformations may intersect, compete, cancel out and complicate each other. Deleuze and Guattari's concepts of order words and incorporeal transformations may seem to suggest that, when an authoritative document – like the United Nations Convention on the Rights of the Child (UNCRC) – declares that children and young people have 'rights', this declaration will incorporeally transform student-subjects and, consequently, the order of schooling. The United Nations, indeed, is an authoritative speaker – like a judge or a teacher, it would be thought that the statement 'you have rights, as a child' might transform the bodies of children and young people into rights-bearing individuals, who are then capable of affecting and authoritatively intervening in their schooling.[9] Yet, as I discuss in the following sections, there are variables left open in this statement imparting 'rights' and competing order words in the context of schooling – including assessments of the 'maturity' (age), 'competence' (ability) and 'reliability' (emotionality) of the child's testimony. This statement of rights comes to rest differently on different bodies; the weight of history bears down on and shapes contemporary common-sense approaches to rights.

Political theorist Sana Nakata (2015) has powerfully explained the politics of children and young people claiming rights, even after they are declared to 'have' them. As Nakata (2015) demonstrates, successfully claiming rights depends on the recognition of the speaker as 'already hav[ing] a political subjectivity that makes for the possibility of being a rights-holder' and that their actions are recognised as political (2). However, children and young people are 'not generally regarded as having any political character, they do not often make rights claims for themselves, but rather other adults do so on their behalf' (Nakata 2015: 2). They, thus, 'are not in the same position to enforce their rights as adults' (28). Even when an authoritative statement is made 'giving' them 'rights', other order words may invalidate the legitimacy of their subsequent speech. This potential cancelling out of the order word declaring children and young people's rights can be understood through considering other historical order words of schooling.

The next section constructs an account of some of the historical order words of schooling, thinking with the puppet scenario. These order words segment students according to their presumed 'age', 'ability', 'emotionality' and purport, in their institutional use, to be politically neutral: just extractible 'data' about particular students. According to common sense, *everybody knows* that human bodies of a certain age can and can't do certain things; *everybody knows* that some people just 'naturally' have more intellectual ability than others; *everybody knows* that some people are 'naturally' more emotional than others (Deleuze 1968/1994, my emphasis). Segregations between particular bodies – in age groupings, ability groupings, and the separation of students with 'behavioural' issues from other students – follow from these ordering words. I have taught and researched in schools marked as 'low socioeconomic' or 'disadvantaged', and with separate 'special units' for students with 'special needs'; students, variously, are ordered as 'ESL/EALD (English as a Second Language/English as an Additional Language or Dialect)', 'refugee', 'disengaged', 'at risk' and 'gifted and talented', in a 'selective stream', on 'green', 'amber' or 'red' traffic-light behaviour levels, and so on. I introduce historical and sociological accounts of the consequences of these ordering words here; these ordering words will be revisited in Chapters 4–7 in analysing the movement of the concept of student voice in and beyond schools. These order words are not unmoveable; there also may be 'pass words' that can interrupt the work of order words (Deleuze and Guattari 1980/1987): that which cannot be ordered and/or refuses to be ordered.

## *The Order of Schooling*

### ORDERING AGE: THE YOUNG VOICE

When the concept of students 'having a voice' is invoked, students' voices may be apprehended through common sense understandings of age. What the student-puppet says may be understood in accordance with his[10] young age, interpreted through a prior framing of his developmental immaturity that makes it easy to dismiss his question. The puppet scenario that opens this chapter also includes a second scene – when the student-marionette's body has now 'grown up' and is in Year 11. The student-marionette, now a few years older, asks the same question:

**Pythagoras (narrator):** Fast forward to year 11. The same question is asked.
**Samantha (teacher-puppet):** Good morning everybody. Um, as you all know, um, Pythagoras was visited in the younger years in order to –
**Johnathan (student-marionette):** *(Tone of voice is deeper in pitch and calm in tone. Remains seated)* Excuse me miss, um, I'd like to ask a question. How does this benefit us in life?

*Figure 3.3* A Year 11 student-marionette sits and asks a question.

**Samantha (teacher-puppet):** Oah! I'm happy you asked that question and I'll be happy to explain it to you. Um, you may not feel that Pythagoras is important, but it is because um, you'll um, it'll be, um, it will appear in all your exams. Blah blah blah blah.

*Figure 3.4* A teacher-puppet answers the student-marionette's question.

In this later scene, the teacher-puppet relates differently to the older student-marionette than they had to the younger student-marionette. Pythagoras said, after creating this puppet scenario: 'if a younger student asks any question, it's just disregarded. It's going to be immature. A senior student does it, it's worth talking about' (focus group). The question itself does not change from Year 8 to Year 11, but something has changed in the student-marionette's physical body, interpreted by the teacher-puppet as a growth in intellectual maturity.

There is a history to the ordering of students' voices and bodies according to age, informed by modernist Western conceptualisations of childhood that overlap, diverge and sometimes contradict one another. As flagged in Chapter 2, 'objective' studies of the child (conducted by European and North American men) aimed to establish the origins of adult behaviour and the stages of 'natural' processes of development: from Freud's psychoanalytic studies of psychosexual development to Jean Piaget's (1977) studies of stages of cognitive development. Later psychoanalytic and linguistic theories, like John Bowlby's (1982) psychoanalytic theory of humans' biological programming for attachment, and Noam Chomsky's (1965) theories of the innate structures and functions of language acquisition, aimed to determine natural, universal processes of social and linguistic development. G. Stanley Hall's (1904) conceptualisation of adolescence as a period of 'storm and stress' naturalised a perception of the emotional volatility of young people of a particular age range: limited self-control (the 'storm') and a sensitivity to stimuli around them (the 'stress'). Hall's conceptualisation of adolescence was inextricable from his recapitulation theory – that is, the theory that the individual human's biological development from infancy to adulthood recapitulates the history of the whole species from 'barbaric' to 'civilised'. Recapitulation theory was profoundly influenced by eugenic theories of race, racial hygiene and evolution that naturalised White supremacy (Lesko 2012). These earlier psychological and psychoanalytic conceptualisations of the child's development oriented the gaze of the adult towards children and young people's physical, emotional and intellectual deficits in comparison to adults and separated the individual from others as a site of observation and regulation (Burman 1994). This common-sense logic that students developmentally progress through stages of 'maturity' over linear time is inextricable from accompanying justifications for classed and racialised segmentations between bodies.

Even as theories of age and the social ordering of generations have been contested and demonstrated to be contingent, contested and unstable, shifting and changing in and within historical periods, societies, cultures and institutions, developmental understandings of children and young people's progression through predictable stages in linear time have pervaded societal common-sense understandings of childhood and adolescence. Bodies are segmented in a binary and linear fashion in the education system, the justice system, and political participation processes. Within schools, young people's words, emotions and actions are commonly understood in relation to normative developmental psychological stages, pathways and/or deviations. Monitoring, controlling and channelling young people's desires in order to develop their character and sense of responsibility are a critical part of developing 'citizen-workers of the future' (Lister 2007: 697) and securing national order and progress (Bessant 2021a). To return to the UNCRC, the views of the child can be 'given due weight in accordance of the age and maturity of the child' (United Nations 1989): a convenient loophole to lighten the weight of the child or young person's view. According to these developmental ways of knowing students, the student-marionette may be interpreted as immature according to his age, lacking expertise in comparison with the older teacher-puppet. Chapter 4 further considers how this order word of age shapes student representation in school governance processes.

ORDERING ABILITY: THE LINGUISTIC VOICE

The student-marionette's words are apprehended not only in relation to the age of his body, but also in relation to his perceived ability, appraised through performance on tests in the dominant language group of the schooling system (in Australia, Standard Australian English). Historically, testing of cognitive capacities and linguistic competencies and theories of differential linguistic 'codes' across groups have (explicitly or implicitly) reinforced a professional common sense that appraises the linguistic capacities and expressions of students who differ from the Western norm in deficit terms. Before and alongside the testing of 'intelligence' (for example, the 1904 Intelligence Quotient tests developed in France by Alfred Binet and Theodore Simon), racialised differences between human bodies and groups were conveniently 'found' through social Darwinist evolutionist practices of eugenics, craniology and phrenology (Rudolph 2018). The European discipline of linguistics ordered and mapped languages onto tree-like diagrams, defining, bounding, describing and sorting languages with the 'scientific' assumption that language is a stable structure, assuming wholeness and original identities, while curtailing multiplicity (López López 2017: 60).

In schools, children and young people's speech has been ordered and managed: working-class children and young people discouraged from speaking vernacular forms of the standard language, and First Nations children and young people forbidden from speaking their language and dialects at school in the interests of 'assimilation' (Bodkin-Andrews and Carlson 2016). Complex mixes of multiple languages – what Glissant describes as 'mutual mutations generated by [the] interplay of relations' (1990/1997: 89) – are unrecognisable in the hierarchical ordering of language groups and the testing of language skills, with implications for how children and young people's vernacular voices are interpreted within the schooling system. Intelligence Quotient (IQ) instruments to assess the cognitive 'ability' of the child and young person were/are informed by such Western 'scientific' ways of knowing that naturalised differences and inequalities between bodies on the basis of race, gender and class as by-products of evolutionary and genetic differences, eliding the cultural specificity and bias of the test instruments themselves and histories of the ordering and suppression of language. Official testing of students has focused attention on deficit – the language of 'disparity', 'disadvantage' and 'failure', rather than on colonial processes of suppressing language and culture, and the devaluing and denial of other ways of knowing and speaking (Fogarty et al. 2018; Rudolph 2018). As Kamilaroi scholar Melitta Hogarth has eloquently put it in the context of Australia, this 'discursive trickery' has normalised notions of 'Indigenous inferiority and implicitly, White superiority' (2018: 667). Questions of the politics of knowledge production are frequently elided – that is, who creates these evaluative instruments and the 'persistence of authorizing non-Indigenous researchers as the knowers' (Shay and Sarra 2021: 11).

Judgements of students' linguistic capacities and related judgements of their 'abilities' have powerful consequences for how students' bodies are ordered, and how their voices continue to be understood and shaped throughout their time in and beyond school. I use inverted commas around 'ability', after the work of educational researcher Becky Francis and colleagues in the UK, to signal a conception of 'a fixed and inherent level of "ability"' that has powerful consequences for students' experiences of school, their self-confidence and sense of their intelligence (Francis et al. 2020: 2, 157). The segregation of students according to prior academic attainment into separate groups or 'sets' – also called 'streaming' or 'tracking' – is still a prevalent practice internationally, despite research that has demonstrated its detrimental effects on students with low prior attainment (Francis et al. 2020). Students' modes of speech, emotional expression and bodily deportment are closely entwined with educational sorting and selecting, shaping students' access to educational opportunities. Students from classed and racialised backgrounds with modes of speech and bodily deportment most similar to those valued by dominant (white, middle class) groups in society are more likely to be grouped in higher 'streams' (or 'tracks') according to prior academic attainment, and to experience academic success and a sense of achievement (Apple 1979; Bourdieu and Passeron 1977; Francis et al. 2020). In 'ability' streams or tracks, students are given or withheld access to knowledge and skills associated with social power and reward (Anyon 1980; Haberman 1991/2010), creating a 'double disadvantage' for students 'from disadvantaged backgrounds who are placed in "low ability" groupings' (Francis et al. 2020: 3). In (so-called) low 'ability' classrooms, where students from non-dominant class, language and racialised backgrounds are over-represented, classroom communication is frequently dominated by teachers' voices (Barnes et al. 1969). *'Blah blah blah blah.'* The classroom experiences that students are offered (or not), in turn, order their voices and shape their conception of themselves as learners and of their capacity to effect change in their classrooms, schools and lives.

Students' subsequent success or failure in school can be understood in relation to their background or internal qualities or deficits; Richard Valencia describes how 'deficit thinking' (1997, 2010) serves to further order and reproduce cycles of classifications according to (so-called) 'ability'. Challenges faced by particular students in schools are then attributed to 'alleged cognitive and motivational deficits', and/or genetic pathology, immoral behaviour, asserted deficits in material family circumstances, and family linguistic and communicative resources (Valencia 1997: 9). The student-puppet's voice in this puppet scenario might be understood, according to such deficit thinking, as lacking communicative resources to diplomatically articulate his opinions – even as this assessment of 'ability' may be filtered through the lenses of his perceived racialised, classed and gendered identity.

ORDERING EMOTION: THE EMOTIONAL VOICE

The ordering of students' bodies according to age and ability, however, does not contain the affective expressions of students' voices. Noise in schools is overlaid with normative expectations of what students' voices should sound like. The student-marionette's voice, if/when apprehended and understood as overly emotional (*'disruptive'*), may be subject to disciplinary or psychological intervention. This order word of emotion murmurs around the call for students to empower themselves by 'having a voice'.

Feminist scholarship over time has mapped how bodies have been ordered and understood according to codes that segment rationality (associated with males) from emotionality (associated with females). Earlier feminist scholars unthreaded taken-for-granted gendered norms surrounding emotion and rationality that construct women as a threat to social order, dialogue and rationality (Jaggar 1989; Lloyd 1984). Feminist and queer scholars have further explored how voices and bodies are known and understood through taken-for-granted conceptions of 'emotion'. These scholars have traced how the subject is commonly understood to be 'energetically and affectively self-contained' (Brennan 2004: 2), 'expressing' emotions from the 'inside-out' (Ahmed 2004: 8–9). These ways of understanding emotions are critiqued for their individualising of feeling, and their marginalisation of the political question of 'who decides' what emotions are acceptable and unacceptable (Boler 1999: 98).

In schools, dominant psychological understandings of emotion have produced explanations, classifications, regulative devices and programmes to remedy the internal issues of isolated individuals, sorting and sifting the (so-called) 'abnormal' or 'at risk' 'emotional' student from the 'rational' student (Harwood 2006). Certain expressions of feeling – associated with classed, racialised and gendered subjectivities – may be considered to be too excessive, too extreme, too heated in emotional expression when judged against the normative standard of white middle-class bodies' expressions of emotion (Youdell 2011). These young people's expressions of emotions are apprehended and interpreted in terms of what they are perceived to lack: control, diplomacy, respect. When students are considered to lack emotional control, there becomes, as Val Gillies puts it, 'no pedagogically acceptable language for voicing the fear, violence, hardship and racism' that shape their lives (2011: 193–4). Psychologising order words effect transformations on young people and their educators and individualise and abstract emotions from their social and political contexts.

Order words imputing emotionality have concrete consequences: students considered unable or unwilling to control their emotions are more likely to be spatially relocated outside of conventional classrooms, experience surveillance, punitive discipline, suspension or expulsion, or to 'drop out' or be 'pushed out' of school (Fine 1991; Smyth and Hattam 2001; Tuck 2012; Youdell 2006), and/or to be diagnosed with a behaviour disorder (Harwood and Allan 2014). The emotional expression and psychological vulnerability of young people with particular religious and racialised identifications may be more closely monitored, with the educator looking out for any interpretable signs of (so-called) radicalisation to violent extremism (Abdel-Fattah 2021). Such psychologising frames of interpretation of emotional expression reconstitute the educator as 'guardian of the mouth', particularly in relation to the 'threat of minority orality' (Niccolini 2009: 41, 42).

In Chapter 6, I explore the enactment, at one school, of a particular school 'reform' programme that orders students' expressions of emotions: Positive Behaviour Interventions and Supports. Programmes like Positive Behaviour Interventions and Supports encourage schools to develop a consensus, across their diverse community of students, parents/guardians and educators, of the school's values and emotional and behavioural norms. Developing a consistent school-wide framework for behaviour support is understood as supporting individual students to 'identify, understand and regulate their emotions, and understand and manage the emotions of others' (Mayes et al. 2020: 4). Such programmes have been criticised for placing the onus on individual students to take responsibility for their feelings, and to then adjust and self-regulate their emotions (Gillies 2011). This imperative to 'take responsibility' for individual emotions is then passed downwards (from leaders to teachers, and teachers to students) (Mayes 2020c). Bodies are compelled to perform their positivity. As Sara Ahmed (2010) has argued, this imperative to positivity positions melancholic, angry or emotionally ambivalent bodies as Other, with these bodies associated with queer, migrant, neurodiverse and politically activist subjectivities. Focusing attention on individualised emotions elides political questions surrounding the conditions that generate 'unacceptable' emotions like anger, and the conditions for acceptable speech in schools.

According to the order word of emotion, the student-marionette's words and actions from the beginning of this chapter might be understood as indicators of his need to learn to manage his emotions more effectively, while the teacher-puppet's response (*'You're being disruptive'*) might be interpreted as rational and justified. Such ways of apprehending and ordering voices condition what students' 'empowered' voices can do. I take up this order word of emotionality further in Chapter 6's analysis of the interweaving of a student voice and a Positive Behaviour initiative at one school.

DATA-AGENCEMENTS: THE ORDER FOR DATA IN SCHOOLS

In the previous sections, I constructed an account of three order words that code multiplicity and instantiate order. In this section, I turn to the production of data about students, teachers and schools. These data form ordering-agencements that constitute another voice murmuring around the call for schools to encourage students to 'have a voice'. Interpretations of the student-marionette's utterances through the grids of his age, perceived ability and emotionality are tangled up with the data that have been produced about him: data about his attendance, academic results, behaviour and so on. Data 'about' the student-marionette become a justification for further intervention. In turn, the imperative to produce and interpret data has reconstituted teachers' work and their professional subjectivities, reshaping the pedagogical relations that are possible between the student-marionette and his teachers.

It has become taken for granted that schools must be 'data driven' – that is, that the strategic direction of schools is to be steered by the data that demonstrate certain problems. Schools are to take up reform interventions that are 'evidence based'; reform interventions are to be evaluated by the generation of further data to evaluate if the intervention 'worked'. In Stephen Ball's (2003) influential piece on the 'terrors of performativity' in education, he writes about the work of data in evaluating educators and schools:

> The performances (of individual subjects or organisations) serve as measures of productivity, or output, or displays of 'quality', or 'moments' of promotion or inspection. As such they stand for, encapsulate or represent the worth, quality or value of an individual or organisation within a field of judgement. (Ball 2003: 216)

Quantitative data are used to construct, know, analyse and govern the practices and performance of students, educators and schools (Biesta 2010). Compelled to produce and intervene into the arrangements of data (data-agencements), educators and school leaders are called to order; they are called to construct progress narratives that demonstrate positive growth over time. Alongside this ascendance of 'governing by numbers' (Rose 1991), it has also become commonly accepted that students (alongside staff and parents/caregivers) should be part of classroom and school evaluation processes (Brown et al. 2020), in the generation of qualitative 'soft data' evaluating teaching and other school initiatives (Simons 2015). Using student voice in whole-school self-evaluation is part of new public management trends towards the self-managing school; educators and schools are compelled to evaluate themselves and to include the positional insights of 'stakeholders' rather than to be (only) inspected from outside (Brady 2016). These processes work to produce new 'teacher assemblages' (Webb 2009): professional subjects who 'openly profess data-responsive attitudes and dispositions' (Lewis and Holloway 2019: 36–7).

The order to generate data has reordered how students are known, how school demographics are re/composed, and the pedagogies that students experience. As I discuss further in Chapter 6, generating and arranging data leads to the cutting up and reconfiguring of complex mixtures of human and non-human bodies and their encounters. The individual subject is rendered '"dividual" material to be controlled', extracted, inserted into other fields (Deleuze 1992b: 7): for example, into collected student achievement data, student suspension data, student attendance data, and so on. Individual and group student data may be interpreted in essentialising ways – for example, explaining student results through recourse to 'inherent deficits' that confirms 'assumptions about students and their families' and ignores 'the unjust context that shapes student outcomes', including 'systemic racism and white supremacy' (Bertrand and Marsh 2021: 35, 36). The public display of school data (on websites like the Australian *My School* website [Australian Curriculum Assessment and Reporting Authority, ACARA 2021], which includes demographic data and aggregated results from standardised test results) has also promoted school 'choice'. School 'choice' has been associated with a 'steady exodus from comprehensive public schools', particularly of socio-economically privileged families (Ho 2015: para. 3). The 'choices' of socio-economically privileged families have been enhanced, while inequalities and informal modes of segregation have escalated across educational systems (OECD 2012; Rowe 2017). This production and strategic arranging of data, and the segregations that accompany subsequent 'school choice' practices, come to amplify the ordering of students: students may then be further grouped by the order words of age, ability and emotionality. In some settings, the increased emphasis on performance, competition, compliance, and the more visible sorting and selecting functions of schools have exacerbated student resistances and forced confrontations between, in particular, students and educators (Mayes and Howell 2018; Youdell 2011). Greg Thompson and Ian Cook wonder, from their survey findings of

Western Australian and South Australian teacher perceptions of the impact of standardised testing on curriculum and pedagogy, whether the language and logics surrounding how 'good' teaching is known are being reshaped: from 'non-statistical ways' of knowing students such as 'student responsiveness, depth of understanding of key concepts and student engagement' to that which can be measured (2013: 254); from 'care to codes' (2012b: 579). This analysis resonates with Michael Fielding's (1999b) question, more than twenty years ago, of the impact of logics of accountability on pedagogical relationships:

> How many teachers [. . .] are now able to listen openly, attentively, and in a non-instrumental, exploratory way to their children/students without feeling guilty, stressed or vaguely uncomfortable about the absence of criteria or the insistence of a target tugging at their sleeves? (280)

To return to the puppet scenario in this chapter, the response of the teacher-puppet to the student-marionette's question might be understood in the context of this sharpened focus on teachers' work and student outcomes. '*[I]t will appear in all your exams.*' In a climate where teachers are continually advised by a cacophony of distant policy makers and politicians about how their work should be done, and evaluated through their students' performances, how might an educator feel when a student adds another voice to this cacophony? '*Please, there's no time for your questions!*' To listen to students' voices may be challenging both for practical reasons (finding the time to listen) as well as psychically. '*Um, you may not feel that Pythagoras is important, but it is because um, you'll um, it'll be, um, it will appear in all your exams.*' The interplay of students' physical voices, educators' voices and the voices of data will be further explored in Chapter 6, where I take up the story of how one school ordered their data in response to the troubling intensities surrounding a student voice initiative.

## *Transforming the Order Words of Schooling?*

This chapter has focused attention on what happens when bodies speak in schools: how words form and are formed in shifting settings, and what order words do to bodies and subjectivities. I introduced Deleuze and Guattari's concepts of common sense, order words and agencements, in conversation with a puppet scenario created by students in Year 11. I introduced accounts from the sociology of education of the ordering of students according to age, ability and

## Ordering Voices and Bodies in the History of Schooling

emotionality, and explored how this order is reinforced through data-agencements. This chapter deliberately leaves hanging two issues that subsequent chapters will explore: the unpredictable effects of authoritative statements and subterranean escapes from the dominant order.

Indeed, this chapter risked painting a picture of schools as tightly ordered, as if there were some fixed 'grammar of schooling' (Mayes 2020a; Tyack and Tobin 1994). Subsequent chapters will explore how a social machine (including, here, a school or school system) is 'defined as a *system of interruptions*' (Deleuze and Guattari 1983: 36, original emphasis). Even as order is instantiated and reinscribed daily, there are always cracks effected, leaks made, and desiring-agencements that scramble the order. Within a school, gaps and leaks in the order are felt every day: voices that will not be quiet, bodies that will not sit still, collective hums that rise in volume in the playground or staffroom. There are those who '[scramble] all the codes' of schooling (Deleuze and Guattari 1983: 15). As Ligia (Licho) López López has eloquently written, bodies that are ordered 'are also moving targets', 'participants in the making process, as they change and refuse fixity' (2019: 162). There are 'pass-words beneath order words': 'words that are components of passage' (Deleuze and Guattari 1980/1987: 110). These pass words alter the political question from how to 'elude' the order word to how to 'draw out the revolutionary potential' of the order word (Deleuze and Guattari 1980/1987: 110). Desire can escape, exceed, refuse order and/or arrange itself in more affirmative modes of ordering. As Fred Moten puts it: 'every day that you go into your classroom, you have a chance not to issue the call to order, and then to see what happens' – to notice and celebrate 'what was already happening' and what might still happen (in Harney and Moten 2013: 127, 129). In Sylvia Wynter's terms, this is also to tell other stories that generate new forms of sociality and new worlds (Alagraa 2018).

In the following chapters, I consider a range of attempts to challenge the order words of schooling via student voice-related initiatives. In Chapter 4, I discuss mandatory student representation on school governance councils; in Chapter 5, efforts to encourage student-led dialogue in classrooms and to listen to (so-called) 'silenced' voices; in Chapter 6, student participation in a school reform process. Across these chapters, I interrogate the logics at work in these various initiatives and how they may reinforce the order words of schooling, and other micropolitical potentialities that are simultaneously at work.

The following chapter, Chapter 4, considers the logics of categorical difference that inform calls for mandatory student representation on school governance councils. While critiquing these logics, the chapter also gestures towards the potential of attending to the 'unrepresented singularity' which does not recognise itself in those ostensibly representing them, 'precisely because it is not everyone or the universal' (Deleuze 1968/1994: 52).

## *Notes*

1. The names used in the transcripts of these puppet scenarios are pseudonyms that each student-speaker wrote for themselves (see Chapter 2 for an account of this process). These three Year 11 students described themselves on sticky notes in the following terms: 'Pythagoras': '16 year old male Pakistani Background. Interests: Everything English related; Leadership (Vice Captain); Thinks independently; Loves to question; Thinks critically.' 'Samantha': '17 year old Lebanese gal. Independent, assertive and a curious learner. Passionate about leadership and excelling in education. Interested in the world around me and love to question everything.' 'Johnathan Rudd' did not write a self-description.
2. To give an account of contemporary common sense in education, the problem arises of where to begin. Did contemporary common-sense ways of ordering schools begin with histories of the establishment of compulsory schooling – schooling as a way to instil respectability, obedience and 'usefulness' into working-class children unable to work when child labour became prohibited (cf. Ahmed 2019)? And/or with the colonial social project that attempted to erase and/or assimilate First Nations children into the 'values' of the coloniser through Christian Missions and/or forced removal from families and communities and, later, through schooling, with dramatically differing aims and quality of education offered to Indigenous and non-Indigenous students (Bodkin-Andrews and Carlson 2016)? And/or when the logics of segmenting and segregating young bodies from older bodies, 'boys' from 'girls', higher and lower 'abilities', began? And/or when the mouth became considered to be a private organ, the possession of an individual human body, with each individual made responsible and accountable for what tumbled out of their mouths (Deleuze and Guattari 1983)?
3. Wynter's theory of the historical production of Man is rich and multifaceted, extending and enriching the work of anti-colonial theorists Frantz Fanon and Aimé Césaire, and correcting Foucault's critique of Man (see da Silva 2015 for a thorough account). According to Wynter, secular rationalist Man 1 (Homo politicus) emerges in the Renaissance with the Enlightenment and, specifically, the European encounter

with the inhabited Americas in 1492. Man 2 (Homo oeconomicus) forms with Darwinian divisions that divides those 'naturally selected' (Europeans) from those racialised as 'naturally' inferior. Wynter's theory of the production of Man and who is considered 'civilised' exceeds biology, combining *bios* (flesh-and-blood) and *mythoi* (the stories told about what 'we' are and where we came from) (see Wynter and McKittrick 2015). While over-represented Man is often front and centre in Western artistic and institutional practices, there are myriad differing, incomplete genres of being human (Wynter and McKittrick 2015).

4. See also Deleuze's earlier works: *The Logic of Sense* (1969/2013) and *Empiricism and Subjectivity* (1953/1991).
5. Deleuze and Guattari's use of 'discourse', in their pragmatic approach to language, is to be distinguished from Foucault's notion of discourse. Deleuze and Guattari's use of the term 'direct discourse' refers generally to the enunciation, while 'indirect discourse' refers to the taken-for-granted ways of thinking that manifest in what people say. Foucault uses the term 'discourse' to refer not only to 'shifting systems of knowledge', but also to 'practices that systematically form the objects about which they speak' (Foucault 1972: 49). Deleuze, in his book on Foucault (Deleuze 1999/1986), writes admiringly about Foucault's work on discourses, focusing on Foucault's concept of the 'statement' and 'discursive formations'.
6. Wynter and Deleuze and Guattari are all taking aim at Lévi-Strauss's (1973/2009) *Structural Anthropology* and his structuralist account of the binary structure of all epistemes across all cultures and their value hierarchies.
7. I spell this word as 'subjectification' after the translator's (Brian Massumi's) spelling used in *A Thousand Plateaus* (1980/1987) and keep this spelling consistent throughout this book. I acknowledge, however, Andrew Murphie's (2001: 1315) distinction between 'subjectification' ('a thoroughly stratified or captured position') and 'subjectivication' ('subjective operations which, although operating within social machines, use the processes of these social machines to form lines of escape from them'). For Murphie (2001), both concepts 'involve one's implication in contemporary social machines' and both are 'pragmatic' (1315).
8. 'Shaniqua' described herself, on a sticky note, in the following terms: 'I am a very positive person and I always like to grow a relationship with my teachers. I'm unique, not as smart but still smart. I'm loud, happy. I find myself to be a bit funny. I love making people laugh. I listen in class so I would call myself a good student.'
9. Of course, I am paraphrasing the statement: 'the right to express those views freely in all matters affecting the child, the views of the child

being given due weight in accordance with the age and maturity of the child' (United Nations 1989).
10. The students who created this puppet scenario used the gendered pronoun 'he'. This pronoun suggests their understandings of the gendered bodies associated with deficient and excessive expressions of voice in school.

## 4

# Representing Difference in School Governance

> *'People in parliament don't look anything like the people they represent. By that I mean there's not enough women in parliament . . . people of colour . . . people with disabilities, or trans people, or gays and lesbians.'*
> 'Samaa, a young woman of colour', speaking at Melbourne's March 4 Justice rally, 18 March 2021

Representation is a fraught concept and practice in contemporary political life. Man – that is, the liberal humanist 'average' adult-white-heterosexual-able-bodied-male citizen who speaks standard English (Deleuze and Guattari 1980/1987: 105) – has been, and continues to be – decidedly over-represented. As Sylvia Wynter puts it, this Western bourgeois conception of Man 'overrepresents itself as if it were the human itself' (2003: 260). For Wynter, the 'struggle of our times' is 'the struggle against this overrepresentation' (Wynter 2003: 262). Samaa, the young woman of colour quoted above (by Issa 2021) – exemplifies the frustration at this over-representation of Man in politics. On 15 March 2021, tens of thousands of people across Australia rallied against gender-based violence, following a wave of allegations of historical and recent sexual assault by Members of Australia's Parliament and their staffers. This emerging national outrage was fuelled by the statements of Brittany Higgins, an ex-political adviser who alleged in February 2021 that she was raped in a minister's office in 2019. This outcry and these protests are evanescent expressions of dissent at work – people refusing those who claim to represent them, speaking and acting beyond sanitised forums in which they are invited by those in power to 'have a voice'.

In Australia, it is well documented that the majority of elected political representatives come from white, middle-class backgrounds and are male. A report by independent think tank Per Capita summarises the 'way' to the Australian Parliament based on demographic data of federal Members of Parliament (MPs): 'to be born male in Australia to a white family, attend a private school, get a university degree and then practise as a lawyer (if conservative) or work in a union (if progressive) before entering politics' (Lewis 2019: 14). Even when more 'diverse' representatives are elected to formal political structures, these structures do not necessarily become more 'inclusive', nor produce better political outcomes for all constituents. The increased representation of women in the Australian Parliament in 2020 did little to raise (then) Australian Prime Minister Scott Morrison's concerns about the culture of misogyny in Parliament – until mass public outrage and protests followed former staffer Brittany Higgins's public allegations. Despite the increased representation of First Nations Australians in Parliament in 2018 (Lewis 2019: 14), there have continued to be multiple reframings, excuses and justifications for not enacting a First Nations 'Voice' to Parliament, let alone a Treaty.[1]

Issues of representation in political life reverberate in the politics of schooling: specifically, who leads and who teaches in schools. In Australia, it has been well documented that 'the Australian teaching workforce does not reflect the cultural and linguistic diversity of the Australian population' – both historically, but also persisting in the present (Australian Institute for Teaching and School Leadership [AITSL] n.d.: 13). According to a report published in 2019, almost a quarter (24.8 per cent) of Australian school students speak a language other than English at home, compared with 8.9 per cent of primary school teachers, 2.6 per cent of primary school leaders, 10.8 per cent of secondary school teachers, and 7.7 per cent of secondary school leaders (Australian Institute for Teaching and School Leadership [AITSL] n.d.: 13). While 5.7 per cent of school students identify as Aboriginal and/or Torres Strait Islander, only 1.1 per cent of primary school teachers and leaders, 0.8 per cent of secondary school teachers, and 0.2 per cent of secondary school leaders identify as Aboriginal and/or Torres Strait Islander (Australian Institute for Teaching and School Leadership [AITSL] n.d.: 13). Student leadership within schools – exemplified by Student Representative Councils (SRC) – also have been demonstrated to be sites where privilege is over-represented. Over many years, there have been repeated studies demonstrating the tendency for students who are already confident, high achieving, popular and articulate (which often align with white and middle-class markers of privilege) to be chosen and/or elected for student voice activities representing their peers (for example, Cox and Robinson-Pant 2006; Whitty and Wisby 2007). It has been argued that these representative structures in schools may reinforce inequalities between students: which students' views are attended to, and which students' views are marginalised (Arnot and Reay 2004; Messiou and Ainscow 2015).

In this chapter, I explore advocacy and research that contributed to a policy change in the state of Victoria in 2018 that made it mandatory for state secondary schools to have student representatives on school governance councils – beyond student representation via Student Representative Councils (SRCs). This mandatory student representation can be understood as a macropolitical strategy to challenge the order and governance of schooling (see Chapter 3) via the integration of students in spaces where significant decisions affecting them are made. This is the first of three chapters that each consider a particular concept associated with student voice – representing (Chapter 4), understanding (Chapter 5), and evaluating (Chapter 6). This chapter interrogates the logics of representation that undergirds this advocacy for student representation on school governance councils (and other governance boards). Indeed, it has become a new norm, in many jurisdictions across the Global North, that school-aged students should be represented on governing bodies of schools, local councils and non-governmental organisations; young people have become another key stakeholder group in forums where decisions affecting them are made. In these forums, student representatives stand in for the broader student body as a proxy, attempting to represent the interest of the broader body associated with the identity marker 'student'. This chapter concentrates on policy enthusiasm for the representation of young people on governance councils of schools, and the rationales and experiences of student representation in these forums, according to students and school principals. I think about the tendency for particular bodies to stick together in the particular symbolic and material spaces and times of governance councils. This chapter employs Arun Saldanha's (2007) theorising of viscosity – attractional pull and surface tension – between particular types of bodies marked with privilege. I consider the possibilities of Deleuze and Guattari's critique of representational logics of difference and recognition for rethinking and reworking representational models of change at work in student voice. This chapter argues that policy changes to mandate the inclusion of student representatives on governance councils may effect a quantitative change (the numerical addition of students) without a qualitative change – an intensive change in the politics of schooling itself. That is, policy changes may be made with little done to alter the way that children, young people and the role of students are conceptualised in society, and little done to alter the logics that schools must be run like businesses. However, this argument does not diminish the micropolitical force of such macropolitical policy changes, which operate in excess of the individual student who represents their peers. In other contexts, political injustices and inertia do not not stop students from taking powerful actions that come to shift educational policy (see Welton et al. 2017 for historical examples in the USA, and Welton and Harris 2022 for contemporary examples in the USA).

## *Students on School Governance Councils*

> 'The school is made for us – we know what's best for our school. We go there; we know what needs to be improved.'
> Student, metropolitan student workshop

> 'Having students [on school councils] – then it won't just be parents who are old and used to their old ways. If students are there, they have a new way of thinking compared to parents.'
> Student, regional student workshop

> '[Students should have a say in] every aspect of the school's operation. [. . .] Ultimately they're a significant, very large percentage of the community so why shouldn't they have not only an opinion but an actual right to change how the school operates?'
> Principal interview[2]

The entry point for this chapter's exploration of the representational logics of student voice is a commissioned study of school students' and principals' views on student representation on school governance councils in the state of Victoria, Australia. While a range of terms are used nationally and internationally to describe school governance bodies (for example, 'school board' in the USA and Western Australia), I employ the term used in the state of Victoria, Australia: 'school council'. School councils meet regularly (often once a month) to make collective decisions about matters impacting on the daily operations of a school. School governance councils' voluntary members may include the school principal, and teacher, parent and community representatives. The school council is a space of 'democratic potential', according to Andrew Wilkins (2016): 'a space that is accessible to a broader, non-expert, non-technical audience' and that nurtures citizens' 'political capacity' to 'shape public institutions and public life' (18). This section of the chapter opens with fragments of statements made by particular students – extracts from the middle of longer conversations and written responses. These two students and a principal made certain affirmative declarations about the potential of student representation: that students 'know what's best for our school', that student representation will enable 'a new way of thinking', and that student representation might enable the 'actual right to change how the school operates' for a 'very large percentage of the [school] community'.

This study – of students' and principals' views of student representation on school councils – was commissioned by the VicSRC (Victorian Student Representative Council), who describe themselves as: 'the peak body representing school-aged students in Victoria', working 'to empower all student voices to be valued in every aspect of education' (VicSRC 2021: para. 1). In 2015, at the VicSRC's annual Congress meeting, students from across Victoria voted for a policy advocacy priority for the VicSRC for 2016: School Leadership and Governance. The students attending this Congress and voting for this policy priority were themselves representatives from their school communities. VicSRC students arguing for this policy advocacy priority considered mandatory student representation on school councils to be a political strategy that could strengthen student voice in school decision-making processes across Victorian schools.[3] As a former teacher and research advocate for student participation in school governance practices, I was commissioned as a researcher to facilitate a study of students' and principals' views on and experiences of student representation on school councils, to support their policy advocacy.

Accordingly, in negotiating the methodology for the study with the VicSRC, the study was designed not only to investigate secondary school students' and principals' views of the benefits and challenges of student representation on school governance councils, but also to intervene politically in current school council policy arrangements – that is, to advocate change in the composition of Victorian government school councils. Six secondary school students (Years 7–11) were involved throughout the research as co-researchers (Research Interns), and were part of designing, creating and analysing the data. Twenty-one students from Years 7–12 participated in two student workshops (one in metropolitan Melbourne and one in regional Victoria), designed and facilitated by Research Interns. A total of 218 students completed an anonymous online survey sharing their experiences, views and ideas surrounding student representation on school councils. Ten principals were also interviewed by Pinchy Breheny (Research Assistant) and me about their experiences and perspectives on student representation on school councils. Student research activities (co-researcher work, student research workshops and online surveys) generated accounts of past experiences of students who had been student representatives on their school's council, as well as speculations of students who had not directly experienced a school council meeting (see Mayes 2016c).

The final report strategically foregrounded the 'benefits' of student representation on school councils, with curated supporting quotations from students and principals (Mayes 2016c):

1. Students have experiential knowledge that other adults may not have.
2. Young people and adults learn and connect through dialogue.
3. Students have a right to have influence on decisions that affect them.
4. Student representation can improve communication between the school council and the broader student body.
5. Student representatives benefit individually.
6. Students feel heard and valued when changes happen.

This summary of 'benefits' of student representation on school councils was followed, in this report, with discussion of the 'challenges' prompted by student representation on school councils:

1. Students' experiential knowledge may not be recognised, trusted or valued.
2. There are relational, structural and spatial barriers to learning from and connecting with each other.
3. It can be a challenge choosing/electing student representatives who will represent the range of students enrolled in the school and take the role seriously.
4. Student representatives can feel caught in the middle.
5. There are time costs for student representatives on school council.
6. Student representation without action is tokenistic and potentially damaging.

The full report explored these challenges in practical terms, with concrete recommendations and implementation ideas for schools and students (Mayes 2016c). The six student Research Interns and I also co-authored a publication aimed at students and schools, summarising the report findings (Mayes et al. 2016a).

The research report published from this study was used as evidence by the VicSRC in their campaign for mandatory student representation on Victorian Department of Education School Councils. In February 2018, a Ministerial Order was signed, establishing the new category of 'student' as mandatory membership category on Victorian government school councils. Those involved in this study and beyond were delighted with this impact – VicSRC student representatives were reported in the Victorian newspaper *The Age* as being 'thrilled' and it being a 'very exciting moment' (Cook 2017). The VicSRC took the report's recommendations up and extended them further, creating resources to support students and schools to enact 'meaningful' student representative involvement on school councils (VicSRC: Student Voice Hub n.d.). Throughout this process of research and policy change, however, I felt and articulated misgivings about such a drive towards mandatory student representation, while understanding the political significance of this policy advocacy.

To be clear, in questioning the logics of stakeholder representation, I am not dismissing the political tactic of campaigning for greater representation of minoritised groups in forums where decisions affecting them are made, nor the yearning to be recognised in one's specificity. Deleuze and Guattari stress that struggles against majoritarian axioms are not without importance; they acknowledge the 'determining' force of political struggles – for example, feminist struggles for the vote, labour struggles and decolonial struggles (Deleuze and Guattari 1980/1987: 471). For Deleuze and Guattari, these struggles 'index another, coexistent combat': people's 'demand to formulate their problems themselves' (Deleuze and Guattari 1980/1987: 471), to not have another 'speak for' them (Alcoff 1991). Students advocating for mandatory student representation on school governance councils could be described as engaging in 'strategic essentialism' (Spivak 1996: 214; see also Braidotti 1994: 177, 189). Spivak (1996) describes strategic essentialism as working with a 'scrupulously visible political interest' (214) – that is, appealing to a visible, shared group identity for advancing particular political purposes. Appealing to a shared group identity (here: student) does not necessarily suggest that this identity expresses an 'authentic' ontological truth of who the people who identify with this group are. Of course, appealing to an essentialised notion of 'student' masks a multiplicity of differences among, between, within and beyond students. Yet, within the context of educational politics, this strategic appeal to an essentialised notion of 'student' makes the concept of 'student' politically legitimate and operative; this appeal can be mobilised alongside critical questions surrounding representation and power in education.

This chapter explores the assumption that, if there is mandatory student representation on school councils, student interests will necessarily be better served. It interrogates the liberal humanist legacies underpinning this assumption and their logics of representation. I consider how student representatives are compelled to resemble other council representatives to be recognisable as legitimate speakers, and students' accounts of feeling caught in between, speaking for others. Throughout this chapter, quotations from students and principals are interwoven with the voices of theory, in exploring the perturbations and possibilities of student representation. The research configurations where student quotations were spoken/typed/written are indicated in brackets; all principal quotations are from transcribed interviews. The following abbreviations are used after quotations: OS (online survey), MSW (metropolitan student workshop), RSW (regional student workshop), PI (principal interview). Two students are named (with pseudonyms[4]): Samuel and Rebecca; other students in these research conversations are named with the label 'student', since their contributions were either anonymised (in the case of the online survey) or made in focus group settings where individual voices were difficult to identify and distinguish. Samuel and Rebecca, both in Year 12 at the same government co-educational school in an outer suburb of Melbourne, had been student representatives on their school's council in different calendar years. Samuel had been a student representative when he was in Year 11; Rebecca when she was in Year 10. Both gave accounts of their student representative experiences during the metropolitan student workshop. As Samuel and Rebecca shared their experiences, participating students spontaneously asked further questions; some of these questions are included in the transcribed accounts below.

## *The Problem of Recognising Difference*

A student representative in a school council dominated by adults could be understood as 'different' from the standard adult representative: teacher, parent or community member. As outlined in Chapter 3, common sense recognises, classifies and measures subjects and objects under representational categories: *this* is a teacher; *this* is a student; *this* is an adult; *this* is a child (Deleuze 1968/1994: 148). People live by such mantras that demarcate categorical difference: 'everybody recognises that . . .' (as one student wrote in a survey question response) 'students are looked down upon and are not considered smart enough to know what we want or to be involved in big decisions' (OS). Such 'acts of recognition exist and occupy a large part of our daily life' (Deleuze 1968/1994: 135). It is efficient and convenient to think in terms of categories of difference – with a classroom of students, it is efficient and convenient to group like with like, creating distinctions and comparisons between them (and tracking their different patterns of growth over time). According to this common sense, a school council meeting runs smoothly and efficiently when all its members resemble each other: 'We're here to get things done' (Rebecca, MSW). This logic of recognition simplifies, streamlines and triages, even as these stable categories subordinate multiplicity and difference to universality and sameness. This constant or standard is called, in Deleuze and Guattari's work, the 'major' – the abstract 'standard measure' by which others are evaluated (Deleuze and Guattari 1980/1987: 105). This 'major' figure aligns with power and domination – the major appears twice, once in the constant and again in the variable from which the constant is extracted (105). The major figure dominates – any other individual is only understood in its comparative similarity to what is recognisable. Difference is understood in terms of either difference *from* the same (for example, the child as different from the adult), or difference *of* the same over time (for example, a child maturing as they grow up). Difference differs *from* something that is understood to be certain and stable. Difference is understood as comparison and negation – this is X, this is *not* X.

Advocacy for student representation on school governance councils seeks recognition of students as 'stakeholders' in school life – to broaden the standard to include and value students. Such a move seeks to expand the dimensions of the pre-existing constant or standard for a political subject – the liberal humanist Man that opened this chapter (Deleuze and Guattari 1980/1987: 105). Liberal humanist politics of difference defend the rights of minorities to be included in the majority – to be recognised, to participate and to represent themselves as an identity category. This stakeholder model of representation assumes that there will be 'minimal hierarchy, social and cultural diversity, equal valuing of specialist *and* lay knowledge, and forms of open participation which allows for conflicting viewpoints as well as scope for difference and deliberation' (Olmedo and Wilkins 2017: 580, original emphasis). The logic, here, is that the physical presence and recognition of diverse interests and demographic groups at the school council meeting table will enable these interests to be better served. It is anticipated that the inclusion of students in school governance processes will enable their standpoint knowledge and capacities to be recognised, legitimated and affirmed (see Chapter 1):

> [S]tudents know the most about what's going on in classes and can give a perspective that the teachers and parents may not necessarily have. (OS)

> Students know stuff that teachers don't know [. . .]. Students don't know some things that teachers know. It's an opportunity for a partnership. (RSW)

In this liberal humanist vision, when difference is included, the school council can collectively make decisions in the best interests of students at the school through democratic deliberation – in 'partnership'.

> [With student representation, adults] would see our perspective, and not impose rules/ideas that negatively affect us. (OS)

> [Student representatives can have] the courage and voice for the students that don't have the courage and voice on matters affecting them. (MSW)

School council meetings are understood to be social and rational – in Habermasian terms, spaces where individual intellects, wills, intentions and interests work towards 'achieving, sustaining and reviewing consensus' through 'the intersubjective recognition of criticisable validity claims' (Habermas 1984: 86, 17).

Yet, multiplicity is muffled under the category of student, just as it is under the categories of teacher, parent or community member. Even before mandatory student representation, it was not the case that adult members of school councils were representative of the demographics of their school community. A student in a focus group spoke about the over-representation of white bodies in their argument for the need for mandatory student representation:

> [M]y school council's members are 100% Caucasian whilst my school is almost entirely not. It would be good to have some form of representation even if it's from students. (Student, MSW)

Previous research has demonstrated the over-representation of white, middle-class and middle-aged school parents and community members on school governance councils/boards in the UK (for example, Ranson et al. 2005) and USA (for example, Howell 2005). This over-representation has been amplified with the ascendance of the demand for 'good governance' (Olmedo and Wilkins 2017: 580). In Australia, Jessica Gerrard and Glenn Savage (2021) have analysed how devolved school governance practices (in the case of Independent Public Schools in Western Australia) valorise parent members' professional 'managerial skills, knowledge and culture' – those 'more likely to be possessed by middle-class parents in white-collar professions' (10). They have pointed to the tension between the Western Australia Department of Education's stated commitment to ensuring that school governing bodies are representative of the school community, and the valorisation of managerial skills, arguing that this privileging has the potential to 'reproduce, rather than disrupt, prevailing norms in parent engagement patterned by class, race, and gender' (Gerrard and Savage 2021: 10). This analysis accords with Wilkins's (2016) research, in the UK, on the alterations in governance requirements that appeal to 'technical knowledge and expertise', contributing to an ascendance of 'professionals, experts, consultants and research people with decision-making skills' in the composition of school councils (506).

Those students who are student representatives on school councils may perpetuate established patterns of privileging those with particular managerial and communicative skills, associated with white bodies and middle-class subjectivities. Of the ten principals interviewed in my study, eight already had student representatives on their school council. Of these eight, in six cases, the schools' student captains were the default choice for the school council student representative(s). One principal, speaking about having the student school captains on the school's governing council, acknowledged that these students were not demographically representative of the diversity of the school community:

> The word 'representative' could be taken in two ways. Do they [student school captains as school council representatives] represent their peers when they go along to these things [school council meetings]? Yes, I do think they do that. I think they represent the thinking that they are aware of to the best of their ability. Are they representative of our students in terms of behaviour, demography, age, skin colour, language? No, not necessarily but then you could argue that Parliament and you go down into Victoria [state government] – everybody down there is a white middle-class man or woman – is that representative of Victoria? Not at all. We face the same challenges around democratic representation that others would. But do they attempt to represent their peers? I think they absolutely do. (PI)

The risk, then, is that mandatory student representation on school governance councils perpetuates existing patterns of over- and under-representation of particular demographic groups – along gendered, classed and racialised lines.

## *The Problem of Being Recognised as Representing Others*

When representation categories are broadened to include students, the student representative can be recognisable, as long as they are not *too* different – as long as they resemble the major in their speech and actions. Difference is subordinated to 'resemblance' (what it is perceived to resemble), to 'opposition' (according to previous predicates), and to 'analogy' (a judgement that compares) (Deleuze 1968/1994: xv). The student representative who resembles other council members may more easily and comfortably slip into these configurations of bodies. Rebecca's father was a long-standing parent representative on the school council:

> I was chosen because I was one of the more senior SRC [Student Representative Council] members and my Dad was on school council – it was convenient to go [in the car together]. He was there even before I was on council so we had discussions at home about it. It is a big commitment, and daunting, so you have to be interested in going. [. . .] My sister was on it [school council] too – she got into the rhythm. [. . .] She said, 'the financial report is not going to make sense, but one day it will'. (MSW)

There is a certain viscosity in these configurations – a holding together of aggregates of bodies – between particular types of bodies marked with privilege (Saldanha 2007).[5] The concept of viscosity hovers between solidity and fluidity, in the haziness of borders, speeds and slownesses, clusterings and expansions, movements in and out. Middle-class, white bodies – like Rebecca's – might more easily move and feel held in such viscous aggregates of bodies.

When a student becomes a student representative on a school governance council, they become recognisable by the extent to which they approximate or resemble the major – the extent to which they speak and act how a standard council member speaks and acts, and follow the communicative norms of the council meeting. Students in this study spoke about how a student representative could learn skills for life and work through being a council member: for example, improving 'students' confidence and speaking skills' (MSW), 'literacy skills', with the experience 'good to put on your resumé' (RSW). A student with current experience as a student representative spoke about benefiting from the 'experience of being in a setting with important people' and being 'treated like an adult' as 'prepar[ing] you for when you leave school – how to handle yourself, talk to people' (RSW). While, of course, these are all helpful skills to learn, the onus falls on the student to integrate to the style of communication of the school council – rather than the council to modify its communicative norms to be open to a multiplicity of ways of speaking, listening and relating. I am reminded of Edward Said (1989) and Gayatri Spivak's (1987) analysis of the 'dialogical' encounter in the colony: one party always needs to modify their communication to speak according to the categories and linguistic norms of the party with greater power. As Chapter 5 further explores, these assumptions about communicative norms and rationality privilege those from particular classed, gendered and racialised positions. Council members are compelled to contribute in a manner that approximates the norms of calm rationality associated with being white and middle class, and to figure out for themselves when it is an appropriate time to speak.

> A lot of conversations – you wanted to talk if you could, but they didn't give you that opportunity. It's hard for a young person to get the courage to speak up if they're not given the opportunity first. (Samuel, MSW)

When students in the Metropolitan Research Workshop questioned Rebecca further about these experiences, Rebecca described some of the habitual patterns of speech in school council meetings:

> **Student:** Do you think you had the same amount of what you got to say as the adults did?
> **Rebecca:** In some ways yes in some ways no. They want to move through quickly. Sometimes it's hard to get a voice. They do want you there and want your input. You picture a meeting and everyone having a say – like this. It is everyone sitting around a table. You have the school council president: agenda 1: this is what we talked about last week, are we going to move this motion? It's an open discussion that's controlled – very formalised. [...] If it's too casual you don't get anything done. We're here to get things done.
> **Student:** [Was there] SRC reporting at council meetings?
> **Rebecca:** A quick, 'anything to say?' You've got to get your moment quickly, get whatever you can in. (MSW)

Yet the conditions of speech are more than discursive. There are material arrangements of human and non-human bodies that generate particular affective intensities. During the metropolitan workshop, Samuel created a seating plan of the school council meetings that he attended. He indicated where he was seated with stickers on

THE POLITICS OF VOICE IN EDUCATION

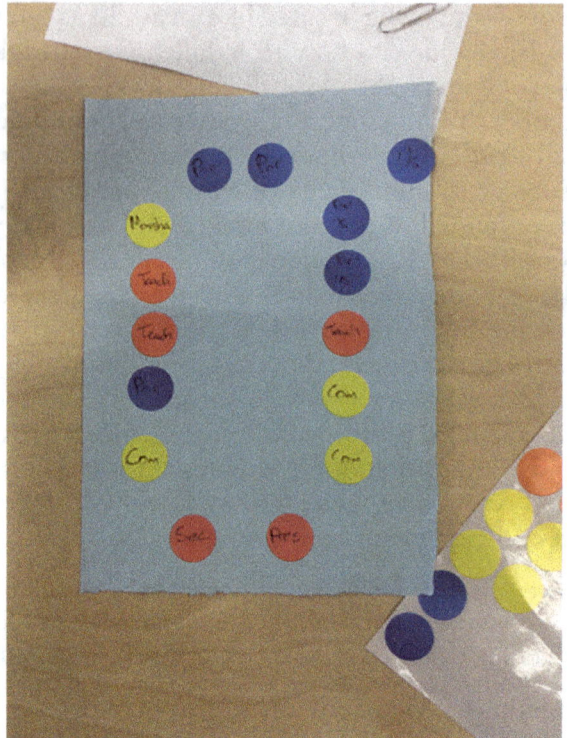

*Figure 4.1* A school council meeting arrangement in stickers.

a piece of paper (see Figure 4.1), and Samuel verbally explained this arrangement of stickers:

> We [the other student representative and Samuel] were put separately from the rest of the school council. We weren't sitting in the same position on the table. We were at the back, slightly off in the corner [the blue sticker in the top right corner]. We just kind of watched what happened. We went into a room like a restaurant. I often sat on the side a bit, from nerves. (Samuel, MSW)

In Figure 4.1, there is a viscous aggregating of sticker-bodies in a rectangular formation on a piece of paper; the blue sticker (that Samuel uses to represent his body) is stuck beyond the perimeter of this rectangle. Samuel gives an account of how his capacity to act (to speak and participate) was constrained not only by discursive norms, but also by the spatial configurations of chairs and bodies in a school council meeting. In his account, spoken in arrangement with paper, stickers, pens and tables in a research event, his discursive position-

110

ing was inextricably entangled with these furniture arrangements and spatial positionings that materialised and amplified differences between human bodies. The chair worked in confederacy with the table, the meeting agenda, the other human bodies, sedimented discourses of who should speak and who should be silent, circulating affects, ticking clocks, to materialise a felt sense of exclusion. Here, political philosoph(ies) of a school council materialised in concrete relations between bodies; the student representative subject forms in and through material-discursive practices (Mayes et al. 2016a).

Representative students are understood in their difference *from* adults, and their difference *from* 'other' students; students are evaluated as council members against the major (liberal humanist Man). Even when a student (like Rebecca) approximates the major (through her father and sister's historical presence, knowledge and relationships), she does not necessarily feel 'relaxed':

> [Y]ou walk in, you've got the principal and other teachers – principal and high up teachers – the people who volunteer are quite often head of faculties. We had a member of parliament [on school council]. You have high important people – people from [a university]. You're not walking into a relaxed setting. (Rebecca, MSW)

The representative student is integrated into the governance space but does not feel comfortable there. These issues with communicative norms and their spatial arrangement are not new for school councils. Helen Young (2017) has analysed the discursive processes shaping decisions made (or not made) in four school councils in the UK, particularly for parent representatives from non-dominant classed, gendered and racialised subject positions. Young (2017) considers 'who talked and on what subject', speakers' 'authority claims' and the 'norms which limit who can speak and what can be said' in these meetings (813, 824). Parent representatives from working-class backgrounds and minority ethnic groups spoke to Young about self-censoring and silencing themselves because of 'social awkwardness and not wanting to challenge norms' – as one parent put it, finding meetings '"quite daunting actually"' (2017: 816).

There is already a theory of change in operation when the student representative steps into a council meeting – that is, beliefs about how to improve a school, and established processes for proposing and enacting change (Tuck and Yang 2014a: 13; see Chapter 2). Principals may feel that, if student representatives are there, then they can effect change by helping other students in the school to comprehend the rationale for decisions made. The sentiments below echoed across a number of principal interviews:

> [E]ven if they're there and they're hearing about the decision, they're getting it almost straight from the horse's mouth if you know what I mean. It's not third-hand and then they don't know why that decision's been made. So if they know why the decision's been made then there's a better understanding and then that gets round to the other students. [. . .] So I suppose that's why I think it's important for the students to be there, to understand that there is policy that we have to follow and there's a line. (PI)

Yet, in some survey responses, students expressed the hope that student representation would lead to, for example, 'less distance between those in leadership and students, an understanding of what the student community wants' (OS). The change hoped for is that the school leadership will understand the student community's desires. Notwithstanding student desire for greater 'understanding' between students and leadership, student representative accounts suggested a tendency for the student representative to take on a mediator role – speaking for and between students and the school council, but also caught between. Rebecca spoke about attempting to raise a SRC concern at a council meeting:

> **Student:** Did you raise [a particular SRC concern] at school council?
> **Rebecca:** I did once but it wasn't received well. They'd already had all the discussions and it was set. It wasn't a time for review. [. . .] But SRC was really focused on it. But school council was like, 'we've done that issue. That is for the 3-year review – put it up then.' [. . .] [I was] in an in-between place – I couldn't make any changes to school council, but the SRC wants you to do something about it. [. . .] You're the one taking back the information and often the students didn't want to hear it. It [information from school council] didn't serve their [the SRC's] purpose. Their purpose was changing uniform, and I had no news on uniform. I had news on maintenance, on grants to do this building, or fix our garden. Then students are complaining, 'we're making garden, but we are not doing this'. But it's explaining to them the grant has to be used for the garden. Sometimes students think, 'why are you spending money on that and not on this?' You have to explain to them that sometimes you don't get a choice. You then speak for students, but then students don't like it. (MSW)

Listening to Rebecca and to other principals, the student representative is to communicate, back to the student body, how student voice is 'taken very seriously', but how not all requests will be actioned:

I also think that it's important that they go back to the student body and say that student voice is taken very seriously. It's not lip service. Everything that is brought to me is discussed. They don't get everything they want. Not everybody does in life, so I'm not interested in ambit claims but I am very interested in considered, concerned enquiries about improvements across the board. I think it's a nice conduit between the two groups. (PI)

Positioned to help students understand or be more receptive to decisions, it could also be argued that the student representative may become an intermediary in the service of better governing the student body (see Bragg 2007; Whitty and Wisby 2007). As one student wrote, 'They give them leadership positions and claim that it gives them a "student voice" but in reality they just use that student to do their dirty work and the students never really have a say in anything' (OS). To adapt Deleuze and Guattari, the student representative is 'given a choice, but on the condition that [their] choice conform to the limits of the constant ("you mustn't choose to change society [or your school] . . .")' (1980/1987: 105). The 'misfortune' here is 'not speaking, but speaking *for others* or representing something' (Deleuze 1968/1994: 52, original emphasis). The changes that students suggest may, then, be adjusted to be 'safe' – that is, remaining within the boundaries of established institutional practices and processes. Such adjustments may 'dilute, redefine or bludgeon' students' political imaginations under the rationale that they are '"out of their depth"' (Clay and Turner 2021: 393). As the student representative comes to understand and communicate back to other students how the school council operates, and how change happens, they may gradually become socialised into these expectations for how change happens (or does not happen). That is, students understand that they can 'have a voice', but that actions creating change are only legitimately made by those in authority. Chapter 5 further explores this problem of 'understanding'.

The student representative may be well aware that they are speaking for other students – flattening differences in their attempt to make a difference (Mayes et al. 2016b). Longing for recognition in relation to the dominant group engenders a double judgement – judgement for being 'different' by those who are the same (adult school council members), and the judgement of other students for not speaking to their difference. The best that Rebecca could do was to coach the SRC in how to write a proposal that would address the school council's requirements:

[I could go] back to SRC, saying, 'they're looking at it from this way. How can we write our proposal to help address what they're thinking about?' (MSW)

The student representative comes to speak for other students, replicating the issues that have previously been analysed of Student Representative Councils speaking for the multiplicities of the student body (Cox and Robinson-Pant 2008; Finneran et al. 2021; Mayes et al. 2019).

## *Speaking to One's Difference?*

There is a looping effect at work in the accounts I have just considered – students are 'given a seat' at school councils in order to avoid adults speaking for students, but then student representatives risk speaking for other students. The student representative may be compelled to come to resemble other school council members in communication style as they become socialised into the norms of this space – needing to lose their difference to be recognisable. Difference becomes muffled; the same is reified. So where is the possibility for change?

Deleuze, in various places, speaks of the potential of speaking to one's difference – a concept that I have found simultaneously full of possibility, but also confounding. For Deleuze, in *Difference and Repetition*, difference-in-itself is not negation (not X) or comparison (difference from X), but affirmation – difference is valued in itself, in its unique particularity. In Deleuze's ontology of pure difference, difference is primary and proliferating; identity cannot contain difference in its teeming multiplicity. Difference is beneath and beyond any identity category. Rather than demarcating categorical differences, Deleuze's thought opens out to difference, moving towards an 'extremity of difference' where there is '[a] single and same voice for the whole-thousand voiced multiple, a single and same Ocean for all the drops, a single clamour of Being for all beings' (Deleuze 1968/1994: 304). Difference is not subsumed within the same or the identical, but is to 'speak for itself'; bodies 'speak to' their difference (Tormey 2005: 141). Representing being (both in artistic form and in political representative form) becomes something to be resisted, since this constrains singularity and undermines creative processes of continuous variation and divergence from the majority.

In a conversation with Michel Foucault some years after *Difference and Repetition*, published as 'Intellectuals and Power', Deleuze further takes up this notion of 'speaking for others' and possibility of one speaking 'on their own behalf' (Deleuze and Foucault 1977: 209). In this conversation, they discuss the Groupe d'Information sur les Prisons (Prison Information Group), an organisation that sought to produce information about the conditions inside French prisons; they discuss the relationship between the prisoners' struggle and the role of the intellectual. Foucault describes the May 1968 protests as having demonstrated to 'the intellectual' that 'the masses no longer need him to gain knowledge: they know perfectly well, without illusion; they know far better than he and they are certainly capable of expressing themselves' (Deleuze and Foucault 1977: 207). Deleuze credits Foucault for teaching intellectuals of his generation 'the indignity of speaking for others' but argues the need to 'draw the consequences of this theoretical "conversion" – to appreciate the theoretical fact that only those directly concerned can speak in a practical way on their own behalf' (Deleuze and Foucault 1977: 209). The role of the intellectual becomes, in Deleuze's summary of Foucault's prison activism, to 'create conditions that permit the prisoners themselves to speak' (206). Foucault describes how 'when the prisoners began to speak, they possessed an individual theory of prisons, the penal system, and justice' – a 'counter-discourse' (209). Deleuze connects the situation of 'prisoners who are treated like children' to that of 'children who are treated like prisoners' – 'infantalised' and made to 'collect three tickets to get into the washroom during the day' (210). Deleuze speaks of children's protests – a pertinent example for the case of student representation on school governance councils, and makes the bold declaration: 'If the protests of children were heard in kindergarten, if their questions were attended to, it would be enough to explode the entire educational system' (209).

Deleuze credits the children in this statement as engaged in 'revolutionary action' rather than 'reform' (Deleuze and Foucault 1977: 209). He decries 'reform' as 'stupid and hypocritical', 'designed by people who claim to be representative, who make a profession of speaking for others' (209) – perhaps one might think here of adult advocates for mandatory student representation on school representative councils in the cause of school reform. Deleuze describes such reform as leading to a 'division of power, to a distribution of this new power which is consequently increased by a double repression' (209) – one might think here of the student representative who comes to tell other students how to frame their concerns to be palatable to the school council. Revolutionary action, for Deleuze, is radically different; it arises 'from the complaints and demands of those concerned' and questions, with the 'full force of its partiality', 'the totality of power and the hierarchy that maintains it' (209). The protests and questions of children, 'heard' and 'attended to', are Deleuze's example of such revolutionary action (209).

While I have found this account inspiring, I have found Gayatri Spivak's critique of Deleuze and Foucault on the politics of knowledge production and the role of the intellectual to be compelling. In short, Spivak draws attention to the colonialist language within which difference-in-itself speaks.[6] In her influential essay 'Can the Subaltern Speak' (1987), Spivak critiques the assumptions of Deleuze and Foucault's declaration that representation is over, that others can now 'speak for themselves', and that intellectuals can withdraw from 'speaking for' others. According to Spivak (1987), Deleuze and Foucault valorise 'the concrete experience of the oppressed', while being 'uncritical about the historical role of the intellectual' (69). She argues that Deleuze and Foucault run together a sense of *representation* as '"speaking for", as in politics' (proxy), and representation as *re-presentation*, 'as in art or philosophy' (portrait) (Spivak 1987: 70, original emphasis). She argues that to run together these two notions of representation leads to a position that suggests 'that beyond both is where oppressed subjects speak, act and know *for themselves*' (Spivak 1987: 71, original emphasis). For Spivak (1987), to make this claim reinstates the 'constitutive subject', and renders intellectuals 'transparent in the relay race'; the role of the intellectual, then, becomes to 'merely report on the nonrepresented subject and analyze (without analyzing)' the workings of power and desire (74). According to Spivak (1987), Deleuze's assumption that the Other can 'speak for' themselves does not account for how the Other must represent herself through the Western terms of representation that are comprehensible to the coloniser. Simone Bignall and Paul Patton (2010) summarise the contribution of Spivak's critique: it is 'not enough for Western intellectuals to resist the imperial temptation to "speak for" the colonised other, since this response carries with it the danger that the other will remain inarticulate, having already been silenced within colonial history' (5). This postcolonial critique has resonances in considerations of assertions of letting school students' 'cries' and 'protests' be heard – particularly Deleuze's 'cries' and 'protests' of context-less children. Whether in the colony or the classroom, the speech of those minoritised may remain outside the bounds of what can be heard by those with institutional privilege (whether as adult teacher, or as privileged student representative). Thinking with Spivak, it is too easy to declare that students can just 'speak to' their difference and explode the educational system.

This chapter has explored policy advocacy for school students to be represented on governance councils of schools, drawing on research conversations with students and school principals. Thinking with Deleuze and Guattari's critique of representational logics of difference and recognition, I have questioned whether integrating students into a structure of governance whose logics of representation remain uncontested may unwittingly perpetuate existing inequalities. That is, if a student representative does not approximate the pre-existing constant or political standard (the adult representative and its classed, racialised and gendered valences), then they may be beyond recognition – unrecognisable as a viable political representative. In turn, demanding such recognisability can mute difference and alterity – any new student member of a council must be integrated to existing frames of reference, and may then come to speak for other students. Working with the accounts of two students who had previously been representatives on their school's council, this chapter explored some of the viscosities of classed and racialised privilege that cluster around the school council table, and their felt material impact on what student representatives bodies can feel-say-do. I considered Deleuze's reference to bodies speaking 'on their own behalf' (Deleuze and Foucault 1977: 209) and Spivak's critique of this notion as naive to the always already colonial language of representation through which a body speaks to their difference.

What could conditions that enable students to 'speak to' their difference in all their multiplicities look like? Returning to *Difference and Repetition*, there is 'always an unrepresented singularity' which does not recognise itself in the one ostensibly representing them, 'precisely because it is not everyone or the universal' (Deleuze 1968/1994: 52). Deleuze suggests the potentiality of noticing moments where:

> someone – if only one – with the necessary modesty not managing to know what everyone knows, and modestly denying what everybody is supposed to recognise. Someone who neither allows himself to be represented nor wishes to represent anything. (1968/1994: 130)

The following chapter further investigates the creation of conditions for student speech in schools, and the conditions for listening to the force of difference-in-itself. I consider the affective sensorium that contours the conditions for speech and listening in schools: the atmos-fears of dialogue. The chapter interrogates the promise of dialogical 'understanding', frequently framed in terms of Habermas's ideal speech situation (see Chapter 1). Thinking with a puppet scenario created by a group of Year 9 students in 2013, I grapple with the imperative to 'understand' in schools – to understand others and to come to a point of consensus across (at times) irreconcilable difference. In this puppet scenario, a chicken-puppet articulates being 'scared'. This articulated statement becomes a prompt to think through the atmos-fears that shape and condition the dialogical encounter that are more-than-individual and more-than a matter of a classroom or school's 'climate'; bodies sense and articulate 'fear' as a discursive placeholder for the 'ungraspable multicausal matrix' of late capitalism (Massumi 1993a: 12). I articulate this fear with the targeting (and creation) of the student (presumed to be) at risk of violent extremism via schools, in a policy context where the preventive logic of 'listening' to students was deployed as a matter of state and national security. Thinking with this puppet scenario, and the policy conditions for the voice of the student who identifies or is identifiable as Muslim and/or Arab, it is not so easy to say that a student's cries and protests can be heard by the institution as revolutionary action (Deleuze and Foucault 1977). 'Radical' is a term that has various histories, present connotations and embodied consequences for differentially positioned students (Gerrard 2014; Mayes 2019a). Indeed, in the case of Countering Violent Extremism (CVE) programmes as they bore down on schools, 'intellectuals' and educators (like myself) 'listening' to the voices and embodiments of students were complicit and implicated in the subjectification of particular student subjects deemed to be 'risky'. While exploring these processes of subjectification in and through dialogue, the following chapter also argues, thinking with Édouard Glissant and Kara Keeling, for the value of opacity and the right not to be compelled to be understandable.

## Notes

1. At the time of the copyediting of this book (September 2022), after a change of federal government in the May 2022 election (to Labor), newly elected Prime Minister Anthony Albanese pledged a national referendum within the parliamentary term, to enshrine a body to advise the government on Indigenous issues in the Australian constitution: the Aboriginal and Torres Strait Islander Voice to Parliament.

2. The research configurations where these statements were made are explained towards the end of this section.
3. In Victoria, under previous legislation, school councils were required to include, in their composition, the principal, parent members, department employee members, and other community members (of no more than one third composition for each respective group). Students could be co-opted into the 'community member' category.
4. In this study, there was not the opportunity for students to write their own pseudonyms or self-descriptions.
5. Arun Saldanha (2007) uses this concept of viscosity in making sense of how white hippies tend to stick and aggregate together and exclude bodies of colour in the Goa trance scene (admittedly, a vastly different setting to a school council meeting!).
6. Previous engagements with Spivak's critique of Deleuze and Foucault in 'Intellectuals and Power' have situated Deleuze's words in his broader oeuvre of work, and attempted to refute Spivak's claims (for example, see Holland 2003; Robinson and Tormey 2010). I am not as interested in these defences of Deleuze and Foucault as I am in what Spivak's critique does for thought and political action in relation to the voice of the student (see Chapter 2).

# 5
# Understanding the Atmos-fear of the Dialogical Encounter

> '[T]he verb to understand *in the sense of "to grasp"* [comprendre]
> *has a fearsome repressive meaning.*'
> Édouard Glissant, *Poetics of Relation*

> Teacher-puppet: *What's your problem, chicken?*
> Chicken-puppet: *Bbb, bbb, I'm –*
> Teacher-puppet: *Yes?*
> Chicken-puppet: *– scared –*
> Teacher-puppet: *Yes?*
> Chicken-puppet: *– of you. Broooaak.*
> Teacher-puppet: *Are you scared of me?* [1-second silence]
> Chicken-puppet: *Yes.*
> Teacher-puppet: *Why?*
> Chicken-puppet: *Mmmm.* [Taps beady eyes on table twice] *Bruuuk.*
> Chicken-puppet scenario, below

> 'Fear is the inherence in the body of the ungraspable multicausal
> matrix of the syndrome recognizable as late capitalist
> human existence (its affect).'
> Brian Massumi, *The Politics of Everyday Fear*

There are 'many politics' (Deleuze and Parnet 2006/1977: 190) in any dialogical exchange – tangled lines of speech, silence, ambivalent desire, impasses, refusal, opacity. In this chapter, I consider the politics and ambivalences of attempts to support students and teachers in schools to 'express' themselves and come to 'understand' each other through dialogue. The opportunity for dialogue between students and teachers has been posited as enabling students and teachers to reach an understanding across diverging positions and perspectives – to see things from each other's view, to understand each other's pressures and desires, to reach an understanding (see Habermas 1984: 44; see also Chapter 1). At times, student voice initiatives jumble school hierarchies and roles: for example, where students conduct interviews or participant observational research with teachers, such initiatives unsettle established assumptions about who asks and who answers questions, and who understands and who needs to understand. When premised on liberal humanist concepts of agency, rationality and the possibility of equality, promises of reaching understanding through dialogue risk eliding the specificities of when, where and under what conditions the dialogical encounter is staged, and the differential experiences of these dialogical encounters.

My attention, in this chapter, is on how institutional policies and everyday practices invite students' voices to speak, or to conduct interviews with teachers, but then turn around and interpret some students' voices, bodies, thoughts and desires to be the problem. Returning to Spivak's (1987) critique of Deleuze and Foucault discussed in the previous chapter, this is to question the conditions for listening when voices speak. While the previous chapter attended to the logics that privilege particular students as representatives on school governance councils, this chapter attempts to listen to the voice and silences of the student who is not recognisable – who is not necessarily privileged, nor 'disadvantaged' – perhaps, an 'unrepresented singularity' (Deleuze 1968/1994: 52).

In this chapter, I consider what happens when the dialogical encounter doesn't feel so 'empowering' (Ellsworth 1989) – when students and teachers do not speak as expected in the dialogical exchange, and where bodies feel (or are imagined or interpreted to be feeling) fearful, frustrated and unfulfilled. This chapter's exploration of the politics of feeling and understanding in student voice begins with a puppet scenario created by four Year 9 students at a secondary school in southwest Sydney in 2013. I introduced this school in Chapter 1; in Chapter 2, I gave an account of research focus groups with students (in Years 7–12) who had been involved in the school's student voice group in the past or present. As I explained in Chapter 2, during these focus groups I invited students to speak, draw or compose a scenario relating to the concept of student voice, offering seven puppets and one marionette as part of a repertoire of objects and materials, coloured markers, paper, postcards and an iPad. I told students that the scenarios could be composed in written, visual or audio-visual form, and that they could be based on their personal experiences or a fictional story. The enabling constraint for the scenario was that it would explore an issue surrounding student voice. Students took this prompt in multiple directions: some re-enacted dialogical events that they had experienced or witnessed, others generated fantastical scenarios of potential imagined future dialogical events, while others performed events that had not necessarily happened.

The particular scenario that I think with in this chapter stages a perplexing dialogue between a chicken-puppet (student) and a teacher-puppet – where the chicken-puppet speaks the words, 'I'm ... scared ... of you.' I have struggled to understand this puppet scenario, and I have struggled with the pedagogical and analytic imperative to understand it. I have wondered how you will understand it, and the imperative for me to help make it make sense to you. This chapter draws on the work of Édouard Glissant, French poet, novelist and theorist from the island of Martinique, who articulated and enacted a poetics and ethics that resisted European colonial attempts to 'understand' the other, and affirmed Relation (Glissant's capitalisation) as an ontology and world imaginary. Glissant notes how the French verb *'to understand* in the sense of "to grasp" [*comprendre*] has a fearsome repressive meaning' (1990/1997: 26). Glissant is writing about the structuring of Western ethnography around the colonialist 'discovery of the other', where the ethnographer is driven towards '[u]nderstanding cultures' and 'the truth of human beings' (1990/1997: 26). The colonial structure of schooling, and its concern for the 'at risk' Other (see Chapter 3), is a primary site of such modes of understanding – those who work in schools are compelled to discover, to grasp, to extract, to understand, and somehow, then, to 'fix' and/or 'empower' their students. Grasping evokes the image of 'hands that grab their surroundings and bring them back to themselves' in 'enclosure if not appropriation' (Glissant 1990/1997: 192). This chapter dramatises the institutional desire to grasp and understand – to pin down what has happened in a dialogical encounter – in order to diagnose what's wrong with the student and/or teacher. I do this through exaggerating an attempt to interpret and understand the chicken-puppet's statement of being 'scared' as an individualised psychological problem – the chicken-puppet's problem, and/or a problem of the teacher-puppet's style of teaching. I consider the possibilities of the concept of classroom and school 'climate' for understanding the perplexities of this dialogical encounter, and the insufficiencies of this concept. I argue that fear is more-than-individual, and more-than a matter of a classroom or school's 'climate'; bodies sense and articulate 'fear' as a discursive placeholder for the 'ungraspable multicausal matrix' of late capitalism (Massumi 1993a: 12). This ungraspable matrix might be called the 'atmos-fear' (see also Verlie and Blom 2021). In discussing the atmos-fears that shape and condition the dialogical encounter, I think with the research of Australian sociologist Randa Abdel-Fattah in her book *Coming of Age in the War on Terror* (2021), as well as Shiva Zarabadi's (2020) affective analysis of the 'pedagogy of fear' in UK classrooms (78). While many things can happen in the dialogical encounter, this chapter argues, with Glissant and Keeling, for the value of opacity and the right not to be compelled to be understandable.

In working with this puppet scenario, my aim is not to represent students who created this puppet scenario in 2013 in a meeting room at a secondary school in southwest Sydney, nor other students, nor myself. Later in this chapter, I pan back to certain affective-material-political currents in circulation around the school in and after the period of this research, reading this puppet scenario with and through policy documents, later research encounters, other researchers' encounters, and theory. Reading these voices, policies and theories across time, queering and traversing temporalities, entangles their affective-discursive-material conditions in an effort to make a different sense of dialogical encounters in schools. I attend to a 'figuration of fear' (Shiva Zarabadi, personal communication)[1] from the puppet scenario – a chicken-puppet's articulation of being 'scared' – rather than 'real voices' of students whom I have been in dialogical encounters with. As I explained in Chapter 2, I have learnt from Eve Tuck and K. Wayne Yang's (2014b) critique of the settler colonial academy's extraction of Indigenous people's sacred stories and objects that there is a flawed theory of change in imagining that, if I just grasp, capture and then share students' 'pain stories on a silver platter', this will necessarily change these patterns in education and beyond (812). This is especially the case as a privileged white feminised researcher and former teacher.

I don't claim that the students who created this puppet scenario were thinking of particular institutional, national and transnational fears in creating this scenario. However, in this and other studies, I have sensed what Brian Massumi (2005) describes as a 'central nervousness', though how this nervousness 'translated somatically varied body to body' (32). This fear may include, but also be more-than, students feeling intimidated or nervous about voicing their views to teachers and the messiness of managing teachers' responses. It may include, but also exceed, the nervousness of the individual teacher, who is anxious that their authority will be undermined through student voice. It may suggest, but not encapsulate, the anxieties of the individual teacher, overloaded with everyday administrative pressures that constrain the time and energy that they have left to listen to their students. It may include, but be something other than, individualised student mental health issues that are perceived to be housed inside students and that students bring with them into classrooms. While these fears are undoubtedly somatically sensed, conceptualising fear as individual risks bolstering a therapeutic conception of student voice for 'well-being' that muffles the political dimensions of feeling in education. Sara Bragg (2007) considers analyses of student voice that foreground teachers' 'fear' to be overly 'psychologising' (344) and locates teachers' responses within a broader educational context of the 'terrors of performativity' (Ball 2003: ch. 6). Extending Bragg's analysis, I situate fear – both students' and teachers' – in the context of its 'saturation of social space' in late capitalism; fear that is not the possession of a subject but 'part of the very process of subject formation' (Massumi 1993b: ix). Massumi, after Deleuze and Guattari, recasts the psychological framing of fear as an individualised emotion. Fear, rather, is political: 'the inherence in the body of the ungraspable multicausal matrix of the syndrome recognizable as late capitalist human existence (its *affect*)' (Massumi 1993a: 12, original emphasis). Massumi wrote about the 'politics of everyday fear' before the events of 11 September 2001 (Massumi 1993a); the young people with whom I have worked (as a teacher and researcher) have grown up in a world that they've 'only ever known to be "at war on terror"' (Abdel-Fattah 2021: 16). Amidst the 'terrors of performativity' (Ball 2003: ch. 6), creeping processes of intrusive surveillance, 'preventive' interventions connected to a fear of terrorism, and the erosion of civil liberties, insecurity has become 'the new normal' (Massumi 2005: 31)[2] – an atmos-fear. Like Marx's superstructural forces, and Foucault's microphysics of power, these affects are 'known principally through their effects', but 'remain none the less real or analytically valid as a result' (Hynes 2013: 561). These fears, anxieties, tensions, suspicions and paranoias are sensed, even if the multicausal matrix that gives rise to them is beyond the teacher-puppet and the chicken-puppet's (or the students', or your, or my) understanding.

## *Bruuuk*

The puppet scenario that I work with in this chapter was created by four Year 9 students from the student voice group that I spent time with throughout 2013, during my doctoral research. These students had been part of dialogical interviews with the principal and teachers in the Human Society and Its Environment department about teachers' preparation for a new Australian curriculum for history. The names used below are pseudonyms chosen by these four students.[3] The puppet scenario that they created dramatically performs a student/teacher dialogue that, in many ways, is hard to understand. In this scenario, a chicken-puppet says 'bok' in a classroom and, following a student-puppet's suggestion to 'have a focus group', the chicken-puppet momentarily becomes intelligible to the teacher-puppet, and says: 'I'm ... scared ... of you.' When the teacher-puppet asks the chicken-puppet a further question, the chicken-puppet returns to chicken-speech.

This performance of a dialogue between a chicken-puppet and teacher-puppet reminds me of the clerk Gregor in Franz Kafka's novella *Metamorphosis* (1915/1992), who wakes up to find himself a cockroach in his family home – suddenly made strange to his family. What has happened – why he is the way he is – is inexplicable to him, and his family and his boss cannot understand him. The chicken-puppet's apparent refusal to explain himself to the teacher-puppet also reminds me of the repeated phrase of Bartleby, the scrivener (copyist) to a lawyer, in Herman Melville's novella *Bartleby, the Scrivener* (1853/2014): 'I would prefer not to' – a phrase that Bartleby repeats throughout the story, and which does not make sense to the lawyer-narrator. These figures, and their strange embodiments and words, have been subject to wide-ranging interpretations – for example, psychoanalytic interpretations of Kafka's work that reduce plot events to the Oedipal triangle, or look for archetypes, or engage in 'so-called free association that always bring us back to childhood memories', or 'interpret, to say that this means that' (Deleuze and Guattari 2006: 7). Melville's Bartleby, similarly, has been the subject of interpretation and debate among numerous philosophers and literacy critics, from Georgio Agamben and Slavoj Žižek to Deleuze. While I am not arguing that the chicken-puppet is a new Gregor, nor a new Bartleby, nor that the students who created this scenario knew Kafka or Melville, I suggest that this puppet scenario shares qualities of what Deleuze and Guattari call a 'minor literature', and that its opacity offers possibilities for considering the politics of dialogue and understanding in schools.

For Deleuze and Guattari, Kafka (and elsewhere, Melville) is among the authors that they praise as composing a 'minor literature':

writers who carve out 'a non-pre-existent foreign language *within*' a major language – from the margins, deterritorialising it from the border (Deleuze 1997: 109–10, original emphasis). The minor is not less in number – indeed, there are more numerous children, women, people of colour, and people who are materially and epistemically minoritised than the major abstract standard. The minor is not less in number, but rather exceeds and escapes from the confines of dominant majoritarian identity categories – particularly those imposed by the major. The concept of minor is multiple: 'minority' can be used in reference to musical, literary, linguistic, political and juridical spheres (Deleuze and Guattari 1980/1987: 105). A 'minor literature' is constructed from a marginal position: in the case of Franz Kafka, a Czech Jew writing in German, or – for another example – Samuel Beckett, an Irishman writing in French (Deleuze and Guattari 2006: 16). These writers disturb and reconfigure the major language's dogmatic image of thought and its grammar from within it. A writer of 'minor literature' becomes 'a stutterer in language', making 'the language itself scream, stutter, stammer, or murmur' (Deleuze 1997: 109–10). Such writing is always political (Deleuze and Guattari 2006: 17). Deleuze and Guattari acclaim Kafka for central Europe, and Melville for America – as writers of a 'minor literature', creating a collective enunciation of a minor people. Deleuze and Guattari refuse to analyse Kafka's work via singular interpretations; they are, rather, interested in a 'Kafka *politics*', 'Kafka *machines*' and 'a Kafka *experimentation*' (7, original emphasis). Bartleby, similarly, is of interest to Kara Keeling, who extends Deleuze's reading of *Bartleby, the Scrivener* in *Queer Times, Black Futures* (2019), for the insights that it 'offers into the politics, possibilities and pitfalls of opacity, incommensurability, radical refusal, and risk' (43). It is important to reiterate that the students did not describe this puppet production as 'minor' – this is my imposition.

In what follows the puppet scenario transcript, I revisit postcolonial and psychoanalytic critiques of the dialogical encounter, considering dialogue's im/possibilities. I then read the puppet scenario as a minor literature, considering its political immediacies. I attempt to grasp the atmos-fears – in the classroom and school's 'climate', and diffusely spreading in and beyond the school in the affective sensorium surrounding the 'war on terror'. I consider what the puppet scenario might have to teach the reader, after Glissant and Keeling, about the right to opacity: the right to refuse to render oneself understandable.

## Understanding the Atmos-fear of the Dialogical Encounter

*The scene is set at the table in the school's executive meeting room. On the left side of the frame, the teacher-puppet is standing, facing the student-puppets. The teacher-puppet is starting a lesson.)*
**Isaac (teacher-puppet):** Okay class, we've been learning about travel. Does anybody have any questions?

*Figure 5.1* The teacher-puppet is starting a lesson.

**xPeke (chicken-puppet):** *[Quietly]* Bok.
**Isaac (teacher-puppet):** Yes, chicken?
**xPeke (chicken-puppet):** *[Loudly]* Braaaaaeek. *[Raises open beak to the ceiling]*
**Isaac (teacher-puppet):** I'm sorry. Can you please repeat that?
**xPeke (chicken-puppet):** *[Loudly]* Braaaaaeek. *[Opens beak to ceiling]*
**Isaac (teacher-puppet):** Um. I don't understand you.
**xPeke (chicken-puppet):** *[Loudly]* Bok bok, braaaaaeek.
**Isaac (teacher-puppet):** Okay chicken, stay with me after class.
**xPeke (chicken-puppet):** *[Plaintively]* Breaara. *[Chicken-puppet slowly collapses forward on table, beak down]*
**Umprikash (student-puppet wearing yellow cap):** It seems we have a communication error.
**Isaac (teacher-puppet):** Okay.
**Umprikash (student-puppet):** Why don't we conduct a focus group to solve this issue?
**Isaac (teacher-puppet):** Sure thing. *[Teacher-puppet moves closer, and student-puppets move closer to each other.]*
**Umprikash (student-puppet):** Why did you put the chicken on detention?
**Isaac (teacher-puppet):** I didn't understand what he was saying in class. *[Chicken-puppet taps beady eyes on table three times.]*

*Figure 5.2* The chicken-puppet says 'bok'.

*Figure 5.3* The chicken-puppet collapses forward on the table, beak down.

*Figure 5.4* The puppets move closer together to talk.

xPeke (chicken-puppet): *[Lifts head from table quickly and quietly says]* Mmrrrra. *[Replaces head on table, face down. Taps table with beady eyes twice. One-second silence.]*

Shaza (student-puppet with orange hair): Maybe you're just misinterpreting what the chicken's trying to say.

Isaac (teacher-puppet): I will try now.

Shaza (student-puppet with orange hair): Go ahead.

Isaac (teacher-puppet): What's your problem, chicken?

xPeke (chicken-puppet): *[Slowly, lifting head from table. Puppet arms are on side of beak. The human voice of the puppeteer still has the cadences of a chicken's squawk]* Bbb, bbb, [pause] I'm [pause] –

Isaac (teacher-puppet): Yes?

xPeke (chicken-puppet): Scared [pause] –

Isaac (teacher-puppet): Yes?

xPeke (chicken-puppet): Of you. [pause] Broooaak.

Isaac (teacher-puppet): Are you scared of me? *[One-second silence]*

xPeke (chicken-puppet): Yes.

Isaac (teacher-puppet): Why?

xPeke (chicken-puppet): Mmmm. *[Taps beady eyes on table twice]* Bruuuk. *[One-second silence]*

*Figure 5.5* The chicken-puppet taps their beady eyes on the table twice.

*Understanding the Atmos-fear of the Dialogical Encounter*

## The Im/possibilities of Dialogue

Something happened in this puppet classroom, but it is not clear what it is that has happened. A teacher-puppet has opened the lesson with a question. A student – a chicken-puppet – responds to the question, but with a form of expression that is unintelligible to the teacher-puppet ('bok', 'Braaaaaeek'). The teacher-puppet attempts to understand the chicken-puppet's question: 'Yes, chicken? [. . .] Can you please repeat that? [. . .] Um, I don't understand you', before saying, 'Okay chicken, stay with me after class.'

Then there is an intrusion to the usual pattern of classroom interactions: a student-puppet speaks without being called on by the teacher-puppet. The student-puppet speaks in an almost exaggeratedly rational tone and robotic mode: 'It seems we have a communication error' – as if speaking about a computer malfunctioning. The student-puppet suggests a focus group: 'Why don't we conduct a focus group to solve this issue?' (Perhaps this student-puppet is a student representative; see Chapter 4.) The teacher-puppet agrees to the proposition and physically moves closer to the student-puppets, who then reconfigure their puppet-bodies into an arrangement closer to a circle. In this different configuration, the teacher-puppet gently asks, 'What's your problem, chicken?' The chicken-puppet responds by haltingly speaking in the language of the classroom. There is a silence after the chicken-puppet slowly articulates a particular feeling in language: 'I'm [. . .] scared [. . .] of you'. There is another silence after the teacher repeats the utterance as a question: 'Are you scared of me?' The teacher asks, 'Why?' – asking the chicken-puppet to elaborate and give an account of itself. The chicken-puppet responds to the question 'why' with silence and bashing its eyes on the desk, and a return to chicken-speech, 'Bruuuk'.

Something about the chicken-puppet's speech and silence prompts me to revisit postcolonial and psychoanalytic critiques of Habermas's ideal speech situation; these critiques interrogate the abstracted premise of dialogue as removed from concrete, situated territories where power, knowledge and desire circulate. Edward Said (1989) lampoons the 'scrubbed, disinfected interlocutor' and the 'entirely academic or theoretical environment' of Habermas's ideal speech situation as 'a laboratory creation with suppressed, and therefore falsified, connections to the urgent situation of crisis and conflict' (210). For Said, neutrality and equality in the colonial dialogical encounter is impossible; one party will always need to speak according to the categories and linguistic norms of the party with greater power ('What's your problem, chicken?'). The colonised will be at first driven to speak within the terms of the other party ('I'm [. . .] scared [. . .] of you'), and may then either have their voice eroded into the categories of the coloniser, refuse to speak, or respond antagonistically (Said 1989: 209–10). The interlocutor may then be dismissed as 'uncivilised' or unworthy to participate in the dialogue. Students, too, may be burdened with the responsibility to 'translate their ideas and experiences into a common language (which is often not their language)' and 'expose themselves (in a manner that puts them at risk of judgment and rejection)' (Burbules 2004: xviii). From a psychoanalytic perspective, as Peggy Phelan (1993) puts it, the expectation for understanding, and the experience of 'always failing to feel and see it', commits the participant, 'however unwittingly, to a concomitant narrative of betrayal, disappointment, and rage', so that the participant accuses self or 'the other of inadequacy, of blindness, of neglect' (194). When you are asked a question that you have not invented, the aim then becomes 'to get out' of the conversation (Deleuze and Parnet 2006/1977: 1). Dialogue, far from being a neutral zone of encounter, is a 'political struggle' (Alcoff 1991: 15) deeply entwined with assumptions about communicative norms and rationality that privilege those from particular classed, gendered and racialised positions and invalidate the speech of others. The dialogical space of student voice might be a dangerous space where the possibility of further subjectification is amplified.

Things are not as they have seemed to be. Perhaps the teacher-puppet felt this classroom to be an open, 'safe' space; perhaps their subjectivity is constructed on an understanding of themselves as a progressive educator who listens to students and allows students to initiate dialogue. It is not just that the teacher-puppet needs to welcome the conditions of a focus group and become-otherwise, or that a student-puppet needs to initiate a focus group where the teacher-puppet and the chicken-puppet can understand each other better, or that the teacher-puppet needs to better understand the chicken-puppet's feelings, or that the chicken student-puppet needs to better understand the teacher-puppet's feelings. What does this statement, 'I'm [. . .] scared [. . .] of you' do for the teacher-puppet? Perhaps the chicken-puppet's statement of being 'scared' startles the teacher-puppet out of comfort and habitual modes of being, alerting them to something not previously apprehended. Perhaps there is an ontological trembling between the ordered interactional dynamics that condition when students are authorised to speak, and the potentiality of this new configuration. Do the perplexities of dialogue negate the possibility of something happening in and through these moments? Perhaps, amidst the questions that the chicken-puppet 'turn[s] in circles among', there are 'becomings which are silently at work, which are almost imperceptible' (Deleuze and Parnet 2006/1977: 1). Perhaps the chicken-puppet's statement effects a crack in the 'rigid segment' of the professional subjectivity of the teacher-puppet. Deleuze and Parnet write that, while a 'profession is a rigid segment', it is 'what happens beneath it, the connections, the attractions and repulsions, which do not coincide with the segments' (2006/1977: 93) that may open up to something new. Yet, what habits lead the teacher-puppet back to the place where they reassert their prerogative to ask the questions and to ask the chicken-puppet to make themselves and their articulation of feeling 'scared' transparent – that is, to ask the chicken to explain why they are scared?

By the end, there seems to be an impasse; a withdrawal. The lines of connection that reached out appear to flee back to a line of rigid segmentarity – that divides teacher from student, intelligibility from unintelligibility (Deleuze and Guattari 1980/1987: 227). Perhaps the teacher-puppet comes to interpret this dialogical intervention through the order words of the chicken-puppet's age and (im)maturity, 'ability' or emotionality (see Chapter 3). Two rigid segments remain: a chicken-puppet whose fear is not understandable, and a teacher-puppet who may not wish to invite student questions or feedback again. Retreating in fear to a molar line (of teacher/student subjectivities) is the danger of the molar line that Deleuze and Guattari elucidate:

> We are afraid of losing. Our security, the great molar organisation that sustains us, the arborescences we cling to, to binary machines that give us a well-defined status, the resonances we enter into, the system of overcoding that dominates us – we desire all that. [. . .] We flee from flight, rigidify our segments, give ourselves over to binary logic; the harder they have been to us on one segment, the harder we will be on another; we reterritorialise on anything available [. . .]. The more rigid the segmentarity, the more reassuring it is for us. That is what fear is, and how it makes us retreat into the first line. (Deleuze and Guattari 1980/1987: 227)

Perhaps words 'cannot say enough – or hide enough' (Mazzei 2007: 35). Perhaps, like Gregor in Kafka's *Metamorphosis*, the chicken-puppet does not understand why their words are not understood:

'It was true that the words he uttered were evidently no longer intelligible, despite the fact that they had seemed clear enough to him, clearer than before' (Kafka 1915/1992: 85). Perhaps in these words and silences, the chicken-puppet senses the impossibility of accounting for – in words – who they are, what they are trying to say, or why things are the way they are; they sense that they are, or have become, an 'affect alien' (Ahmed 2017: 57). The chicken-puppet articulates being 'scared' in this student–teacher relation, but perhaps this fear is viscerally apprehended in spatio-temporal-material configurations – beyond these particular individuals, in the classroom and school 'climate'.

## A Political Immediacy

> '"Did you understand a word of all that?" the chief clerk asked [Gregor's parents], "surely he's not trying to make fools of us?"'
> Franz Kafka, *Metamorphosis*

One characteristic of a minor literature is the connection of the individual to a political immediacy; in a minor literature, 'the political domain has contaminated every statement' (Deleuze and Guattari 2006: 17). At this school, in the context of the production of this puppet scenario, there was an institutional political immediacy in the wake of the students' research findings: contestations about the concept of 'respect' between students and teachers (see Chapter 6). You walk into a classroom, or a school foyer, and feel the 'affective atmosphere' (Anderson 2009; Brennan 2004): a stifled prissiness, a chaotic jangle of bodies-in-motion, a heavy languor, ripples of joy, a thick tension, a diffuse nervousness. While the notion of a classroom or school climate has been said to be too 'ethereal' (Solvason 2005: 85), and the definition, measurement and strategic approaches towards changing 'school climate' (or 'culture', 'atmosphere', 'ethos') to be too politically contested and empirically problematic, it has become another target for educational reform – something that can be expediently 'improved' with minimal financial cost (Bragg and Manchester 2011). School Effectiveness and School Improvement (SESI) research and psychological approaches have framed school climate as 'a *problem* to be "improved" and smoothed out towards a common sense of "positive" feelings across a school community' (Mayes et al. 2020: 2, original emphasis).

A school leader or researcher influenced by SESI and psychological approaches might hear the chicken-puppet's words and wonder about what these words signify about this classroom and/or school climate: is there a problem with interpersonal socio-emotional communication patterns between teachers and students? Improving the classroom or school 'climate' (or 'ethos' or 'atmosphere') might involve sending out a survey to measure individual perceptions of the school's climate, ethos or atmosphere, generating data about the 'gaps' between the declared school climate and the lived experiences and perceptions of school climate from differently positioned students and staff. For SESI scholars, these dissonances are problematic, and school leaders are encouraged to develop a 'distinctive' climate to unite and drive the school (see Chapter 6). Yet, Voight et al. (2015) have raised doubts about the 'positivist ontology' that seeks a 'single unified representation of climate' (254). They demonstrate, through their study of racial disparities of students' experiences of school climate, how universalising approaches to climate mute the different experiences of subgroups within a school who 'may have significantly different experiences of safety, connectedness, relationships with adults, and opportunities for participation' (263). In recent years, phenomenological qualitative approaches to school climate have similarly explored how individuals apprehend the common phenomenon of a school's climate, expanding on survey results – for example, in this puppet scenario, the chicken-puppet articulating being scared of their teacher. This approach to climate assumes that people internally experience a common atmosphere, even if differentially apprehended, that the school is a self-contained site, and that the researcher (or teacher) is set apart from the phenomenon of the school's climate (Mayes et al. 2020).

But who gets to say what a school, or a classroom, feels like? Whose account is considered to be legitimate? When asked how one feels at school, how is what can be said politically constrained and shaped by the conditions of the dialogical encounter? The atmosphere/atmos-fear is not 'grasped' 'at all in the same way' (Deleuze and Parnet 2006/1977: 13); at this school, different interview and research configurations with me produced different accounts of the atmosphere and the possibilities of the dialogical encounter.[4] Even as fear may collectively attune and even shock a multiplicity of bodies, reactions of bodies vary according to each body's 'lived past' and each body's angle of participation in the (classroom) event (Massumi, in Massumi and McKim 2009: 2).

## THE POLITICS OF ATMOS-FEARS

Yet, where does this atmos-fear begin and end – does it have geographical and temporal boundaries? What might it do to think fear, beyond the psychologised human subject, as dynamically generated and plugged in beyond the student–teacher dyad, and beyond the school? Fear is an 'ordinary affect' – everyday, ubiquitous, micropolitical, localised (Stewart 2007) – and everywhere, micropolitically modulated, globalised, yet differentially sensed. Fear is more-than-institutional, yet micropolitical – the extension of other social bodies, spaces and things, registering in multisensory and multitemporal ways. Fear is calibrated and modulated in objects, texts and relations that activate the body: measures of performance, security cameras, large metal gates, school policies, modes of speaking, listening, relating and being (Massumi 2005). Fear, when it is named in language, is connected with collective agencements of enunciation at social and infra-individual scales (Guattari 1985/1996: 269). Schools are open systems, continually leaking local, transnational and global social, economic and political fields and flows that entangle with the feeling of a school or educational space (Deleuze and Guattari 1983: 95–6). Of course, fear has always been a potent affect – the fear of teachers is plugged in with cultural and historical memories and representations (old movies and popular cultural references, parents' and grandparents' stories of corporal punishment, one's own experiences). Many fears circulate as I write – pandemic fears, eco- and environmental fears, immigration fears, internet safety fears, civil society fears, economic fears, political fears, existential and religious fears, aesthetic and literary fears and so on. These affective currents in circulation – atmos-fears – leak into schools, with material effects and affects.

Rereading this puppet scenario, I think of the geopolitical politics of feeling following the 'war on terror' – what the late Lauren Berlant has called 'the first war on an emotion' (2005) and its ripple effects in counter-terrorism measures that seeped into schools during and following the period when this puppet scenario was created. Clusters of affects – moral outrage, fear, insecurity, frustration – formed and modulated around the war on terror. This fear was and is affectively produced and modulated (Massumi 2005), but it is not just the fear of potential violent subjects or violent acts, but also a 'fear of being feared' (Aly and Green 2010: 279). As Zarabadi has put it, there is a vague feeling of 'threat that is sometimes hard to explain, hard to locate', with an 'autonomy to remodulate relations between students and peers and students and teachers' (2020: 74–5). The chicken-puppet's 'frightened face' looms up, 'looks at something out of the field' (Deleuze and Guattari 1994/2009: 19) – circulating institutional, national and transnational atmos-fears:

> There is, at some moment, a calm and restful world. Suddenly a frightened face looms up that looks at something out of the field. The other person appears here as neither subject nor object but as something that is very different: a possible world, the possibility of a frightening world. (Deleuze and Guattari 1994/2009: 19)

This school (and others where I subsequently worked as a teacher and researcher in the 2000s and 2010s) is located in a region where 'suspect communities' were created (Kundnani 2012: 4) in the wake of the 9/11 attacks in the USA, the 7/7 London bombings, the 2002 Bali bombings, and later acts committed by those claiming identification with and inspiration from the so-called Islamic State in Iraq and Syria (ISIS). In this period, 'radicalisation' to violent extremism became a 'new lens through which to view Muslim minorities' and people who could be identifiable as Muslim (Kundnani 2012: 3), and Muslim communities became subjected to disproportionate restrictions on civil liberties and increased surveillance. In this period, the field of 'terrorism studies' mushroomed – described by Jasbir Puar and Amit Rai (2002), invoking Foucault, as a Western 'will to knowledge' to *'understand* the terrorist psyche' (125, my emphasis). Ilyas Mohammed's (2021) analysis of seven terrorism journals between 2015 and 2019 has demonstrated that 'publications and knowledge production on terrorism are dominated by scholars with Western heritage and institutions based in Western countries' (12). This Western-dominated knowledge production has closely influenced 'the policies of governments and international institutions, the media, the public imaginations on terrorism, and interethnic and inter-religious relations' (Mohammed 2021: 12). During this period, the will to 'understand' the pre-/radicalised subject also infiltrated schools (Abdel-Fattah 2021; Zarabadi 2020).

Governmental politics and funded programmes relating to countering 'radicalisation' to violent extremism had a direct impact on some schools in Australia from 2014, though these policies and programmes have been unevenly felt in their effects. While young people move through intersecting, heterogeneous identifications and subjectifications, those identifying (or identified) as Arab Australian and/

or as Muslim came to 'bear the consequences of an over-determined subject position' following September 11 (Abdel-Fattah 2016: 329). Abdel-Fattah has powerfully mapped how a 'pre-emptive logic of countering the "becoming terrorist"' emerged over this time in Australia, constituting young Australian Muslims in binary form as either 'moderate' or 'extremists' (Abdel-Fattah 2019: 372; cf. Morsi 2017). In the period closely following the production of this puppet scenario, the overarching Australian government policy strategy, 'Living Safe Together', described its aim as to 'build resilient communities that take action against violent extremism'[5] (Commonwealth of Australia 2020b: para. 1). This aim was to be partially achieved through funding 'deradicalisation and diversion' programmes. The logics of Australian government approaches to Countering Violent Extremism (CVE) echo approaches adopted in the UK government's 'Prevent' programme (Her Majesty's Government 2011). In the UK, measures to 'channel' (Her Majesty's Government 2012) those 'at risk' or 'vulnerable' to recruitment to violent extremism through state interventions, including schools, have been demonstrated to target children and young people of Muslim faith (Coppock 2014).

Notwithstanding early criticisms of UK approaches to counter-terrorism, the Australian government's attorney-general's department's booklet, *Preventing Violent Extremism and Radicalisation in Australia (PVERA)* (Commonwealth of Australia 2015), was sent to community organisations and schools after the period of fieldwork – though authors of this booklet have argued that it was never intended for use in schools (Safi 2015). Newspaper articles (which I deliberately do not cite) reported schools being told to be on 'student watch' for signs of radicalisation, authorising principals to report concerns about particular students' (perceived) 'anti-social' or 'inappropriate' behaviour to police or CrimeStoppers. In the *PVERA* booklet, the process of radicalisation is framed in terms of individual psychological and social 'vulnerability' – those with 'personal welfare problems' or who 'have encountered social marginalisation' (Commonwealth of Australia 2015: 3). This attention to 'vulnerability' is consistent with broader counter-radicalisation approaches that Aislinn O'Donnell (2018) has critiqued for their 'softer, quasi-therapeutic approach' that renders 'emotional and existential vulnerability' an 'explanatory paradigm' (983). Yet, the line between vulnerability and radicalisation is unclear, especially since preventive action operates on a pre-emptive logics of apprehending the becoming of the terrorist-subject before any evidence of violence

(Abdel-Fattah 2021). Indeed, a report by Rights Watch UK (2016) has demonstrated, in relation to the UK Prevent strategy, how teachers may be 'concerned with compliance but inadequately equipped', leading to 'a culture of over-referral and excessive scrutiny of children, particularly Muslim children' (5). Schools thus became part of processes of trying to understand and intervene into the lives of the potential student-becoming-terrorist that create, modulate and amplify institutional racism and Islamophobia – fostering what Shiva Zarabadi calls a 'pedagogy of fear': that 'we live and are schooled next to a potential terrorist and risky other' (2020: 78).

## DIALOGUE AND COUNTERING VIOLENT EXTREMISM

Dialogue has become part of 'soft' (preventive) approaches (compared with 'hard', interventionist approaches) to countering the (apparent) 'problem' of radicalisation – though these approaches 'overlap and are inextricably linked' (Spalek and Imtoual 2007: 190). Developed in 2016, the NSW Department of Education and Training *School Communities Working Together* strategy document simultaneously advocates fostering 'resilient, respectful and inclusive learning environments' for a 'positive school culture', while advocating 'reaching out to students and noticing changes in behaviour' to 'assist in identifying the early signs of when a student may be vulnerable to anti-social and extremist influences' (NSW Government: Education n.d.). What is left unsaid is whether the experience of being 'reach[ed] out' to necessarily feels 'respectful' or 'inclusive'. The *PVERA* booklet (Commonwealth of Australia 2015) makes a recommendation that those 'vulnerable' to radicalisation to violent extremism participate in interventions designed to support those who 'feel disconnected' or that they 'don't have a voice in society' (23). 'Voice' here, is a strategy to reconnect the young person presumed to be at risk of radicalising back to 'mainstream' society. Abdel-Fattah, in her analysis of programmes funded through the Living Safe Together grants programme (2014–15), notes how many of the funded programmes avoid the language of violent extremism and 'were presented as positive, empowering and educative initiatives', despite coming under the remit of the government's CVE strategy (Abdel-Fattah 2021: 83). Project descriptions included 'school-based activities such as group discussions, assignments and creative team projects to promote "mentoring" and "opportunities for young Muslims to [. . .] voice their opinions"' (2021: 83). Such contexts for dialogue can elide broader inequalities and injustice and pathologise dissent – against Islamophobia and moral panics, extreme displays of White nationalism and racial vilification, the racialised politics of offshore processing of asylum seekers, and the Australian government's divisive foreign policy sympathy towards Israel (Low 2016). 'Student voice' could be interpreted to be, and enacted as, a way to 'help' 'vulnerable' students 'have a voice' and divert them from violent extremism.

In 2016, a principal of a government boys' secondary school in western Sydney invited Remy Low, Nicole Mockler and me to partner with her in research relating to this school community's resistance to discourses of radicalisation. This principal spoke about wanting her students to be 'radical': radical in the sense of critically questioning the status quo (Low et al. 2019; Mayes 2019a). Remy, Nicole and I developed a research proposal for the University of Sydney Faculty of Education and Social Work Research Program Grant funding scheme, with the title 'Religion, Radicalisation and Critical Education'.[6] We articulated the aims of the research as to 'critically analyse the political, policy and media framing of recent counter-extremist policies and their interpretation and enactment in Australian schools' (Low et al. 2016: 3). The proposal foregrounded 'both the constructed nature of the "problem"' of radicalisation (citing critiques cited in this chapter) and 'a discourse of possibility that can point to more egalitarian and democratic approaches' in education (Low et al. 2016: 3). The proposed research included three dimensions: a policy and media text analysis, an interview study with school principals, and a case study (including interviews with staff and focus groups with students) at this school relating to particular school programmes (including student voice programmes and an 'interfaith dialogue' programme with other schools). The proposal included the acknowledgement that:

> A risk of researching the construction of the 'problem' of radicalisation is that this project may further reify and perpetuate the propagation of this 'problem'. We deliberately will work with a case study school where the principal is actively resisting discourses of 'radicalisation', in order to map alternative modes of making sense of current local and global concerns. (Low et al. 2016: 6–7)

On one of the first days that I visited this school for the purposes of this research, a Muslim staff member asked me directly if the research programme was being funded through government CVE funding. It wasn't. At the same time as I declare here, and declared to him at the time, that this research was not funded through government CVE money, the granting of $14,000 of university seed funding for a project with 'radicalisation' in the title is suggestive of the socio-political-affective appetite in 2016 for research contributing to greater 'understanding' of Muslim-identifying/identifiable students and schools, even if from a 'critical' perspective. This staff member's question – and the silences between and after his question and my answer – has lingered with me. In the 2016 context where the Australian government was funding programmes that appeared to be about engagement and 'voice', with the veiled agenda of 'deradicalising' the presumed pre-radical student subject, it is unsurprising that this university-funded research would be interpreted as another CVE-funded project. Student voice and 'critical' research, under such policy funding conditions, may be harnessed as extensions of state surveillance or, at least, may propagate uncertainty about whether one's community has been placed under further surveillance. As a teacher and researcher, I have been entwined and implicated in these conditions for 'voice' and 'dialogue'.

These 'soft' dialogical approaches to countering violent extremism in schools take place in particular spatial and material configurations that may also circulate fear. In the context of devolved responsibilities to individual school leaders, including for safety, 'schools have undergone rapid growth in securitisation, in a bid to placate fears, whether real, imagined or curated' (Taylor 2018: 312). Before, during and after this period of fieldwork, Australian government federal funding was committed to support the construction of 'protective' security infrastructure (including closed-circuit television and security lighting). The Schools Security Programme (launched in 2007 as the Secure Schools Programme) has provided millions of dollars of 'non-recurrent funding for security infrastructure, such as closed-circuit television (CCTV) systems, lighting and fences, and for the cost of employing security guards' (Attorney-General's Department, cited in Taylor 2018: 317). The prevalence and forms of surveillance technologies in schools are unevenly distributed between schools, aligning with racialised and classed demographics.

Students at the school where this puppet scenario was created spoke about the differences between their school's security gates and the open borders of the leafy green private school that they had visited as part of their student voice research. Other students from this school, in another focus group,[7] made references to their school's CCTV and high gates. These students spoke about feeling 'spied at' (Abu George), feeling like they are 'walk[ing] into a jail' (Abu George) and feeling like their school thinks that they will 'plant a bomb or something' (Onetwothree; all student quotations are from Mayes 2020b: 389). These material conditions made one student, Abu George, articulate feeling 'more insecure'; another student, Sarah, said, 'I get it for like safety reasons. [...] But they overdid it' (Mayes 2020b: 389). Emmeline Taylor (2017) argues that surveillance technologies can be 'ushered in with promises of safeguarding children', to 'enhance a sense of security', but they can also 'conjure feelings of anxiety, loss of privacy and mistrust' (424). Fear swarms within and between the material conditions of schools. Notwithstanding potential alternative interpretations of the function of security cameras, lighting and gates, their function and affective intensities were apprehended and interpreted by the students in arrangement with a 'cumulative assemblage and repetitious circulation of laws, public debates, media headlines, political discourse, social and educative practices' and pedagogies (Abdel-Fattah 2021: 114).

It is perhaps no wonder, then, that there is a 'spiral to silence' – Elisabeth Noelle-Neumann's (1974) phrase for silencing one's voice from a fear of being isolated or criminalised for one's views. Abdel-Fattah (in Sydney, Australia) and Zarabadi (in London, UK) have perceptively mapped the consequences of these atmos-fears for the 'pedagogy of speaking politics as a Muslim' (Abdel-Fattah 2021: 257). Their analyses include accounts, from Muslim-identifying young people they spoke with, of being censored but also self-censoring; having one's tone policed, but also policing one's tone. Abdel-Fattah describes the 'fear *of* and fear *for* the Muslim student' (247, original emphasis): with adults and teachers cautioning students to monitor their own speech, embodiment and faith practices. One politically passionate student, Jihan[8] (Year 12, public school), gives an account of being told not to be too '"angry in my voice"' (in Abdel-Fattah 2021: 119); this 'pressure to self-censor in classroom contexts' is a 'common theme' among many of the Muslim students Abdel-Fattah spoke to (257). Pressure to self-censor becomes internalised; as one Muslim-veiled student (Farah, Year 12) said to Zarabadi:

> [W]e have to take into account everything that we say; we can't be too extreme and I felt like if I say something then people ... I have to hold myself back, or else they might think 'oh I am becoming extremist' which obviously I am not. [...] (in Zarabadi 2020: 73)

Similarly, Abdel-Fattah (2021) quotes from Muslim-identifying young people who give accounts of being worried about things that they say being misinterpreted in classrooms across multiple contexts in Sydney. As Fadi, 'a 17-year-old devout Muslim boy at Inner West Islamic School', put it: '"I'm not afraid of terrorism. I'm afraid of being *accused* of being a terrorist"' (in Abdel-Fattah 2021: 21, orignal emphasis). Farah, speaking with Zarabadi, describes a particular moment of self-censorship in an English lesson:

> And in one of my English lessons, I remember a White boy said something and then the teacher said something and when I was saying something back my friend was like you have to be quiet, because you know it's different for them, they don't understand these things. (in Zarabadi 2020: 74)

According to Zarabadi, there are 'invisible but present forces' that silence Farah's 'voice and hold her body back'; her 'affective entanglement with threat micro-materially changes her relations to her body, other bodies, and her environment' (2020: 74, 78). There is fear in these dialogical situations – fear that 'threads through relationships of trust (fear of your teachers' or friends' suspicions, for example) and through political participation (fear of expressing your opinion, fear of being seen as "too angry" and so on)' (Abdel-Fattah 2021: 18). A student's repression or redirection of their speech and energies is firstly a social and affective relation before it is a conscious decision; desire is blocked or redirected in social relations that may become internalised in psychic repressions. Desire comes to desire its own repression (Deleuze and Guattari 1983).

To return to the puppet scenario, perhaps the chicken-puppet fears articulating dissent – and so spirals into silence (Noelle-Neumann 1974). Perhaps the chicken-puppet does not want to be classified as psychologically vulnerable and placed under psycho-therapeutic monitoring. Perhaps the chicken-puppet would prefer not to be part of the opportunity to speak about their (presumed) 'problem' and why they feel the way they feel.

## Towards the Right to Opacity

> 'Bartleby,' said I, gently calling to him behind his screen. No reply. 'Bartleby,' said I, in a still gentler tone, 'come here; I am not going to ask you to do anything you would prefer not to do—I simply wish to speak to you.' Upon this he noiselessly slid into view. 'Will you tell me, Bartleby, where you were born?' 'I would prefer not to.' 'Will you tell

*me anything about yourself?' 'I would prefer not to.'*
Herman Melville, *Bartleby, the Scrivener*

Perhaps the chicken-puppet would prefer not to participate in these dialogical interventions that aim to understand him. In a minor literature, 'language is affected with a high coefficient of deterritorialisation' (Deleuze and Guattari 2006: 16). The dominant language is scrambled and something escapes. Usually, language is written or spoken to make sense; the minor literature, however, does not make recognisable sense (Deleuze and Guattari 2006: 21; Lecercle 2002: 195). Deleuze and Guattari (2006) speak of the deterritorialisation of language in Kafka's work:

> Gregor's warbling and the ways it blurred words, the whistling of the mouse, the cough of the ape, the pianist who doesn't play, the singer who doesn't sing and gives birth to her song out of her nonsinging, the musical dogs who are musicians in the very depths of their bodies since they don't emit any music. [. . .] [A] language of sense is traversed by a line of escape – in order to liberate a living and expressive material that speaks for itself and has no need of being put into a form. (Deleuze and Guattari 2006: 21)

In the case of this scenario, the utterances of the chicken-puppet do not reterritorialise in sense; the chicken-puppet momentarily speaks in the language of the classroom, but their answer seems to still be illegible to the teacher. There is a disorganisation in the expression machine that assumes that a focus group (as a form of content – an organisation of bodies) necessarily will generate a certain form of expression ('dialogue' and understanding between students and teacher). The chicken-puppet's use of words perhaps does not (only) account for an internalised fear (being 'scared'); the words gesture towards the limits and insufficiencies of the dominant language (Bright 2020: 22–3). This strange speech – and momentary clarity – stymies speech, and arrests, alters and redirects affective flows. The chicken-puppet withdraws from engagement and makes the dialogical speech situation 'topple into silence' (Deleuze 1997: 72). No understanding is reached, there is no resolution; the chicken-puppet does not make itself transparent and understandable.

In a minor literature, 'everything takes on a collective value' (Deleuze and Guattari 2006: 17). The 'individual concern' – perhaps, here, the chicken-puppet's statement of being 'scared' – is 'all the more necessary, indispensable, magnified, because a whole other story is vibrating in it' (Deleuze and Guattari 2006: 17). Everything that is said 'is necessarily political, even if others aren't in agreement' (17). There is no individual subject – for example, the chicken-puppet as representative of an individual student or 'type' – only collective agencements of enunciation (Deleuze and Guattari 2006: 17) – conjunctions of forms of content (configurations) and forms of expression. The collective agencement of enunciation makes it possible – even momentarily – 'to express another possible community and to forge the means for another consciousness and another sensibility' (Deleuze and Guattari 2006: 17) – even if it is not clear what this other consciousness and sensibility are. Erin Manning, writing about the 'minor gesture' (2016), after Deleuze and Guattari, posits that the minor makes a difference, whether or not this difference is perceived (255, n.1). The effects of the minor may be felt in other registers – at other times – in the moment of blinking (Deleuze and Parnet 2006/1977: 1).

In the chicken-puppet's minor inflections, there is ungraspable heterogeneity, multiplicity, unknowability and non-understandability, and the potential for honouring opacity and refusals to be the subject of dialogical interventions. I wonder what it might look like to honour opacity, and to stop trying to grasp – to understand – speech and silences in (and beyond) schools. Glissant (1990/1997) explains the Western 'process of "understanding" people and ideas' as based in the 'requirement for transparency' (189–90): 'In order to understand and thus to accept you, I have to measure your solidity with the ideal scale providing me with grounds to make comparisons and, perhaps, judgments. I have to reduce' (Glissant 1990/1997: 190). In this mode of understanding, according to Glissant, difference is understood by its relation to Western norms. Glissant (1990/1997) wonders about the possibilities of displacing 'all reduction', agreeing 'not merely to the right to difference' but also 'to the right to opacity' as 'irreducible singularity' and 'exultant divergence' (190). The opaque, according to Glissant, is 'not the obscure', but is 'that which cannot be reduced' (191) or grasped. Perhaps dialogue becomes something else, then:

> I thus am able to conceive of the opacity of the other for me, without reproach for my opacity for him [sic]. To feel in solidarity with him or to build with him or to like what he does, it is not necessary for me to grasp him. (Glissant 1990/1997: 193)

Glissant (1990/1997) argues for opacity as a basic condition for political legitimacy – for 'understanding' the impossibility of reducing anyone to a truth they could not have generated on their own (194).

Reading Glissant and Bartleby, Kara Keeling argues that 'Bartleby's opacity, his refusal to signify in accountable and politically meaningful ways, is the story's greatest resource' (Keeling 2019: 192). The chicken-puppet's strange speech and silences in 2013 have lingered with me across temporalities, policy mutations and school and research configurations – teaching me the value of opacity. While becoming-imperceptible is an oft-quoted Deleuze and Guattarian political tactic, opacity is always already imperceptible and illegible according to majoritarian common sense (Keeling 2019: 191). A politics of opacity, in Keeling's extension of Glissant, is not a reformist politics that reifies existing structures. A politics of opacity, rather, asserts the right not to be compelled to make oneself transparent, and to remain unaccountable, refusing 'to be bound by dominant standards of measure, recognition, and evaluation' (Keeling 2019: 46). Valuing and legitimising opacity throws into relief the repressive logics of reform that had been in operation and compel the formation of different logics of relating (see Chapter 7).

This chapter has drawn attention, via a puppet scenario, to the limits of dialogue in voice endeavours, and the intractability of understanding. The chicken-puppet's speech and silences, in this scenario, lie somewhere between sense and nonsense; the sense that is sensed does not make sense. The dialogical encounter might offer the conditions for a relational encounter that might shift and transform pedagogical relations, but students and teachers are not necessarily rendered comprehensible to each other through the dialogical event. I turned from the student (as a site of deficit and risk) to the politics of seeing, listening and attuning in schools – with particular attention to contemporary atmos-fears. Thinking with the puppet scenario has raised the political question about whose understandings are privileged in classroom and school life, the affective sensorium surrounding classroom events, and the subjectifications effected in the dialogical encounter. Thinking beyond classroom and school 'climate', I considered the targeting (and creation) of the student (so-called) at risk of radicalisation to violent extremism via schools through the preventative logic of 'listening' to students. I considered the spirals of silence and the self-repression of speech in situations where certain bodies and identifications are interpreted as grasping onto cultural, religious or political attachments that are considered to be risky or extreme. As Abdel-Fattah (2021) astutely puts it: 'the ideals of relational trust and "open classroom climates" within schools sit in tension with the wider discursive and racialised construction of young Muslims as "politically risky" subjects or "would-be terrorists"' (306). These varied mis/uses and diverging experiences of the enactment of dialogue in the classroom challenge universalising statements of the value and possibilities of dialogue and voice as necessarily empowering. Advocates of voice in schools might take care with whether and how students and teachers are compelled to give an account of themselves and how the dialogical event is interpreted and grasped as a way to monitor and govern students. These compulsions and interpretations may, inadvertently, smooth dissenting views and block flows of interest – desire for connection. At the same time, institutional patterns of subjectification do not contain desire; desire exceeds and escapes interpretations of what a body is feeling, believing, saying and doing. The question is how to stop grasping, to refuse to grasp, to refuse fixity and to value movement and dynamism, valuing more affirmative climates-in-the-making (Mayes et al. 2020).

The following chapter extends this consideration of what exceeds and escapes complex movements of desire in and through the open system of schools. I turn to the institutional imperative to evaluate educational reform interventions (such as student voice) through the collection of 'data' as evidence of whether or not an intervention has 'worked'. At the school where this puppet scenario was created, the students as researchers (SaR) initiative that had been funded through targeted funding for 'low socioeconomic school communities' was evaluated by the school leadership as having made 'little or no progress' towards the target: 'Decrease in student incident interviews by 10%'. I tell a story of how students' early research with other students – where students had declared that they did not feel 'respect' from their teachers (perhaps, for some, an oblique reference to institutional racism and Islamophobia) – became entwined with a Positive Behaviour Interventions and Supports programme, where students were given behavioural tokens ('RESP tokens') by teachers when they were thought to be demonstrating 'respect'. The chapter attends to what, in Keeling's (2019) terms, exceeds 'dominant standards of measure, recognition, and evaluation' (46). I map the movements of these small tokens for the molecular flows, micromovements, disruptions and connections that exceeded the definitive statements made in the school's reform evaluation documents. I argue that the movements and uses made of the RESP token indicate some of the virtual forces that leave micropolitical traces, even when voices are ostensibly muted.

## Notes

1. Shiva Zarabadi used this phrase to account for the chicken-puppet, in her response to an earlier version of this chapter. Acknowledgements and thanks to Shiva Zarabadi for reading an earlier version of this chapter and for this eloquent observation.
2. Returning to Massumi's words in 2020 and 2021, when the COVID-19 pandemic is widely described as inaugurating a 'new normal', this new 'new normal' is another eternal return of previous affects in circulation – fear again, circulating what Achille Mbembe (2018) has called a 'racial affect' that fears and polices some bodies more than others (para. 4).
3. The students described themselves on sticky notes in the following terms: xPeke – 'Unique (my way)'; Isaac – 'I don't really know how to describe myself'; Umprikash – 'Short year 9 boy'; Shaza – 'A year 9 male, with a passion for sports and challenge for keeping high ranks in learning'. As Chapter 2 explained, while the students give, withhold and perhaps laugh at racial, cultural, religious, gender and virtual/actual markers of identity in their self-descriptions, they are each multiply positioned across gender, social class, cultural and academic rankings; there are complex sites of subjectifications and multiple axes of inequalities that intersect and interrelate in their experiences of school.
4. Indeed, at the school where this chicken-puppet scenario was created, there were multiple accounts of the dialogical encounter and its atmosphere(s) (Groundwater-Smith et al. 2014; Mayes et al. 2013). Isaac, one of the students who created the chicken-puppet scenario, spoke at another time about his experience of interviewing a history teacher:

> In class it's not as comfortable to talk to the teacher, and there are lots of other people around. The interview was more personal. The teachers all were a little bit nervous, but it was also much more comfortable – in class they might be more stressed or frustrated with students. A teacher is a different person in class, because there's a different amount of students. An interview is a good opportunity for them to meet us, for us to understand each other. (Isaac, Year 9 focus group)

The head of the Human Society and its Environment department, in an interview with me, gave another account of a meeting (planning for the new curriculum) when the department's teachers were observed by the student researchers:

> For those brief moments when [the students] were watching us, it created connections between teachers and students. You are still aware of them, conscious of their thoughts as you talk: their own thoughts, your actions and how you think in terms of what we were dealing

with that day, planning for the programs. I felt that connection was really positive. You couldn't really absolutely ignore that they were there, and you didn't really want to: a connection came in. We were moving away from that student/teacher relationship – there was a collegiality between teacher and student – I've never experienced it before. We only touched on it but it was nice. (Interview)

5. This previous version of the aims is no longer available online; the website wording has been updated. The updated (2020) *Living Safe Together* website now includes the statement: 'Together we can build community resilience to violent extremist ideologies and keep Australia safe' (Commonwealth of Australia 2020b: para. 1).
6. Helen Proctor and Susan Groundwater-Smith were also listed on this grant application as mentors/critical friends.
7. This focus group was with three Year 11 students. The students described themselves on sticky notes in the following terms: 'Abu George': 'Small & weak & can't lift anything'; 'Onetwothree': 'Smart.' 'Sarah': 'Understanding'.
8. All names used by Abdel-Fattah (2021) and Zarabadi (2020) are pseudonyms. I keep these names and the description of these young people given by the authors.

6

# Evaluating the Perplexing Outcomes of School Reform

> *[T]hose who evaluated things in macropolitical terms understood nothing of the event because something unaccountable was escaping.*
> Gilles Deleuze and Félix Guattari, *A Thousand Plateaus*[1]

It has become common sense that educational reform interventions (such as student voice) must be evaluated to know if they have worked or not. The data-driven school sets (or is given) targets to meet through reform interventions; for example, to reduce suspension rates by a certain percentage, or improve attendance rates by a certain percentage, or improve the percentage of students attaining a particular standard of academic performance. As I foregrounded in Chapter 3, Stephen Ball (2003) has written about how data come to 'stand for, encapsulate or represent the worth, quality or value of an individual or organisation within a field of judgement' (216). It is taken for granted that reducing suspension rates is right, because a reduction in suspension is supposed to signify that bodies are speaking, feeling and behaving in a manner that is morally agreeable to others and that is right according to the principles of morality. It is taken for granted, in reporting the outcomes of particular reform interventions, that these outcomes are true – that reported outcomes correspond with the intervention. It is taken for granted that reported outcomes stick to bodies and sediment and congeal in schools: that a reduction in suspensions manifests an improved school, and that the school can continue to progress and build on these outcomes in future reform efforts. According to this common sense, collecting data as evidence of whether or not an intervention has worked enables the school to be accountable and transparent to funding bodies. Data thus become desired (Thompson and Sellar 2018) – particularly data that will demonstrate positive growth over linear time, as judged against predetermined normative standards of what particular reform interventions were intended to achieve.

These straight lines between problem, intervention, data and evaluation begin to crack when a reform produces perplexing affects and effects. Things don't always turn out the way we[2] would prefer them to turn out. Voices may say things that some may not like to hear; the experience of 'having a voice' may not feel 'empowering'; students having a voice may not engender the changes that are desired, and different changes may be desired by differentially positioned bodies. In this chapter, I deliberately work with an example of a perplexing outcome of a student voice initiative – when students 'had a voice' and said that they did not feel respected by their teachers, and the response was the production of behaviour tokens for teachers to give students as a reward for when students showed 'respect'. A behavioural token (RESP token; see Figure 6.1 below) is perhaps a quintessential example of a tool for majoritarian evaluation; that is, an evaluation that judges a body according to the normative standard of the major – liberal humanist Man (see Chapters 3 and 4). With the behavioural token as a majoritarian evaluation tool, the teacher judges and rewards a student body for deporting itself in accordance with predetermined institutional norms for how a body should speak, act and feel. This chapter explores how this token became a way to evaluate students at one school; this school was introduced in Chapter 1 and this study is also discussed in Chapters 2 and 5. I also explore how the role of this token in a Positive Behaviour Interventions and Supports (PBIS) initiative was evaluated by students and by school leaders, alongside a discussion of alternative modes of evaluation.

This chapter is concerned with this logic of evaluation in and of schools, particularly evaluations of and with student voice. I discuss two modes of evaluation. One mandates accounts of growth according to predetermined targets; the other evaluates what happens according to the immanent modes of existence that it implies. The chapter narrates what happened during one school's evaluation of two reform interventions; this school's evaluation demonstrates majoritarian logics of change – looking for growth according to predetermined targets. At this school, one of these four-year interventions was a 'students as researchers' initiative (the group that students called the 'Steering Committee', but which was abbreviated in school leadership evaluation documents as Students as Researchers – 'SaRs'). Students as researchers initiatives involve students becoming apprenticed as researchers (here, by an academic partner), in order to conduct their own research inquiries into the conditions of learning and teaching in their classrooms and school (Fielding and Bragg 2003, ch. 1). Throughout this chapter, I use 'Steering Committee' when referring to the group's research and conversations with students; I use 'SaRs' when referring to the school's evaluation processes and documents. This student voice initiative was evaluated by the school leadership according to whether it had met the target: 'Decrease in student incident interviews by 10%.' It was assessed to have made 'little or no progress' towards this target, and the initiative was consequently discontinued at the end of the period of school reform funding. In the same evaluation, by contrast, a Positive Behaviour Interventions and Supports initiative was evaluated as having made 'sound' progress towards the target: 'Decrease in student suspensions by 5%.' This PBIS initiative was to be maintained beyond the end of the reform funding.

Thinking with Deleuze and Guattari's analysis of desire as productive, as well as with the concept of minoritarian evaluations, I turn from the majoritarian evaluation typed on A4 pieces of paper to a smaller piece of paper: a RESP token (see Figure 6.1). Working with this RESP token, I explore an immanent, minoritarian mode of evaluation that notes moments of joy when bodies' capacity to act compound (Deleuze 1988; Deleuze and Guattari 1980/1987). As the previous chapter explained, the minor exceeds and escapes from the normative major standard that seeks to define and delimit (see Chapter 5). Minoritarian evaluations, I suggest, are evaluations that exceed or escape from the targets or criteria for success set by a dominant party (for example, a school or educational system). Rather than only noting how a majoritarian school reform evaluation document divides data and inhibits future relations, cartographically mapping the movements of a small RESP token suggests the molecular flows, tiny movements, shocks, ruptures and repairs that exceed school reform evaluation documents. The movements and uses made by/of the RESP token indicate some of the micropolitical forces that leave felt traces, even when students' voices are misapprehended.

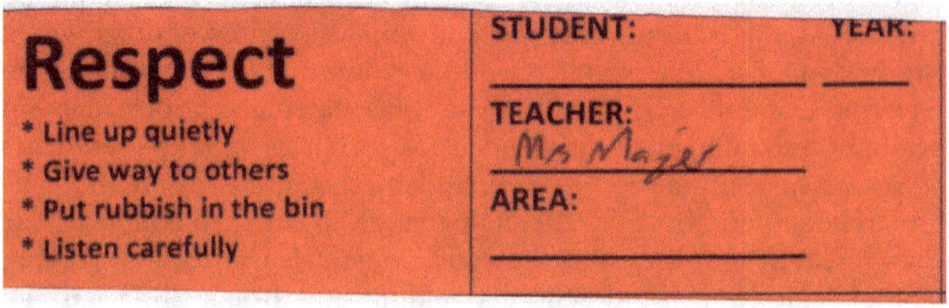

**Respect**
* Line up quietly
* Give way to others
* Put rubbish in the bin
* Listen carefully

STUDENT: _____  YEAR: ____

TEACHER: Ms Mager

AREA: _____

*Figure 6.1* A RESP token.

## Majoritarian Evaluations

In recent years, teachers and school leaders have reported a significant increase in the demand to collect, analyse and report on numerical data in their classrooms and schools (Bertrand and Marsh 2021; McGrath-Champ et al. 2018). Both locally and globally, numbers are used to construct, know, analyse and govern the practices and performance of students, teachers and schools (Ozga 2015). Policy sociologists have thoroughly mapped the consequences of contemporary performative modes of accountability and evaluation: for example, the codification of 'best practice' and the undermining of teachers' professional knowledge, the simplification of ontological questions about what constitutes 'evidence', the reinforcement of deficit discourses about particular students and communities, and the constitution of new types of teachers, school leaders and student subjects (see Chapter 3).

As data are created, knowledge about students and teachers is generated and divided up. Deleuze wrote in 'Postscript on the Societies of Control' that individuals become reconfigured as '"dividual" material to be controlled' (Deleuze 1992b: 7). While the affective intensities accompanying data in an evaluation are ambivalent, their effects are real. The imperative to construct and arrange data can be harnessed to meet a school's affective needs: to manage unsettling affects, to restore a certain affective order, to engender a certain sense of calm – particularly when a reform intervention has unsettled the status quo. To put it plainly, sometimes it's easier to say, 'the data say that this student voice initiative isn't working' than it is to say, 'I don't like what the students are saying.' It is perhaps easier for schools to assemble 'dividuated' data to quietly invalidate and justify the discontinuation of particular reform strategies that are uncomfortable. As Greg Thompson and Ian Cook describe in their study of teachers' manipulation of high-stakes testing data, 'disembodied patterns of data points' are reassembled to 'tell the right 'story' (Thompson and Cook 2012a: 137), in order to meet the demand for the fabrication of developmental, teleological tales of growth over time. At this school, one school leader described their approach to arranging data for accountability reporting:

> **School leader:** And we manipulate the figures because we want the data to show something positive.
> **Eve:** Because you have to show –

**School leader:** You have to show, yeah. You have to show some positives and we did.

In processes of generating and arranging data, bodies, encounters and connections are cut up and reconfigured. Individual or numerical bodies, in the society of control, are substituted with divided material: student incident interview data; student suspension data. This dividual material can be extracted and inserted into other fields. Dividuated data about students are easier to manage, move around and map to a target on an A4 Word table than the mobile, ever shifting and changing flesh and bones of a student who speaks. These processes of strategically selecting and managing dividuated data are of interest, not just because they are reductive (of complex social realities), but also because of how they are productive – that is, how they are 'put to work' (Sellar 2014: 139) by those in positions of power in schools.

Beyond numbers alone, 'soft' data have also become part of processes of dividualisation – qualitative data managed, moved and configured, while maintaining the same logics of evaluation and reform. As Chapter 3 explained, alongside this ascendance of 'governing by numbers' (Rose 1991), it has also become commonly accepted that students (along with staff and parents/caregivers) should be part of classroom and school evaluation processes (Brown et al. 2020). Indeed, it may be seen by some as a triumph that, in certain jurisdictions, student voice has become a policy priority that shapes school leaders' strategic planning and evaluation processes. For example, in Victoria, Australia, the Department of Education and Training's (VicDET) Framework for Improving Student Outcomes (FISO) identifies four priorities for schools, one of which is to develop a 'positive climate for learning' (VicDET 2020). Within this priority, the dimension 'empowering students and building school pride' details student voice practices expected of schools (VicDET 2020). This policy of prioritising of student voice has led to many schools in Victoria prioritising student voice as a reform initiative in itself within their annual strategic plans, and as a mode of evaluating their other reform initiatives – including the positional insights of 'stakeholders'. Qualitative, 'soft data' (Simons 2015) have become valued as 'evidence' that schools can also use in their evaluation processes – for example, quotations from student focus groups speaking about how they experienced particular school programmes or interventions. These 'new(er), more qualitative configurations of evidence' are then used to 'complement' and even '"improve" numerical forms of performance data' (Lewis and Holloway 2019: 38) rather than necessarily challenging their logic of evaluation.

I have worked with such soft data in evaluation. I have observed and have been part of evaluations of student voice initiatives and evaluations of reform initiatives that have included students' voices. Between 2017 and 2020, I led (with Rosalyn Black and Rachel Finneran) an evaluation of a VicSRC (VicDET-funded) programme for schools – Teach the Teacher – exploring how five schools gave an account of the 'impacts' of this particular student voice initiative on student engagement and learning, student/teacher relationships, teacher professional learning, teaching and learning practices and school improvement at their schools (see Black and Mayes 2020; Mayes et al. 2019, 2021). When students, teachers and school leaders were asked to 'give an account' (Lingard et al. 2017) of the 'impacts' of this programme, they often gave quite contrasting accounts. These contrasting accounts, from differentially positioned subjects, suggest diverging theories of change (Tuck and Yang 2014a: 13; see Chapters 2 and 4). For example, students often gave an account of teachers' changing teaching practices, while teachers often gave an account of students' increased confidence, engagement and leadership. Asked whether student voice had supported teacher professional learning (as is implied in the programme name: Teach the Teacher), we were frequently met with perplexing silences (cf. Mayes et al. 2021; cf. Mazzei 2003). Notwithstanding the ascendance of policy enthusiasm for student voice practices, stated or implicit 'goals' for student voice often seem to orient towards a change in student attitudes to school and their 'behaviour'. In the Teach the Teacher evaluation study, some teachers spoke of using student voice in their classrooms for their own learning; they described defining or negotiating their own professional development goals with their students, and then inviting students to evaluate their 'improvement' as a teacher. These practices maintained the logic of establishing a predetermined target for improvement for later evaluation. The risk is that such practices maintain an orthodox image of students, teachers and education and implicit presuppositions of what student voice is meant to do – maintaining the same image of students, teachers and education that pre-existed the reform.

Both 'hard' (quantitative) and 'soft' forms of data can be majoritarian in their logics, in Deleuze's terms – that is, entwined with dominant systems of power and control, with particular modes of recognition and modes of representing change. Majoritarian modes of evaluation set measurement standards, and judge and divide according to established standards of 'success' or 'failure', 'right' or 'wrong'. Majoritarian modes of evaluation maintain pre-existing norms – what Maarten Simons (2015) has called an 'immanent normativity' (720). Schools may identify a goal for improvement of its 'current state in line with a normativity that is inherent to that system' (Simons 2015: 719): for example, 'Decrease in student incident interviews by 10%.' Initiatives for change (like student voice) are oriented towards predefined systemic norms, with the knowledge subsequently generated purported to be a dispassionate, objective evaluation. Yet, in modes of evaluation that operate with the logics of immanent normativity, the current logic for 'student incidents' is not questioned – the image of thought of what student 'behaviour' is meant to look like, and the logics of the value of interviewing and/or suspending a student from school, are maintained.

But what exceeds these majoritarian expectations of what is supposed to change through a reform intervention?

## *A Partial Narrative of a Reform Evaluation*

I begin with an account of how one school's four-year student voice initiative was evaluated. This school, introduced in Chapter 1, had received funding through National Partnership for Low Socio-economic Status School Communities federal and state funding. The funding agreement described the aims of this funding as to 'transform the way that schooling takes place in participating schools', and 'improve student engagement, educational attainment and wellbeing in participating schools' (Council of Australian Governments [COAG] 2012: 1–2). Towards the end of the final year of National Partnerships funding, schools receiving this funding were required to report the outcomes of the reform strategies in an A4 table. Particular 'targets' from the school's Annual School Plan were to be aligned with a particular reform strategy, 'outcomes' aligned to correspond with the 'targets', and an assessment made as to whether the progress towards the target was 'limited (little or no progress)', 'sound (target achieved)', or 'high (target exceeded)'. In 'implementing the reforms', schools were to focus on:

- using data collected through the rigorous situational analysis/environmental scan to identify the outcomes that need to be achieved in each school;
- putting in place new strategies that can effect measurable change, with teacher quality as a key element;
- identifying and addressing individual needs of students;
- accountability for achieving outcomes with transparent planning and reporting;
- ongoing evidenced-based evaluation of reform to refine implementation and identify future priorities. (Australian Government et al. 2010: 19)

The lines of connection to be drawn in schools' evaluation documents between targets, strategies and outcomes were to accord with the future of each reform strategy beyond the funding period. Strategies demonstrated to be successful were to be sustained; strategies where 'little or no progress' was made were to be discontinued. This evaluation document was submitted to the institutional body overseeing the National Partnerships initiative as an accountability mechanism.

The particular students as researchers initiative (the Steering Committee) that was evaluated in this final year (2013) had run for these four years of reform funding. The work of the Steering Committee was not without challenges, and I am entangled and implicated in what happened over these four years. In 2010, this group was formed (by adults, including me) to involve students in considering what reforms the school should undertake with this National Partnerships funding. In 2010, approximately twenty Year 9 students (14-year-olds) from across the school's range of classes, 'ability' groupings, friendship groups and cultural and linguistic backgrounds were apprenticed into a SaRs inquiry undertaken over a whole school year: 'The School I'd Like'. That year, Year 9 students researched how they and their peers were feeling at school, including the reforms that students desired, and presented their research findings to staff. A key finding that the Steering Committee stressed to staff was the importance that students placed on a felt sense of mutual respect between adults and students. This articulated feeling of disrespect seemed to index other embodied experiences and concerns: deficit discourses, classism, institutional racism and Islamophobia – though these were not explicitly named in the students' presentations (cf. Clay and Turner 2021; Welton et al.

2017). This key word – *respect* – was contested; some teachers responded, when students presented their research findings to staff, that students needed to first respect teachers if they wanted to be respected.

Following this staff presentation, the school's senior executive (that is, two deputy principals and the principal) invited the Steering Committee to be part of a Positive Behaviour Interventions and Supports (PBIS) process of negotiating the school's values. As Chapter 3 explained, PBIS is an educational reform programme that aims to encourage whole-school communities to explicitly teach, identify and reinforce 'positive behaviours' among students. In this reform programme, school values and accompanying normative behavioural expectations are to be established through consensus negotiated with all stakeholders. Even while the criteria for positive behaviour are established through consensus, these criteria establish normative standards by which to determine the individual words and actions deemed to be right, as well as the words and actions deemed to be wrong. These values become, as I discussed in Chapter 3, order words – words that order, arrange and reinforce political arrangements and classifications of bodies in relation to other bodies, spaces and things. These behavioural expectations are then to be explicitly taught and teachers are to provide students with 'systematic positive reinforcement for meeting and exceeding performance criteria' (Luiselli et al. 2005: 184).

At the time that the SaRs and PBIS initiatives began to interweave (2010), I was a facilitating teacher of the Steering Committee. I raised concerns with key senior executive teachers over whether the reform's focus was shifting from students speaking (and teachers listening) to student behaviour. Nevertheless, in late 2010, the Steering Committee became part of the PBIS process of negotiating school values and the performance criteria for demonstration of these values, through facilitating focus groups with students and parents. In focus groups, students and parents selected six 'core values' from a list of sixteen values and ranked these values in their order of perceived importance. Teachers facilitated teacher focus groups, where teachers also selected six 'core values' from a list of sixteen values and ranked these values in their order of perceived importance. The PBIS teacher committee pooled and analysed the results from the student, parent and teacher groups. New school values, decided on through this process, were instantiated in the acronym RESP:

Respect
Equity
Safety
Positivity.

A PBIS teacher committee, along with the Steering Committee, subsequently developed explicit performance criteria for the demonstration of each of these values in specific areas (for example, corridors, classrooms, the canteen) – that is, behavioural indicators for adults to recognise and affirm students' demonstration of RESP values. The Steering Committee reviewed these performance criteria that had been written by the teacher committee.

In 2012, the Steering Committee were involved in launching the new RESP values, with a celebratory day of assemblies, performances and games facilitated by students and teachers. RESP values were displayed around the school on expensive colourful signs. A token system was introduced, in which tokens (see Figure 6.1) were to be given by teachers to students when students demonstrated Respect, Equity, Safety or Positivity. Students were to collect and deposit their accrued tokens in RESP bins in the school foyer. Every week, at school assemblies, a member of the school leadership team transferred these deposited tokens from the RESP bins to colour-coded paper bags. During the assembly, an executive teacher (that is, a head of department) or deputy principal drew several tokens out of these bags and read out the names of students written on them. Students whose names were drawn out walked to the front of the assembly, shook a deputy principal's hand, were given an ice lolly that recess time as a reward, and invited to a barbeque with the school principal during class time at the end of the school term.

As I explained in Chapters 1 and 2, in 2013, I returned to the school as a researcher (though frequently mistaken to be back teaching again), visiting the school 2–5 days a week for one year. Over this year, I spent time (in formal focus groups and interviews, and in informal conversations) with students previously and currently involved as researchers in the Steering Committee, as well as with school staff, generating accounts of student voice and the school reform process. A total number of 100 students, staff members and parents were involved in sixty-eight formal interviews and focus groups. In that same year, as I explained above, the SaRs initiative was evaluated as unsuccessful – and discontinued. However, PBIS was evaluated as meeting its intended outcomes, and continued after the end of the National Partnership for Low Socio-economic Status School Communities funding cycle.

## *Evaluating This Evaluation*

When I spoke to students in the fourth year of this reform (2013), when it was being evaluated, there seemed to be two dominant accounts of what had happened over this four-year period of reform. One group of Year 11 students spoke about the installation of the RESP signs as an indication that the school had 'completely changed'. These students had been directly involved in the launch of the RESP values, where their work was acknowledged by the school community. In a focus group, when I asked them about their definition of student voice, they articulated the significance of the RESP signs:

Eve: What is student voice [. . .]?
Pythagoras:[3] I think instead of just having students talk about what they want or write about it, they actively do something to change something – an aspect of school.
Eve: Were there active changes that came?
Pythagoras: Yeah, I think so. But I think it's more actually feeling like you're doing something – that was more than whatever happened. [. . .]
Eve: So what did change for you then?
Pythagoras: Well, RESP happened. And then from that, it seems like a lot of the relationships for students and teachers have been more casual, more open.
Eve: And what was it about RESP that kind of helped that process?
Samantha: It like put all the qualities together and it like created this kind of environment where everyone – it's fair and everyone feels comfortable. I think it's important to feel comfortable.
Pythagoras: And seeing the school put up all those RESP sign things – cause you could tell the school were serious about it and it would happen –
Johnathan: No one thought it was actually going to have an effect –
Pythagoras: It's like, 'we started that' and the teachers –
Samantha: It actually continued – like sometimes you think when they bring something in – is it going to last? Like you're a bit iffy at the beginning but to see that, every assembly people are being read out by –
Johnathan: The RESP awards, yeah. [. . .]
Eve: And you see that as directly a result of your work?

# Evaluating the Perplexing Outcomes of School Reform

**Samantha:** It's good when they follow through on things. [. . .]
**Johnathan:** As a result of *our* work.
**Pythagoras:** Usually when we do this type of thing – like teachers ask what do you want to change – nothing really happens –
**Johnathan:** They forget about it.
**Pythagoras:** But now it's like the whole school is completely changed because of it. It's like RESP is part of [the school's name].
**Johnathan:** And *we* did that. [. . .]
**Pythagoras:** RESP changed everything for me. It proved to me that you can do it.
**Samantha:** How long do you think – do you think it will last?
**Pythagoras:** RESP? They got the boards up – they're not going to take it down. I think it's going to stay.
**Johnathan:** They're printed in colour. (Year 11 focus group)

For these students, the materiality of the RESP signs signified that the school was 'serious about it': the signs were 'printed in colour' and are 'permanent'. It was a 'visible victory' (Mitra 2009: 322) – a sign that their work had made a material difference to the structures and rules of the school. Financial resources had been invested in producing colourful, durable signs, engendering affective investments in the value of student voice: social-production entwined with desiring-production. According to them, students' questioning of majoritarian terms like 'respect' had achieved something: 'We started that.' Their work had been displayed on the walls of the school.

Another group of Year 12 students, who had been involved in the 2010 research on 'The School I'd Like' and the initial negotiation of the RESP values, articulated a different understanding of what had happened:

**Lauren:**[4] [Teachers] sort of changed it to be RESP for students instead of about, teachers and students. [. . .]
**Faisal:** So now they are rewarding us in class for, 'their behaviour's being good and respectful and safe and positive', but they're not really putting it to themselves.
**Rebecca:** Yeah. Because that is what they liked. [. . .] It's not really student voice anymore. It was about student voice, students having a say, but it was changed around.
**Lauren:** You know why I think they took credit? Because they changed it, you know, put it on the students instead of us thinking about teachers' and students' relationship.
**Faisal:** As soon as voice – it changes over time.
**Abdul:** Now it's more about mediocrity, you know like, 'this student was equitable today,' or 'this student was safe today' [. . .]. You're getting

rewarded for not doing what you're not supposed to do rather than doing what you should be doing.

**Rebecca:** Teachers are still the top dogs. We wanted it to be about student voice and us making a change in the school that would benefit the students. And maybe this RESP thing is good and it does benefit the students and it gives them the incentive to, you know, be better but our focus was not on the students –

**Faisal:** Our focus was on more so education and students actually wanting to come to school and learn rather than being rewarded for behaviour. It was more about learning then just simple behaviour. [I] mean, I could sit there quietly and not learn anything. You know? It's more about – I actually sat there one day just daydreaming and I got a RESP award, just being quiet.

**Abdul:** The thing about encouraging mediocrity is that like, it makes people passive. Like it makes students passive and they won't like think forward and try and, try and add to what is being taught and try and state their opinion. They will just sit there and be, mediocre, be average.

**Faisal:** I'd rather no Merit system and teachers just teaching and the student actually interested in that. That's really what I was hoping for from the start –

**Rebecca:** That's what we kind of aimed for. As Faisal said, we were aiming for improved education. We wanted people in the school to learn. Let's face it: this school kind of has a reputation of people like not doing very well at school. And we wanted to change that reputation. (Year 12 focus group)

For these students, it was not that the school had 'completely changed' (as the previous group had suggested), but rather that 'students having a say [. . .] was changed around' 'over time'. To these students, the reform process had morphed to refocus on student behaviour, and fostered 'mediocrity' and 'passiv[ity]'. Student voice in school reform, in this account, had been appropriated and reworked to become, as Rebecca said above, 'what they [teachers] liked'. Potentially disruptive affects, voices and actions were reordered and defused in force.

## Evaluating Differently

The RESP token was simultaneously a tool for majoritarian evaluations of student behaviour, as well as part of other minoritarian evaluations. The logic of token economies is developmental and teleological, aiming to produce recognisable targeted behaviour. According to the PBIS model, students are rewarded through a recognition system that reinforces pre-established 'identified target behaviour' (Yeung et al. 2013: 2). The token is an object for student development towards an established standard for student speech, emotional expression and behaviour – standards that accord with white, middle-class standards of 'civility'. Tokens are reminiscent of Melanie Klein's partial objects (the mother's breast as a separate part of the mother's body, or the child's 'blankie' as a developmental attachment tool). Deleuze and Guattari's discussion of Klein's partial objects extends their critique of interpretosis that I introduced in Chapter 2.[5] For Klein, according to Deleuze and Guattari (1983), partial objects are objects of consumption, part of the child's evolution. According to the logic of the token, the student will desire the reward and control their body according to predetermined behavioural expectations in order to earn the reward. According to the logic of the token, the student will gradually internalise the behaviours needed to gain the reward. The token, in turn, is intended to remind the teacher to praise the student, to become more positive in pedagogical speech.

However, the token seemed to do far more than serve as an object of evaluation and reward. I now turn my attention to analyse the RESP token as a partial object and a component of minoritarian evaluations, according to Deleuze and Guattari's critique and retooling of Klein's concept of partial objects. Deleuze and Guattari credit Klein with the 'marvellous discovery of partial objects', but lament that she 'failed to grasp the logic of these objects' (1983: 44) – their potential to subvert the Oedipal complex in their connections, conjunctions, syntheses and disjunctions with desiring-machines. I examine the partial object of the RESP token for its potential to subvert order words that recognise students according to their age, ability, respectful emotional expression, and data produced about them (see Chapter 3). A partial object like a RESP token, for Deleuze and Guattari, is not (only) a tool for achieving pre-established structural stages of development, nor for modifying students' voices, emotions or behaviour. Rather, partial objects are 'political options for problems, they are entryways and exits, impasses the child [and adult] lives out politically, in other words, with all the force of his or her desire' (Deleuze and Guattari 1980/1987: 13).

As Chapter 1 introduced, in Deleuze and Guattari's reworking of psychoanalytical interpretations, desire becomes the primary point of analysis, with power understood to be 'an affection of desire' (Deleuze 1994) and a component in complex desiring-agencements. Deleuze and Guattari's desire is closer to Foucault's conception of power as reaching into 'the very grain of individuals' (Foucault 1980: 199) than it is to Foucault's discussion of pleasure (Foucault 1992). Desire is affirmative and productive – force and capacity seeking connection in mundane everyday processes (Deleuze and Guattari 1980/1987: 229). Rather than separate from power, desire 'creat[es] relations through which power might operate' (Colebrook 2012: 215). The student does not intrinsically lack what a behavioural token represents, and then seek out the token to fill this gap. Desire, rather, 'is always assembled' (Deleuze and Guattari 1980/1987: 229): a RESP token infiltrates desiring-agencements, and potentialises flows between bodies, which may shift and turn in various directions. Desire moves and follows material conditions of existence (Deleuze and Guattari 1983: 27). Desire insinuates itself into (human and non-human) bodies, exceeds capture and control, and metamorphoses those it is assembled with. While at times imperceptible, desire is revolutionary; capable of calling into question the established order of society, 'no matter how small' (Deleuze and Guattari 1983: 116). To analyse desire is to map these almost imperceptible moments where flight fleetingly evades fixity, where regulation randomly ruptures a social field. New arrangements of bodies, objects, sensations and intensities potentialise breaks from segmentary formations, providing alternatives to patterns of social reproduction. The analyst looks for such 'transversal flashes' of desire (see Guattari 1995: 93; Renold and Ivinson 2014: 364); suggestions of something different happening in a concrete social configuration, even if these moments are quickly re-regulated and reintegrated to a dominant order (Ringrose 2015).

Moving with the trajectory of the RESP token through the terrain of the school, with the desiring-agencements that it forms and is formed within, affective constellations are glimpsed. The RESP token affects and is affected by the hands that grasp it, discard it, tear it, fold it into their diary, thread it into an artwork, and speak about it. The question is not (only) what the RESP token meant or represented in this school, but rather what new possibilities the RESP token offered for desiring, speaking and acting that had not previously been available (Guattari 1985/1996). This is not to say that I was (or am) happy about the introduction of a token economy into the life of this school, nor that I am attempting to rationalise it as ultimately 'for the best'. The RESP token simultaneously compounded and constrained capacities to act in different configurations. Bodies experimented with minoritarian uses of RESP tokens, immanently evaluating what

*Evaluating the Perplexing Outcomes of School Reform*

a RESP token could do. In the following section, I compose and connect nine fragmented partial narratives that include the partial object of a RESP token as part of desiring-agencements. I then evaluate these desiring-agencements in a minoritarian manner.

## *Partial Narratives of a Partial Object*

**Partial Narrative 1:** On the whiteboard, 'RESP awards' is written, with a ☺, and a solid line underneath the heading. Students' names are listed underneath.

**Partial Narrative 2:** Through the narrow hole in the top of the padlocked RESP bins where RESP tokens are supposed to be deposited, I glimpse a chip packet wrapper, and an empty juice box, strategically twisted to fit through the narrow hole.

**Partial Narrative 3:** In the classroom, a teacher has written names of students onto RESP tokens, and given the tokens to two students to distribute. These students walk around the room, individually placing the token on the recipient's desk. The students who have received tokens pick the tokens up, unzip their bags, take out their school diaries, slip the tokens under the plastic flap, and return their diaries to their bags.

**Partial Narrative 4:** The executive teacher who organises RESP walks to the front of the assembly. She is carrying four brightly coloured small paper bags with rope handles. Each bag is colour-coded with the RESP colours. She stands, microphone in hand. Students sit on the concrete at her feet. She announces that she is going to draw the latest RESP prizes, and says that following our RESP values 'makes for a nicer place'. There are some 'oooohs'. It is hard to know if the tone of these 'oooohs' is affirmative or sarcastic.

She reaches in the red paper Respect bag to pull out a token with a student name. The first token that the executive teacher pulls out from the red Respect bag is the name of a Year 12 student, Samir.

Samir jumps up and runs to the front of the assembly. The Year 12 students erupt in laughter and cheering. The executive teacher reaches her hand into the bag again. The second token she pulls out from the same bag also has Samir's name on it, and then the third one as well. Students are clapping and laughing.

The executive teacher says, somewhat conspiratorially, that Samir emptied all his tokens from his diary into the bins at the one time. Samir and the executive teacher laugh. The cheering of the assembly takes a few moments to subside.

**Partial Narrative 5:** A small stack of RESP tokens sit in the locked desk drawer, unsigned. The teacher says to me, 'They're literally token.'

THE POLITICS OF VOICE IN EDUCATION

**Partial Narrative 6:** The Year 11 students tell me, grinning, '[name of teacher] gets us to write *her* RESP tokens.'

**Partial Narrative 7:** At the RESP barbeque, the senior executive teacher sits at a picnic table alongside students. She asks a Year 8 boy, 'Are you a little bit naughty? You look like you could be a little bit naughty.' The students and the senior executive teacher smile.

**Partial Narrative 8:** Passing classrooms, I hear voices say: 'You're not being very RESP right now' and, sarcastically, 'Gee, you're really displaying our RESP values.'

**Partial Narrative 9:** In a classroom in the school's Support Unit for students diagnosed with autism, students and teachers sit next to each other. Students' and teachers' hands wind woollen threads and fold pieces of fabric around balls, hula hoops and metal nests. They are crafting works of art that will be combined with the art of other students, teachers, and other community groups into a bigger art work and exhibited at a regional art gallery (see Figure 6.2).[6]

A teacher holds up a RESP token to the group of students. She says that they might like to twist or fold a RESP token into their artwork. She

*Figure 6.2* A photograph of part of the 'Hiromi Hotel: Moon Jellies' exhibition, commissioned by Hazelhurst Regional Gallery and Arts Centre. The exhibition was a performance installation involving local community participation, including students from this school, brought together by artist Hiromi Tango. Photo credit: Greg Piper.

*Evaluating the Perplexing Outcomes of School Reform*

demonstrates folding up a token, winding woollen thread around it, and then hiding the wrapped token within the folds of a small piece of fabric. A student laughs. The RESP token has become imperceptible.

## *Mapping the Movements of the RESP Token*

Mapping the movements of the RESP token, there are impasses, strange detours and breakthroughs, as well as paths that the token was designed to pass through. There are pass words beneath the order word of 'respect' (see Chapter 3). RESP tokens are supposed to be given by teachers, accumulated by students, deposited in RESP bins, and drawn and acknowledged at school assemblies. The intended movements and trajectories of the RESP token can be noted in some of these partial narratives. The RESP token, developed to foster more positive student behaviour and more positive student/ teacher interactions, at times appears to achieve these purposes. In Partial Narrative 1, RESP facilitates a teacher writing a ☺ and a list of students' names who will receive RESP tokens. The RESP token potentially replaces, or supplements, a disciplinary habit where the names of students who display 'negative' behaviours are written on the board. The RESP token may enable 'positive' behaviours that were previously unnoticed and unacknowledged to be recognised and verbally affirmed. In Partial Narrative 3, new configurations of bodies in school classrooms are enabled through the RESP token: students hand out tokens written by the teacher to other students. In Partial Narrative 7, at the RESP barbeque, a new configuration is formed: a senior executive teacher and students sit side by side at a picnic table.

Coinciding with these intended trajectories of the RESP token, the RESP token shifts and moves away from its intended trajectories, put to minoritarian uses. In Partial Narrative 2, the RESP token bin is repurposed for rubbish – where students might, as Paul Willis's (1977) lads might say, 'have a laff' at what a piece of rubbish can do in a RESP token bin. This re-engineering of the RESP bin is perhaps resistant, subversive of the purpose of the RESP bins and tokens. In Partial Narrative 4, a Year 12 student, Samir, pushes the normative, regulative logic of the token to its limit – hoarding RESP tokens, depositing them all at once in the bins, and multiplying the number of recognitions that his respectful behaviour can receive. His actions amplify the 'incentive regulation' (Foucault 2007: 354) of students through RESP, who have been positioned as in charge of accruing tokens as a sign of their value as students. Samir's actions exaggerate the sign (receiving a token = 'good' student) to the point of laughter. Students' laughter accompanies expected assembly behaviour (clapping). In teachers' and students' shared laughter at his use of the token, Samir is simultaneously recognisable as a 'good' student and encountered as something otherwise – subversive, cheeky, clever.

The RESP token is simultaneously nudged back towards previous relations. The RESP token is brought back towards its normative purpose as teachers experiment with what a RESP token might do: in Partial Narrative 6, a teacher experiments with what might happen if students give her tokens, jumbling the order of who is supposed to identify examples of Respect, Equity, Safety and Positivity. In Partial Narrative 7, a senior executive teacher moves from her office to a picnic bench, sitting next to a Year 8 student, eating sausages. In this moment, she reminds him and bystanders of the function of the RESP token, refocusing the conversation back to behaviour: 'Are you a little bit naughty? You look like you could be a little bit naughty.' Encouraged to use the language of RESP in the classroom, in Partial Narrative 8, teachers take the language of RESP back towards (but not identical to) previous classroom interactional habits: 'You're not being very RESP right now'. In Partial Narrative 5, a teacher refuses to accord with the encouragement for teachers to distribute RESP tokens, keeping the stack of tokens securely locked in a desk drawer. In Partial Narrative 9, another teacher takes the RESP token elsewhere – the RESP token becomes an element in a work of art formed between students and teachers. The partial object of the RESP token, intended to form the responsible, self-controlled individual, becomes part of a work of art. The RESP token, and the students' names written on tokens, become folded over by soft wrinkles of wool and fabric. The name of the student, which is supposed to be publicly read out and applauded at assembly, is rendered imperceptible, opaque.

There were many politics felt in the movements of the RESP token. To interpret the affects surrounding the RESP tokens only through the lens of celebration, governance or even resistance diminishes their potentiality. The RESP token was a sign that memorialised part of the students' work in the Steering Committee: a remnant and material remainder of the reform strategy. But it was not only that. The RESP sign and tokens were used to mould students' words, emotional expression and behaviour to become more respectful. But they were not only used to do that. Students and teachers, at times, suggested resistance in their uses, misuses, and refusals of the tokens. But to suggest that these minoritarian uses of RESP tokens were always resistant is also not true. Resistance, and its traditional analytical use, suggests a conscious, oppositional intent of an individual or group, and looks for words and actions that are recognisable as conscious and oppositional (Hynes 2013). Resistance, following Paul Willis (1977), has been previously analysed as ultimately self-defeating; the lads' 'resistant dignity' (39) consigns them to marginalisation at school. But humour and laughter, in some of these narratives, is not necessarily resistant or subversive, but is affirmative and experimental, generative of different modes of being. The RESP token, as an additional element in complex school desiring-agencements, enabled students and teachers to test out different subjectivities and relations. What the RESP token did, and what was done with the RESP token, was sometimes humorous, sometimes shocking, sometimes joyful, sometimes poignant, sometimes clever, sometimes rude, sometimes beautiful – sometimes many of these things simultaneously. The RESP token, a partial object in these desiring-agencements, has a 'flexible and plastic quality which makes [it] inherently political' (Surin 2010: 203).

## Towards Minoritarian Evaluations

When a school (and a researcher) is asked to give an account of a school reform process, it is not necessarily possible to tell a complicated story about how a process of student voice produced excessive affects, unsettled teachers' subjectivities and troubled habitual pedagogical relations. The authorial voice of a school evaluation document, even after conducting collaborative evaluation (and research) processes, must construct a coherent and singular account, drawing conclusions, effecting cuts and folds to the world, making some things come to matter and others to not. Majoritarian school reform evaluations value 'contract, clarity and closure' (Fielding 2006: 310): the identification of targets, the devising of an intervention and the measurement of outcomes correlated to represent the value of an intervention. Theories of change in current accountability processes seek correspondence (or the construction of correspondence) between predetermined targets, a reform strategy and a specific outcome. But, after Marx, via Deleuze and Guattari (1983), we 'cannot tell from the mere taste of wheat who grew it; the product gives us no hint as to the system and the relations of production' (24). The 'products' of this reform period – some students who became school leaders, some teachers who made changes to pedagogical practices, many RESP signs and tokens, some change in suspension data – give us little hints as to the multiplicitous voices and relations that produced them, the multicausal dimensions of the desiring-agencements within which these products were formed, and what the reform account itself produced. This school, like other schools across diverse contexts in an accountability- and market-driven era, experienced external pressure to evidence improvement and to discontinue reform strategies with more ambivalent outcomes. I, too, as a teacher and researcher committed to student voice, have sensed that I should write positive accounts of school improvement and disregard more ambivalent data, to advocate for the adoption of student voice as a reform strategy.

The imperative to reform one's school, one's teachers, one's students, and one's very self does not necessarily increase the capacity of bodies to act. Reform can simultaneously 'erode' bodies (as one school leader from this school described the intensities experienced in leading reform efforts at this school) and compound tensions between bodies. Ceaselessly driven towards teleological targets by 'supposedly necessary reforms' and 'perpetual training' (Deleuze 1992b: 4, 5), bodies in and beyond schools can become exhausted. The demand to be certain, to understand what has happened, to be responsible and change may putrefy relations and life. The imperative for students, teachers and schools to reform themselves, and to produce accounts of how they, or their students, or their teachers, or their schools have reformed along segmentary lines (of identity categories, or class groupings, or teacher accreditation steps, or arrangements of numerical data on A4 Word evaluation tables) may cut off or render mute what is excessive or unspeakable and produce unforeseen effects and affects.

Yet, school reform evaluation accounts (and my research accounts) were unable to contain or explain more ambivalent affects in circulation. I have not been able to account for 'what exactly happened' here (Deleuze and Guattari 1980/1987: 199). In this chapter, I have experimented, instead, with an alternative mode of evaluation, after Deleuze, that evaluates what is said, thought and done according to the immanent mode of existence that it implies: what is enabled and constrained from happening. Forces and relations are distinguished according to their effects and affects – whether they are affirmative or negative at the level of life itself; whether a relation compounds or diminishes a body's capacity to act. Joy accompanies encounters that affirm life and enhance potentiality. According to Deleuze, thinking with Spinoza, when a body encounters 'a body that agrees with [its] nature, one whose relation compounds with ours, we may say that its power is added to ours; the passions that affect us are those of joy, and our power of acting is increased or enhanced' (Deleuze 1988: 27–8). Joy brings 'us near to action, and to the bliss of action' (Deleuze 1988: 28). This mode of evaluation does not predetermine in advance of the encounter what will augment or diminish the body's capacity to act. The capacities of a body, and what will enhance or decrease its capacities to act, are only known in immanent desiring-agencements. What produces joy and augments a body's capacity to act on one day will not do so the next day. Augmentations and decompositions of capacities felt in the encounter are fleeting, rising and falling in transition.

Educators know this: the pedagogical activity, text or explanation that generates joy, engagement and learning with one class cannot be guaranteed to work in the same way with another class. The RESP token that fostered engagement and connectedness in one classroom configuration may be met with bored stares in the next. The research activity that 'elicited' 'authentic' voices in one research focus group may generate little 'data' with another group. Rather than judging initiatives according to predetermined standards or targets, what might happen if they were evaluated as differing relationalities emerge, with the evaluator remaining within the relation, inextricable from it? In a minoritarian mode of evaluating, the evaluator seeks to notice, listen and attend to the differential attunements of bodies to a partial object, configuration, text or strategy: the 'often ambiguous, partial, changing' interminglings of 'joys and sadnesses, increases and decreases, brightenings and darkenings' (Deleuze 1997: 145). As bodies are tuned to particular affective keys, desire shifts and moves, variously affirmative, subversive, composing and decomposing relations.

Minoritarian evaluations of these reform interventions were constituted between bodies at this school at the same time as majoritarian evaluations were composed. Students' voices simultaneously did nothing within and after the majoritarian evaluation document, while also doing many other things before, during, after and in excess of the official evaluation document. Desire attaches itself to objects (here, a RESP token), insinuates itself into bodies, exceeds capture and control, and metamorphoses those it is arranged with.

What a voice, or a RESP token, could do was not only a question for the summative evaluation, but a lived experiment created with other voices, bodies and partial objects in desiring-agencements – 'what can [we] see and what can [we] say [and do] today?' (Deleuze 1999/1986: 98). Sometimes the capacity to speak, to act and to be encountered differently were augmented through a partial object (like a RESP token) that shifted a desiring-agencement – extending what could be taught and learnt, said and done. Moments of augmented power were sometimes fleeting, sometimes sustained, sometimes perceptible, sometimes imperceptible. These immanent experiments were sometimes resistant, sometimes regulative, sometimes predictable, sometimes creative. Students' and teachers' minoritarian uses of the RESP token immanently evaluated the reform strategies through experimentation, exploring what a RESP token could do here, now, in this configuration. Minoritarian evaluations are constructed within a major evaluation, in the borders, and have the potential to forge 'another possible community [. . . and] another consciousness and another sensibility' (Deleuze and Guattari 2006: 17). Minoritarian evaluations happened in the midst of the relation. Immanent modes of evaluation do not move towards an anticipated target or goal, but rather towards affirmative, productive difference. What happened was beyond celebration or co-option, or 'limited' progress towards a target. Indeed, the target was 'exceeded', because the target did not know in advance what voices and RESP tokens could do. Mapping its movements, dynamic trajectories are glimpsed, and perhaps even lines of escape from habitual patterns of relating.

My discussion of this dynamic enfolding, unfolding and refolding of multiplicitous affects in desiring-agencements is not relativistic, as if to suggest that reform strategies and their outcomes are all a matter of one's perspective. Such relativism would lead a student, teacher or researcher to detach themselves from others, hope for the best, and abandon responsibility for how others feel and respond. Forces at work in any desiring-agencement are to be distinguished, rather, moment by moment, according to whether they are affirming or denying of life itself (Deleuze 1992a: 102, 218). Rather than diminishing a student, teacher, school leader or researcher's responsibility, the multiplicity of possible affects and effects that could actualise in any relation heightens *response-ability* (Barad 2007). It becomes even more urgent to attend to what is happening in any pedagogical or school or research event – to ask, 'What is happening in this moment?' (Davies 2014: 738; Mayes 2016b: 118). To interrogate what affects are produced in an immanent relation, and by the partial objects enfolded in it. To question whether what is happening enhances or diminishes the capacities of bodies to act: to engage, to feel good about school and life, to feel connected, to feel knowledgeable and able, to feel in control, to feel a sense of belonging, to feel that they 'have a voice'. To experiment with objects and supplements, seeing what extends and bolsters agency and change. To ask what might be done through these alliances and augmentations, and what we might we become in relation to others (Mayes 2016b: 119).

This chapter has argued for the potential of minoritarian evaluations in schools. I have critiqued the logics of majoritarian school evaluation processes and have arranged stories about one school's evaluation of a student voice initiative and a positive behaviour initiative. I mapped the movement of the material remnant of a reform process – a RESP token – and the desiring-agencements formed with it, attempting to 'stick as closely as possible to the event[s]' associated with this token and to the verbal and non-verbal 'expression of the masses' (Deleuze 2004: 217) about it. Working with the RESP token has taken the focus off individual agency or structural governance, individual oppressions or resistances, laughter and disappointment, to intertwined lines of regulation and lines of liberation that shift and change in contingent configurations. I have mapped the immanent minoritarian evaluations of a RESP token – its minor movements and politics, and what flees from all sides (Deleuze 1994). This chapter has made the case for an alternative mode of evaluation that attempts to listen to minoritarian experimentations with what a RESP token – and what student voice – can do. These desiring-agencements provoke another mode of thought surrounding the intersections of student voice, schools in 'disadvantaged' communities, and school reform. Paying attention to desire-in-motion extends and elaborates the insights gained by analysing what might be celebrated and critiqued about student voice, but also raises questions about the limits of educational reform.

While I offer these thoughts about minoritarian modes of evaluation, I have serious doubts about the notion of school reform. In Chapter 1, I quoted Deleuze's words from his essay 'Postscript on the Societies of Control' – that institutional reforms (including of schools) are 'stupid and hypocritical' not only because they are made by 'people who claim to be representative' and not those directly affected (Deleuze, in Deleuze and Foucault 1977: 208–9), but also because those making the reforms fail to apprehend that 'these institutions are finished' (Deleuze 1992b: 4). Reforms tinker at the edges but keep the dogmatic image of thought – and institutional common sense – intact (see also Ball and Collet-Sabé 2021). But how do those wanting to learn and teach, and relate differently, refuse to reform – that is, refuse the logics of reform? In the following chapter, I consider the micropolitical potential of contemporary student activisms. In the last few years, some students have refused school, refused contemporary common sense about how the world should be, and have been part of immanent experiments in creating other modes and forms of educational life, affirming that another world is possible. Taking the particular example of student climate justice activisms, I explore what is being created as students face the end of the world as it is currently known.

## Notes

1. Deleuze and Guattari are discussing the events of May 1968. Clearly, the events discussed in this chapter are entirely different. I encourage the reader to read my misreading of this quotation with a sense of humour.
2. I leave this 'we' deliberately open-ended: school leaders? teachers? students? researchers?
3. The reader may remember these students' pseudonyms from the puppet scenario that they created, discussed in Chapter 3. As explained in Chapter 2, students who participated in research activities requiring signed consent forms were invited to choose their own pseudonym late in 2013, after focus groups had been completed, during collaborative analysis days. These three Year 11 students described themselves on sticky notes in the following terms: 'Pythagoras': '16 year old male Pakistani Background. Interests: Everything English related; Leadership (Vice Captain); Thinks independently; Loves to question; Thinks critically.' 'Samantha': '17 year old Lebanese gal. Independent, assertive and a curious learner. Passionate about leadership and excelling in education. Interested in the world around me and love to question everything.' 'Johnathan Rudd' did not write a self-description.
4. Since these Year 12 students were unable to attend the collaborative analysis days, I have given them pseudonyms.
5. In short, interpretosis is the process of attempting to capture and stabilise a subject's pathology, identity, or the meaning of what they say or do in time according to a particular interpretive framework (Deleuze and Guattari 1980/1987: 114).
6. The artist Hiromi Tango, who assembled these works of art from multiple settings and hands, describes this process as Art Magic (see Hazelhurst Regional Gallery and Arts Centre 2013a, 2013b). The Art

## Evaluating the Perplexing Outcomes of School Reform

Magic Education Package for schools describes the process of creating Art Magic as '[w]eaving collective personal memories that are embedded in wrapped objects'; according to Hiromi Tango, in weaving and wrapping memory, 'individual transitional emotions' come to be 'stored in an art object' (Hazelhurst Regional Gallery and Arts Centre 2013b: 2).

# 7

# Conspiring with the Trees

*We can't breathe money.*
Cardboard placard, Kuala Lumpur,
global strikes for climate, 21 September 2019

*I speak for the trees so the earth can breathe.*
Cardboard placard photographed in Melbourne,
global climate strike rally, 20 September 2019

Breathing – absorbing oxygen, releasing carbon dioxide – can be dangerous, for some more than others. In Australia, the 'unprecedented' Black Summer bushfires in southeastern Australia in late 2019 and early 2020 burned up to 24 to 40 million hectares across multiple states and territories (Commonwealth of Australia 2020a: 1.12, 1.14). Smoke infiltrated borders of the skin, of fur, of steel and brick and mortar, killing nearly 3 billion vertebrates by incineration, asphyxiation and starvation (World Wildlife Fund 2020). The fires were the direct cause of thirty-three human deaths; their respiratory effects contributed to over 400 other human deaths (Borchers Arriagada et al. 2020). Blanche Verlie (2022a) writes about these fires: 'In breathing the smoke, we inhaled incinerated ecosystems, and the tiny particles of charred multispecies bodies made their way into our lungs, our blood, our organs, our brains' (297). These fires, and their effects on breath, fuelled further mass climate justice activism that had already been happening in Australia and across the world.

Before climate justice activism amidst the Black Summer fires in Australia, there had already been other protests against climate inaction in the midst of poor air quality and pollution, and other protests met with respiratory assault; asphyxiation and suffocation were no new phenomena. In Kuala Lumpur, Malaysia, a protester at the September 2019 global strike for climate held a cardboard placard declaring, 'We can't breathe money' (Tee 2019). On the same day, in Delhi, India, a young protester said:

> 'We are out here to reclaim our right to live, our right to breathe and our right to exist, which is all being denied to us by an inefficient policy system

that gives more deference to industrial and financial objectives rather than environmental standards,' said Aman Sharma, a young protester in Delhi. (Laville and Watts 2019)

Aman Sharma's eloquent words reverberated later, in the midst of the COVID-19 pandemic, when philosopher Achille Mbembe (2020) proposed a 'universal right to breathe' for 'all life', including and exceeding humans (61–2). Mbembe (2020) reminds readers that capitalism, colonialism and their liberal humanisms had already 'constrained entire segments of the world population, entire races, to a difficult, panting breath and life of oppression' (61) – before the choking Black Summer fires, and before COVID-19 was rapidly spreading via infectious respiratory fluids expelled with breath.

While many people in eastern Australia were suddenly struck by the horror of respiratory distress with the Black Summer bushfires, and then COVID-19, there had been previous respiratory horrors, and they did not stop with these fires. Respiratory violence has long been deployed against First Nations peoples and racialised bodies, including young people. In Australia in 2016, in the Northern Territory youth detention centre Don Dale, footage was aired on the ABC's *Four Corners* of 17-year-old Indigenous young man Dylan Voller being tear-gassed and shackled to a restraining chair by his wrists, ankles and head and in a spit-hood (Teece-Johnson and Burton-Bradley 2017). The correctional services officer who placed the spit-hood on Voller's head said that he could not recall Voller saying, 'I can't breathe, I'm choking' (Murphy 2017). In May 2020 in Minneapolis, George Floyd was murdered after police officer Derek Chauvin knelt on his neck for 9 minutes and 29 seconds. Another 17-year-old, Darnella Frazier, video-recorded the murder with her phone; Frazier's decision to post the video on social media 'propelled the movement for racial justice [Black Lives Matter] into a global social movement' (Welton and Harris 2022: 60). The viral video capturing George Floyd's words 'I can't breathe' was watched across the world by millions in pandemic-induced quarantine; viewers connected Floyd's words to the words of others before him, including Eric Garner in the New York in 2014 and Dunghutti man David Dungay Jr in Sydney in 2015. Yet, respiratory violence accompanied subsequent mobilisations for political change, in the form of tear gas and pepper spray deployed as chemical weapons against Black Lives Matter demonstrators in US cities (Choy 2020).

I open this chapter with glimpses into collective, but uneven, moments of respiratory vulnerability, and entanglements of breath and protest in the past and present, to introduce the concerns of this final chapter. From the second half of 2018 until early 2020, school-aged young people in Australia and across the world gathered in mass numbers to protest against government inaction on climate change, before the Black Summer fires of 2019–20 and before the public health emergency of COVID-19. Collective youth and intergenerational networks like Seed (Australia's first Indigenous youth climate network) and Pacific Climate Warriors, young Indigenous activists in other settler colonial nations, and young activists from the Global South had been campaigning for climate justice for many years before Swedish school student Greta Thunberg began sitting outside the Swedish parliament building during school hours in August 2018 when she was 15 years old (Unigwe 2019). In communities where environmental degradation intersects with colonialism, capitalist exploitation and racism, young people have long played vital roles incaring for Land/Country, and in political struggles foregrounding the importance of Indigenous sovereignty and Land rights,[1] even if their activism has not necessarily been recognisable to the mainstream environmental movement (Birch 2018; Ford and Norgaard 2020).

Notwithstanding these long histories, in recent years, the notion of the voice of school-aged students has become associated with the figure of the young climate activist. Young climate strikers have noted the intergenerational injustice that their generation, which has done the least to contribute to the climate crisis, will be dramatically affected by its devastating effects (de Moor et al. 2020). Greta Thunberg is a particular figure of inspiration – indeed, Jessica Ringrose has described Greta Thunberg, after Rosi Braidotti (2002), as a 'feminist figuration' – 'ruptur[ing] her pathologization' from her diagnosis of Asperger's and selective mutism and calling her autism her '"superpower"': 'Greta with a megaphone amplifying her voice at rallies jars against the individualising pathologizing diagnosis of mutism' (Ringrose, in Strom et al. 2019: 17).

Returning to the limits of school reform discussed in the previous chapters, do these student strikes suggest that students have burst the boundaries of constrained institutional forms of voice? Are students now coming to speak on their own terms on matters that urgently concern them (Deleuze and Foucault 1977)? Chapter 1 introduced long-standing critical pedagogic calls for 'empowering' students and educational policy enthusiasm for student voice and agency in classrooms in schools. Yet, these embodied flare-ups of fervent feeling for the climate, outside schooling spaces but within school-time, seemed to come from somewhere else. While some students said that they were striking because of what they had learnt at school about climate change, other students seemed to be striking in spite of their schooling, in defiance of official disapproval from educational department representatives (Lobo et al. 2021: 10). This final chapter attends to the eruption of mass protest from school-aged students in the transnational movement known variously as Fridays for Future, Youth Strike for Climate and School Strike 4 Climate, where many of these young people have refused to attend school on Fridays.[2] Student strikers in Australia may have aligned themselves with various networks – including School Strike 4 Climate (SS4C), Seed Indigenous Youth Climate Network, Pacific Climate Warriors, the Australian Youth Climate Coalition (AYCC) and XR Youth (among many others). Some students involved in this movement have variously spoken about their activism in terms of 'having a voice' and speaking 'for the trees so the earth can breathe', as the cardboard placard that opens this chapter declares.

In this final chapter, I argue that the School Strikes for Climate share many of the issues that have been discussed in relation to student voice in school reform across this book: including problems of speaking for others and the role of schools in attempting to grasp and steer what students say and do. I argue that, in this emerging movement, there are many lines of movement – many voices, many politics – and much micropolitical potential. Amidst the multiple, compromised and ambivalent trajectories of the movement, I suggest that there are molecular forces at work that have the potential to crack open some of the aporias facing contemporary education. Throughout this chapter I re-turn to concepts and conversations from other parts of this book. As discussed in Chapter 2, according to Karen Barad, 're-turning' is:

> a multiplicity of processes, such as the kinds earthworms revel in [. . .]: turning the soil over and over – ingesting and excreting it, tunnelling through it, burrowing, all means of aerating the soil, allowing oxygen in, opening it up and breathing new life into it. (Barad 2014: 168)

After further contextualising this movement, this chapter is structured in three parts, that each re-turn to concepts and conversations from earlier chapters of this book, and bring these into relation with this movement. I re-turn, too, to a particular phrase repeatedly drawn on painted on student strikers' signs – though with differences: 'I speak for the trees.' This phrase comes from the Dr Seuss children's book *The Lorax* (1972/2012), which was also reworked in a 1972 television special (Pratt 1972) and 2012 Universal Pictures feature film (Renaud 2012).[3] It is my aspiration that, in re-turning to concepts and conversations discussed earlier in this book, reading them with and through the heterogeneous youth climate justice movement, that these readings might effect cracks in some of the walls[4] that are felt – even if not by all voices-bodies – in schools. I re-turn to the problems of speaking for others, and the work of schools in steering students' voices and bodies, before considering the possibilities for conspiracies. Trees, and their work producing oxygen to breathe and speak, become part of these concluding thoughts; indeed, one cannot 'have a voice' or communicate in more-than-linguistic modes if there is no breath. Invoking the term 'con-spiracy', I work with anthropologist Tim Choy's (2016, 2020, 2021) discussions of the political implications of the etymology of the Latin *conspirare* (*com*, 'together' + *spirare*, 'breathe'): *breathing-with*. Conspiring (breathing-with) is a more-than-human endeavour; it exceeds human organs: plants and trees make human breath possible, and other species have other ways of breathing (Myers 2019). Conspiring is by no means straightforward, nor necessarily affirmative. I suggest that this concept might invigorate micropolitical movements through the impasses of contemporary education – from reform to regeneration and *respair*. To respair – an older word that functions as both a verb and a noun – is to hope again after a period of despair. The components of this word connect to other words in this book – RESP tokens,[5] resp-ect, air, respiration; *respair* offers regenerative possibilities for other pedagogical and worldly relations.

## *Striking Voices*

While it is not novel for children and young people to be part of social movements (Bessant 2021a), the mobilisation of large numbers of school-aged students in protest actions outside the boundaries of schools in recent years largely caught researchers by surprise. School strikers have cried out for political leaders to take urgent action on climate change to ensure 'a future' (Wahlström et al. 2019), emphasising the need for 'climate justice' – that is, a fundamental restructuring of society that acknowledges that climate change is inextricable from colonialism and capitalism (Rowles 2020).[6] The numbers of strikers gathered across locations progressively increased from when Greta Thunberg began her strikes in August 2018 to late 2019; it is estimated that approximately 6 million people across the world participated in the week of global climate strikes in September 2019 (Taylor et al. 2019).

Commentary from politicians, journalists and academics on the 2018–19 strikes abounded. The legitimacy of the climate strikes was hotly debated in the Australian Parliament, in media reporting, and in public attitudes expressed on social media – particularly following comments, before the November 2018 strikes, by the conservative Australian prime minister that there should be 'more learning in schools and less activism in schools' (The Guardian ParlView 2018). In some Australian news coverage, young people participating in the 2018–19 strikes were variously described as 'intoxicated with their moral superiority' (Bolt 2018), vulnerable to 'the anxiety-producing mass hysteria of the Greta phenomenon' (Shanahan 2019), 'yell[ing] inappropriate and violent comments' (Beaini et al. 2019), as well as marked by 'bravery' and to be 'congratulated [. . .] for standing up' (in Gregory 2019). Researchers have sought to grasp and understand the dynamics of this movement, and to develop new methods to 'capture' its dynamically changing forms of content and forms of expression. There have been, for example, surveys given to student strikers in the midst of their strike actions (de Moor et al. 2020; Wahlström et al. 2019), qualitative interviews conducted in the midst of strikes asking strikers to explain their signs and their reasons for being there (Bowman 2020) and discursive analyses of Greta Thunberg's speeches (Holmberg and Alvinius 2019), and special issues dedicated to exploring the dynamics and educational implications of student climate justice activism (e.g., Verlie and Flynn 2022).

I have been part of this flurry of research activity surrounding the school strikes. In 2020, Michael Hartup and I undertook a corpus media analysis of 500 Australian articles published in Australian national, state (New South Wales and Victoria), and a select sample of regional and rural newspapers over a 17-month period (August 2018–December 2019), with particular attention to the representation of young people's emotions and actions (Mayes and Hartup 2021) and the reported roles and responses of schools as reported across the newspaper corpus (Mayes and Hartup 2022). Throughout 2020, amidst COVID-19 lockdowns and disruptions to schooling, I interviewed three current and past students and seven teachers from across Victoria and NSW about the roles and responses of schools to the 2018–19 strikes (Mocatta et al. 2022). In 2021, journalism studies scholars Kristy Hess and Gabi Mocatta and I interviewed five journalists from regional and rural Victoria and NSW about their coverage of the school strikes (Mocatta et al. 2022). I have been thinking, like and with others, about how education needs to urgently change (Brennan et al. 2021; Dunlop et al. 2021; Lobo et al. 2021; Mayes and Holdsworth 2020; Rousell and Cutter-Mackenzie-Knowles 2020). As the Common Worlds Research Collective have written in a Working Paper for UNESCO (United Nations Educational, Scientific and Cultural Organization):

> [E]ducation needs to play a pivotal role in radically reconfiguring our place and agency within this interdependent world. This requires a complete paradigm shift: from learning about the world in order to act upon it, to learning to become with the world around us. (Common Worlds Research Collective 2020: 1)

These urgent changes needed are ontological – that is, matters of being and relationality – learning to live-with climate change in entanglement within damaged ecosystems, unlearning Western Man's extractivist habits of being, and deeply listening to and learning from the wisdom of Land-based Indigenous relational ontologies in their pluralities (Bawaka Country et al. 2020; Poelina et al. 2022; Tynan 2021; Verlie 2022b).

This chapter is not simply arguing 'Listen to the kids!' (a phrase that may intend to be encouraging but may be apprehended as patronising) – though, of course, their words and actions are frequently inspiring, funny, earnest and thrilling. Like Verlie (2022b), I am interested in how the climate strikes indicate the formation of 'climate capable collectivities' around 'intimate kinships with the more-than-human world' (13), as well as with the politics and perplexities of these political collectivities. In the following sections, I think through the possibilities and ambivalences of young people's climate justice activism which, like student voice in schools, is a tangled moving mesh of many politics and many lines – some straight and segmentary, some molecular (slightly diverging), and some leaking and fleeing as lines of flight (see Chapter 1). Thinking-feeling-speaking-acting with this tangle, as part of the tangle, is necessary for the '(re)generative formation of other pedagogical futures' (Lobo et al. 2021: 11).

## Speaking for . . .?

The problem of speaking for others – a phrase associated with Linda Alcoff's (1991) significant article – has been a central problematic across the chapters of this book. As Chapter 1 explained, addressing the problem of adults speaking *for* school-aged students has been a long-standing rationale for student voice in schools – that is, for students to speak for themselves about matters affecting them at school, rather than others presuming to know what students need (Fielding 2004). Yet, as Chapter 4 explored, institutional structures of governance and their representational logics can reinforce long-standing hierarchies that segment students – such that some students come to speak for the multiplicity of a student community. Indeed, as Alcoff (1991) eloquently expounds, it can be difficult to demarcate the boundaries of an 'oppressed' group – particularly when subjects 'have membership in many conflicting groups' (8). Gayatri Spivak's (1987) essay 'Can the Subaltern Speak?' adds to the challenge of whether, even if the 'subaltern' were to speak for themselves, they are compelled to speak the dominant language – that is, to translate their speech into sanitised terms that will be intelligible to the dominant group. I have wondered how students might, as Deleuze and Foucault discussed (1977), speak for themselves, when inscribed within these school-bound conditions for speech (Spivak 1987).

### SPEAKING FOR THE CLIMATE STRIKER?

The climate strikers, perhaps, speak to this ongoing problematic – how students (across their multiple, variegated and shifting subjectivities) can speak for themselves, speak to their difference and make a difference. Beyond speaking and taking action within schools, students refused school: they initiated, organised and participated in political action during school hours beyond institutional borders. When Australian prime minister Scott Morrison said that he would like to see less activism and more learning in schools, striking students referenced, reworked and rearticulated his words on their cardboard placards (see Mayes and Center 2022): for example, 'LESS ACTIVISM MY ASS' (Tegg 2018: capitals on placard) and 'WE'LL BE LESS ACTIVIST IF YOU BE LESS SHIT' (Noonan 2018: capitals on placard). Less directly reworking Scott Morrison's words, but still speaking to him, the cardboard sign in Figure 7.1 proclaims:

THE POLITICS OF VOICE IN EDUCATION

*Figure 7.1* A young person holds a cardboard sign: 'I SPEAK FOR THE TREES (They say DO BETTER SCOMO)', 21 May 2020, Sydney School Strike 4 Climate rally. Creative Commons 2.0 by School Strike 4 Climate. Original image cropped.

'I SPEAK FOR THE TREES (They say DO BETTER SCOMO)'.[7] Returning to Chapter 5's discussion of Bartleby, young people have not just said that they would 'prefer not to' go to school; they have taken political action to lampoon the (then) government's apathetic climate inaction (lampooning a governmental stance that the government 'would prefer not to' take too much action on climate change right now). In explicitly foregrounding the demand for 'Resourcing Aboriginal and Torres Strait Islander-led solutions that guarantee land rights and care for Country' (SS4C 2021), Australian youth climate organisations' demands have resonated with decolonial and Indigenist politics of refusal of the colonial state as the primary recognising agent (Birch 2018; Simpson 2014). There is 'political potency' in these 'young people's refusals of "common sense" politics-as-usual and the colonial extractivist state' (Mayes 2021a: 88) as they, collectively, shape 'alternative political subjectivities and imaginaries' (Rousell et al. 2021: 2).

Yet, there are ambivalences in any statements that students spoke for themselves and to their difference in these strikes. Indeed, media accounts variously framed and reframed students' statements, and framed and reframed which students' faces and voices appeared in media coverage. While Australian youth climate justice organisations and networks, in their own accounts (on their webpages and blog posts), have often foregrounded First Nations-led solutions, mainstream media representations of their demands and actions have been, at times, quite different. Young strikers were represented, across various newspaper representations, with recurring tropes of 'ignorant zealots', 'anxious pawns', 'rebellious truants' and 'extraordinary heroes'; many articles barely mentioned the movement's political demands (Mayes and Hartup 2021). The 'extraordinary heroes' foregrounded in media accounts were frequently, though not always, white girls. Beyond Australia, when Vanessa Nakate – Uganda's first Fridays for Future activist, and founder of NGO Youth for Future Africa and the Rise Up Movement – gave a news conference in January 2020 at the World Economic Forum in Davos, Switzerland, alongside Greta Thunberg and Isabelle Axelsson (from Sweden), Loukina Tille (from Switzerland) and Luisa Neubauer (from Germany), she was photographed by an Associated Press photographer. However, in the subsequently published photograph and news report, the face, body and words of Vanessa Nakate – 'the only black person and representative of the "Global South" in the original picture' – were cropped from the photo and text in subsequent press reports (Bessant 2021b: 2), and none of her comments from the press conference were included (Evelyn 2020). In this reporting, there was a visual preference for the viscous clustering together of whiteness (Saldanha 2007) when representing these young climate activists. Nakate spoke out on Twitter, asking: 'Why did you erase me from the photo? I was part of the group! You didn't just erase a photo. You erased a continent' (Nakate, cited in Bessant 2021b: 2). Nakate connected this media erasure with the erasure of the work of climate activists of colour within the movement: 'Very many African activists have been doing a lot of work [. . .] trying to get their message heard and listened to' and yet '[c]limate activists of color are erased' (Nakate, cited in Bessant 2021b: 2).

Not only is there a risk of media speaking for the young strikers, but academic commentary (including my own) risks speaking for the multiplicity of the strikers' bodies, actions and their historical-geographic-scientific-affective-material entanglements. As

Alcoff (1991) noted, there is a porous boundary between speaking 'about' and speaking 'for' others: 'conferring information about' others is necessary to craft a coherent account, but conferring information can easily slip into 'speaking in place for them' (9). Many scholarly questions have been asked about who the strikers are (identities), their trajectories into activism (political socialisation) and their intentionality (political demands). But, indeed, there were a multiplicity of bodies-in-motion, trajectories and demands at work as students gathered at these strikes in 2018 and 2019. As Benjamin Bowman (2020) writes, student climate justice activism is a 'polyphonic movement' with 'exceptionally complex' politics (1). Climate justice is an evolving and contested concept, meaning 'different things to different people' and 'different things to the same people depending on a particular time and space' (Jafry et al. 2018: 3). The heterogeneous youth climate justice movement carries with it the histories of environmentalisms' dividing lines of exclusion – white privilege, class privilege, able-bodied privilege – and the tensions and uneasy alliances between 'Green', 'Black' and 'Red' climate activisms (Vincent and Neale 2016). There may be new strategic alliances, friendships, intimacies formed in striking together; there may, too, be uncomfortable politics of solidarity (Land 2015), particularly in the context of the long-standing failure of settler colonial governments and peoples to listen to Indigenous people's voices (Birch 2018). There may be 'subaltern' politics at work in the movement, as Bowman (2020) contends – alongside the risks of particular (white, middle-class, articulate, attractive, able-bodied) students speaking for other students, and adults speaking for students (even if benevolently). There were and are unequally distributed opportunities to strike; the prominence of strikes in the affluent Global North 'maps onto uneven global distributions of resources and power' (Walker 2020: 6). There may be interesting sociological questions to ask about young people's changing forms of political socialisation and modes of politically participating, but these may be of little interest to those striking. As Greta Thunberg is reported as having said to the US Senate Climate Change Task force: '"This is not about us. This is not about youth activism," she said. "We don't want to be heard. We want the science to be heard"' (Associated Press/Reuters 2019). Yet, such demands – for the 'science' to be heard – may not resonate with all striking bodies; for some, this demand may be criticised as reinforcing scientistic understandings of climate change as a 'problem to be solved by technocratic governance in accordance with the knowledge of scientific elites' (Bowman 2020: 4).

How might the adult journalist-academic-teacher refuse to speak for the school strikers – to refuse, in Deleuze and Guattari's terms, the 'Royal Science' of politics (1994/2009), which is concerned with forms of political participation that are recognisable and categorisable, and which appropriates 'new' modes of political expression into its existing categories? In this Royal Science, certain bodies are recognisable, certain modes of activism are familiar, certain demands are intelligible, certain political responses are considered possible. The polyvocality and multivalencies of the movement make it challenging to pin down who these strikers are and what is happening. But perhaps grasping and understanding the strikes in this way does little to trouble dominant modes of thought. As Marcelo Svirsky (2010) argues (in relation to the Occupy movement), to analyse activism in terms of the connections between individual psyches and actions (for example, explaining the 'origins' of a student's activism according to their parents' political leanings, the student's educational attainment, and so on) 'explain[s] very little concerning the empirical relationships between bodies and things' (166). These explanations 'do not account for the body of the activist, the field of action, the assemblages involved, and the multitude affecting and being affected' (Svirsky 2010: 166): the swirling movements and combinations of legs walking out of school, the 'Skolstrejk för klimatet' badge, the cardboard placard drawing of the Lorax, the David Attenborough documentary, the TikTok feed, the plastic wrapper in the playground, the memory of fire, the painted yellow flower, the encouraging teacher, the floods in Kolkata, Donald Trump mocking Greta, the taste of bushfire smoke on the tongue, adults in blood-red cloaks with painted-white faces, drought-driven dust on a settler colonial farm, the YouTube channel livestreaming the Amazon burning, the politically conservative parent, the Uluru Statement from the Heart, the smile of a police officer, the 'no' of the prime minister, the melting permafrost, the wildfires in California, and and and ... variously enabling and constraining, pushing-and-pulling: the influx and efflux of student climate justice activism.

SPEAKING FOR THE TREES?

And then there is the issue of 'speaking for the trees because they can't ('they don't have any tongues') (see Figure 7.2). Students

*Figure 7.2* A young person holds a cardboard sign: 'I speak for the trees because they can't (they don't have any tongues)', 21 May 2020, Sydney School Strike 4 Climate rally. Creative Commons 2.0 by School Strike 4 Climate. Original image cropped.

aligning themselves with the global student climate justice movement have spoken from these collective modes of enunciation at a time when the geological record 'speaks' of the impacts of extracting and burning carbon-rich fossil fuels, deforestation, industrialisation and intensive large-scale agriculture over a relatively short period of time. However, declarations of the responsibilities of some universal 'Anthropos' for these changes in the geological strata have been profoundly refuted. Kathryn Yusoff (2018) has called for greater specificity about '*what* and *who* gets marked in Anthropocene origin stories' (28, original emphasis). Macarena Gómez-Barris argues that there can be no universalising idiom and 'viewpoint' term of 'Anthropocene' that addresses '"humanity" as a whole':

## Conspiring with the Trees

[T]he problem is far more specific: colonial capitalism has been the main catastrophic event that has gobbled up the planet's resources, discursively constructing racialized bodies within geographies of difference, systematically destroying through dispossession, enslavement, and then producing the planet as a corporate bio-territory. (Gómez-Barris 2017: 4)

Claire Colebrook (2020) writes, too, of this 'specific historical threshold where something like "Anthropos" recognises itself as a toxic substance, but manages to then speak for the world precisely by way of this confession' (332). Once again, over-represented Man (Wynter 2003; see Chapter 4) comes to speak for not only all other human life, but also for the more-than-human and the world itself.

So, can school students speak for the trees? As Alexandra Lasczik and Amy Cutter-Mackenzie-Knowles (2022: 6) ask, 'Who can speak for the Earth?' When a child or young person holds a sign, invoking the Dr Seuss children's book (and its television and film remakes), there is a risk of invoking the historical, Romantic association of the innocent white child with nature (Yusoff 2018). There is the risk of reifying Hollywood-style environmentalisms still bound up with capitalism (the 2012 film *The Lorax* grossed a worldwide total of $348.8 million).

In settler colonial Australia, there is the risk of the (white/settler) young person usurping the place of Traditional Custodians for Country, whose relationality with Country, as tebrakunna[8] scholar Lauren Tynan (2021) writes, is 'bound with responsibilities with kin and Country' and 'grounded in Indigenous metaphysics' (2). The question of which trees get spoken for and who is authorised to speak for particular trees is of profound significance and sacred responseability. As a non-Indigenous person, I cannot speak authoritatively on these issues; this section draws on the struggle of Djab Wurrung peoples over the 'Directions Tree' and the Ngarrindjeri concept of Yannarumi: Speaking as Country. Djab Wurrung and Ngarrindjeri are two different, distinct peoples with their own culture, customs, language, laws and lore. What is pivotal in this chapter is their distinct but resonant struggles over who speaks for Country in relation to the settler colonial state.

On 26 October 2020, when Melbourne was celebrating the lifting of a long COVID-19 lockdown, a particular fiddleback tree widely known as a Djab Wurrung 'Directions tree' was cut down and removed to make way for a Western Highway extension, about 180 km west of Melbourne (Perkins 2020). The Djab

Wurrung people had previously established a Djab Wurrung heritage protection embassy to protect these sacred birthing trees, where Djab Wurrung children's placentas are mixed with the seed of the tree, becoming the child's own 'directions tree' (Djab Wurrung man Zellanach Djab Mara, quoted in Perkins 2020). Chelsea Lovett-Ahern from the Djab Wurrung Protection Embassy said on Facebook:

> This Djap Wurrung Directions Tree was the holder of the DNA of our ancestors. She had a strong and staunch woman's energy, where she proudly stood tall with branches stretched wide holding her given space on women's country. We are heavily grieving her loss culturally, physically and spiritually. We need her body back, not turned to mulch like our other trees. We need respect and answers for what has been done! (quoted in Mahomet 2020)

There are ongoing contestations about who can speak for the cultural significance of these particular trees (Higgins 2021). These ongoing contestations are inextricable from histories of settler colonial laws made to compromise and undermine Indigenous sovereignty.

In South Australia, on other Country, the Ngarrindjeri concept of Yannarumi: Speaking as Country has gained traction with the settler colonial state.[9] The Ngarrindjeri concept of Yannarumi is described by Ngarrindjeri scholar Daryle Rigney, Ngarrindjeri scholar Steve Hemming, and settler scholars Simone Bignall and Katie Maher, as 'speaking lawfully as Country', inextricably connected to 'understandings of peaceful relations and wellbeing' (Rigney et al. 2018: 1187). They write that Yannarumi is particular to Ngarrindjeri Country while acknowledging that 'the spirit of Yannarumi is shared by many Indigenous nations in Australia and internationally' (Rigney et al. 2018: 1206). As Bignall, Hemming and Rigney write, Yannarumi 'conveys a Ngarrindjeri philosophy in which being is expressed (or "spoken") through processes of ecological connectivity'; since Ngarrindjeri are 'inseparable from the lands and waters that define their existence', they 'experience the wellness or ill-health of the environment as an aspect of their own cultural health as an Indigenous Nation' (Bignall et al. 2016: 469). Yannarumi: Speaking as Country 'cannot be claimed by non-Indigenous settlers on Indigenous lands, however, the principle of environmental and relational responsibility expressed by the concept of Yannarumi is widely accessible' (Hemming et al. 2019: 224). Ngarrindjeri Speaking as Country has become a political programme for advocating for Country and protecting their lands and water, particularly in state and federal governmental processes; in Speaking as Country, Ngarrindjeri 'express in an amplified voice their expectations for the protection of their Country and its well-being' (Bignall et al. 2016: 468). The South Australian government and all agencies on Ngarrindjeri Country now 'share the responsibility to sustain the ecology of relationships that foster healthy life in this region' (Hemming et al. 2019: 224). Ngarrindjeri Speaking as Country has become a 'transformational public pedagogy' that asserts an 'Indigenous educative authority' as 'agents of ethical interconnection' (Rigney et al. 2018: 1188, 1189).

Learning from the contestations surrounding the Djab Wurrung directions tree, and from the Ngarrindjeri concept of Yannarumi, non-Indigenous school strikers cannot claim to speak as Country – or speak for the trees. Yet, Yannarumi creates a vision of 'all people Caring, Sharing, Knowing and Respecting the lands, the waters and all living things' (Hemming et al. 2015: slide 4), where 'the aim of teaching and learning is not to "target" and "train" students, but to respectfully and creatively weave connections' (Rigney et al. 2018: 2105). Students speak and move with the oxygen that trees generate; perhaps the trees speak through the students, through enabling them to breathe and speak? The students' signs gesture to a desire for more-than an extractivist mode of relating to Country and a desire to be relationally responsible to Country speaking. I can't speak for the various networks and groups associated with youth climate justice activism and how they might respond to the notion of 'speaking for' the trees. However, this movement has – in various ways – grappled with what notions of 'climate justice', 'solidarity' and being an 'ally' might look like across situated Indigenous/non-Indigenous, classed and gendered subjectivities and generational locations (Mayes 2021b). In the lead-up to the 15 May 2020 online climate strike, I attended online SS4C zoom workshops ('Climate strike school') which explored, for example, Climate Justice and COVID-19, climate and COVID-19 worker solidarity, and First Nations justice. Following teaching from First Nations climate justice leaders, attendees untangled histories of key events in Aboriginal and Torres Strait Islander resistance and explored the role of allies in break-out groups led by students; attendees grappled with complex questions of the dynamics of speaking and listening, speaking for and speaking with, and how to form political alliances that do not eviscerate, appropriate or colonise difference.

While the issues of speaking for others and for Country are certainly not resolved, there seems (to me) to be a desire to attune to microfascisms amongst many pursuing climate justice. As discussed in Chapter 2, microfascisms are the danger that accompanies the molecular line – that is, the line that slightly diverges from binary, segmentary lines – where there is a troubling of gendered, classed, racialised, sexualised, ableist and ageist lines of demarcation between bodies, and of the lines between the human and more-than-human. The molecular line, while diverging from the molar, risks 'reproducing in miniature the affections, the affectations, of the rigid' line; there can be a 'fascism of the Left and fascism of the Right' (Deleuze and Guattari 1980/1987: 228, 214). Guattari notes how an activist group may resist exploitation, alienation and oppression, 'while at the same time, within the problems of the group, there may be micro-fascist processes on the molecular level' (Guattari and Rolnik 1982/2008: 185). Microfascisms in the climate justice movement might be at work when a climate group declares that it is only concerned about action on climate change (and that it doesn't have time for other intersecting justice issues) – demarcating issues from each other as if they are separate (see Whyte 2020: 56). There may be a microfascism in speaking for the trees – that is, a potential reproduction of disrespect for the relationality and agency of Country in seeking to intercede for Country. But there may also be microfascism in a group becoming fractured by finger-pointing, ostracising the student who painted a Lorax cardboard sign because they 'spoke for' the trees. I return to these tensions of solidarity in the final section, thinking with the concept of conspiring. But before then, I return to the atmos-fears of schools in the formation, ordering and movement of students' voices.

## *Schools and Students' (Striking) Voices*

Climate change is shifting the affective atmosphere/atmos-fear in classrooms and schools. As Blanche Verlie and Simone Blom (2021) beautifully phrase it in conceptualising 'climactic-affective atmospheres', 'climatic conditions can waft into classrooms, ignite changes, and spark alternative worldings' (2). A classroom and school's 'climate', as Chapter 5 explored, is more-than-individual (the teacher or individual student's psychological state) and more-than institutional – that is, contained within a school's boundaries. Climate change, as 'a socio-meteorological force that includes gaseous conditions and student climate activism, infiltrates, disrupts, and contributes to educational atmospheres' (Verlie and Blom 2021: 3–4). Meteorological and climatic forces have transcorporeal effects and affects on bodies (Neimanis and Walker 2014); bodies in classrooms (both students' and teachers') may feel variously disempowered, overwhelmed, hopeful, frustrated, underprepared, anxious and betrayed through what is taught or not taught about the changing climate in their classroom, and from political responses to climate change beyond their classrooms (Jones and Davison 2021; Verlie 2022b). Verlie and Blom (2021) explore how, in the wake of Australia's 2019–20 bushfire crisis, classroom climates, meteorological atmospheric conditions, and national and global 'political storms' intermingled, with distinct effects and affects on students and teachers (10).

In the 2018–19 School Strikes for Climate, before Australia's 2019–20 bushfire crisis, students also felt and acted on the transcorporeal effects and affects of climate change, and schools responded in a range of ways to their concerns. Newspaper reports described schools as 'divided over allowing students to support the strikes' (Chrysanthos and Baker 2019). In a corpus analysis of 500 newspaper articles, Michael Hartup and I (Mayes and Hartup 2022) mapped a spectrum of school and educational departmental responses reported across this sampled newspaper coverage: from non-support with disciplinary consequences, to non-support for striking during the school week, to permission to strike on school grounds only, to parental discretion, to active support. Here, I focus on two particular responses – where students were permitted to strike on school grounds, and active support. I draw on these two examples to reinforce, as Chapters 5 and 6 discussed, how students' voices and bodies can be institutionally curtailed and institutionally recaptured, but with a micropolitical remainder.

Reported examples of students being given permission to host climate change 'events' or 'protests' on school grounds suggest the institutional steering of students' political voices, with diverging affective connotations. Two elite independent girls' schools in Sydney were reported as 'hosting student-led climate change events within the school's grounds':

> [Independent girls' school principal] said the school 'sought to balance support for student voice, the environment and the immense value of education' by encouraging student-facilitated, in-school action.
>
> Students at [another independent girls' school] have also organised a climate-focused event on school grounds. (Chrysanthos and Baker 2019)

A school in the Northern Territory where the majority of the students are Indigenous was reported to have permitted students to 'protest in their schoolyard':

> Students in the remote Northern Territory town of Tennant Creek did not go on strike, but staged a protest in their schoolyard which faces a major highway.
> School attendance is a huge issue across the NT, and the school community decided it was inappropriate to encourage students to skip school for the day. (ABC News [No author] 2019)

The contrasting description of these school-approved student actions ('student-facilitated, in-school action' and 'a protest') is striking: one action suggestive of 'student voice' obediently expressed within pre-agreed boundaries, and the other invoking the negative connotations of 'protest'. The account of 'the school community' deciding it 'was inappropriate to encourage' non-attendance is vague; it is not clear who decided that student participation in the strikes would be 'inappropriate' and whether students, parents and community were part of this decision-making process. The rationales for containing students' political expression within school grounds diverge across these differing geo-social contexts and imply racialised and gendered understandings of where and how these young people should express their political concerns.

A small number of schools were reported, across the newspaper corpus, to have actively supported their students participating in the school strikes. One article noted the privilege of the schools which were actively supporting the striking students: 'Some of Sydney's most exclusive private schools are throwing their support behind students choosing to attend today's climate change rally, with some pupils encouraged to "become the changes they seek to see in the world"' (Collins and Coleman 2019). The response from one elite boys' school headmaster, originally published on the school's website, was republished in full in the *Sydney Morning Herald* as a feature article (Parker 2019). In this full response, after summarising his understanding of the scientific findings of the 2014 Intergovernmental Panel on Climate Change ('a pretty reliable group of scientists'), the headmaster details the arguments made by the Year 11s who came 'into my office asking me to support the climate strike', how he countered their arguments, and how they then responded. The headmaster foregrounds that: 'I stay neutral and allow all points of view – sometimes to a fault' – avowing the supposed political neutrality of teachers and schools. The students' responses ultimately are demonstrated by the headmaster to be sensible, well considered and actively shaped by the school's ethos and programmes:

> I ask what's going to happen when they want to march about immigration or abortion or any other issue. What's to stop them marching out for that?
> They say I am committing a 'slippery-slope fallacy' (damn those critical thinking lessons we teach them) and that climate change is different in kind to any of these issues because it affects the lives of everyone. [. . .]
> I point out the lessons that students everywhere will be missing – that they all need to be in school to get an education.
> They say to me the very vision of [school name] is for boys to make an active and positive difference in the world. Going on a march for the climate fits the school's vision better than one more regular day around the classrooms, they tell me. (Damn the school's vision – I should have seen that one coming.)
> Why not Saturday? I ask. Show your commitment that way.
> 'It's not a strike if it's on a Saturday,' they say. They get passionate now. They say they have no voice, no vote, that those in power have deserted their generation.
> They say all they can do to be heard is to stop doing the thing the government expects them to do that day – going to school. This isn't going well. [. . .]
> Students who have shown they care about this should be able to march [. . .] If their parents have allowed them to be absent to go to the strike, then the least we can do is give them the school's support too. (Parker 2019)

While the headmaster's rhetorical support of the school strikes is an admirable example of political advocacy, it is simultaneously a savvy marketing opportunity (see Chapter 1) – to showcase how the school's students apply the school's lessons in 'critical thinking' and live out the school's 'vision' to 'make an active and positive difference in the world' with 'passionate' yet logical and rational arguments. There is an institutional capture here – even if altruistic – rearticulating an understanding of the students' political demands in the service of institutional promotion.

Schools and school systems responded differently to the 2018–19 School Strikes for Climate across gendered, classed and racialised lines, though not in clear-cut ways.[10] Reported responses suggest a tendency for those who are already advantaged – that is, students from elite independent schools (and, in particular, boys) – to be more likely to be supported by their schools to strike; the 'passion' of these students was recognised as legitimate expressions of political agency. Reports of students' climate actions being constrained to school grounds came from a school in a Northern Territory town and from two independent girls' schools. These responses are suggestive of the uneven distribution (across geographic and socio-economic contexts) of opportunities for students to 'have a voice' on government inaction on climate change (Brennan et al. 2021; Mayes and Hartup 2022). It is also suggestive of when, where and how representational injustices discussed in Chapter 4 begin: these school responses are part of young people's political socialisation and sense of who belongs in political debate and whose participation is to be contained.

However, these reported responses are not exhaustive, and institutional constraints and/or institutional capture cannot enclose desire. Indeed, students who were not officially permitted to strike still went to the strikes; one blog post described the May 2021 strikes as about students 'extending their voices beyond the stifling grasp of schools' (Variyan et al. 2021). Chapter 5 explored this institutional grasping – how adults may seek to 'understand' students, with varying consequences and subjectifications effected in and through this grasping. Chapter 6 mapped the movements of a RESP token as a partial object in a school reform process. I reviewed how Deleuze and Guattari (1983) credited psychoanalyst Klein with the 'marvellous discovery of partial objects', but lament that she 'failed to *grasp* the logic of these objects' (44, my emphasis) – their potential to subvert the Oedipal complex in their connections, conjunctions, syntheses and disjunctions with desiring-machines. Partial objects affect and are affected by the hands that grasp them; partial objects have a 'flexible and plastic quality which makes [them] inherently political' (Surin 2010: 203).

To re-turn to students' signs that intertextually invoke the Lorax's 'I speak for the trees . . .', each is a particular partial object in its own, moving affective constellations and desiring-agencements, making its own minoritarian evaluations. Some signs that quote this phrase from the Lorax – in Figure 7.2, for example (and I am just speculating) – could be institutionally recaptured: perhaps a school could use this photo in a school newsletter as an example of a student from their school boldly standing up and speaking for the trees, 'making a difference' in the world. Other signs that rework this phrase might move in other directions – like Figure 7.1's direct address to 'ScoMo' (then prime minister Scott Morrison) to 'do better'. Others still – and here I am taking some poetic licence – might become somewhat of a minor literature. As discussed in Chapter 5, a minor literature connects the individual to a political immediacy, deterritorialises language (and may not make recognisable sense), and takes on a collective value (Deleuze and Guattari 2006). The 'language of sense' that is 'traversed by a line of escape' is exemplified, for Deleuze and Guattari (2006), in Kafka's work:

> Gregor's warbling and the ways it blurred words, the whistling of the mouse, the cough of the ape, the pianist who doesn't play, the singer who doesn't sing and gives birth to her song out of her nonsinging, the musical dogs who are musicians in the very depths of their bodies since they don't emit any music. [. . .] [A] language of sense is traversed by a line of escape – in order to liberate a living and expressive material that speaks for itself and has no need of being put into a form. (Deleuze and Guattari 2006: 21)

Perhaps there are forces more elastic and evasive that can be glimpsed in the partial objects of student strikers' signs that evade the adult (teacher, school leader, reporter, researcher) interpreter's sweaty grasp. Read the sign in Figure 7.3. Perhaps you interpret it as a sign of immaturity and/or 'adolescent' rage or rebellion (see Chapter 3). Perhaps you gasp in air in surprise at the swear word (perhaps you don't spend much time with young people). Perhaps you exhale and your ribs contract with a short laugh. Perhaps there is nonsense at work that somehow makes sense. Perhaps there is a password beneath the order word. Perhaps your exhaled breath laughs with the world at the extractivist hubris that ever thought that the shifting agencements of a sign – and a voice – and a student – and a teacher – and a school – and a world – were ever able to be grasped at all.

## *Con-spiracies*

Con-spiracies form with the huddling together of bodies, the intimacies of shared breath and shared tactics in the thick of troubled and troubling atmospheres (Choy 2016). Recent conspiracies include that COVID-19 is a hoax and that climate change is a hoax; these conspiracies – which are multivalent in their origins and trajectories – are frequently bound up with vested interests in maintaining the status quo. COVID-19 conspiracies in circulation in 2020, at least, seemed, for their proponents, to solidify and harden the sense of the 'rights' of the asserted 'sovereign citizen' to not wear a mask, get a vaccine or to comply with community public health lockdown

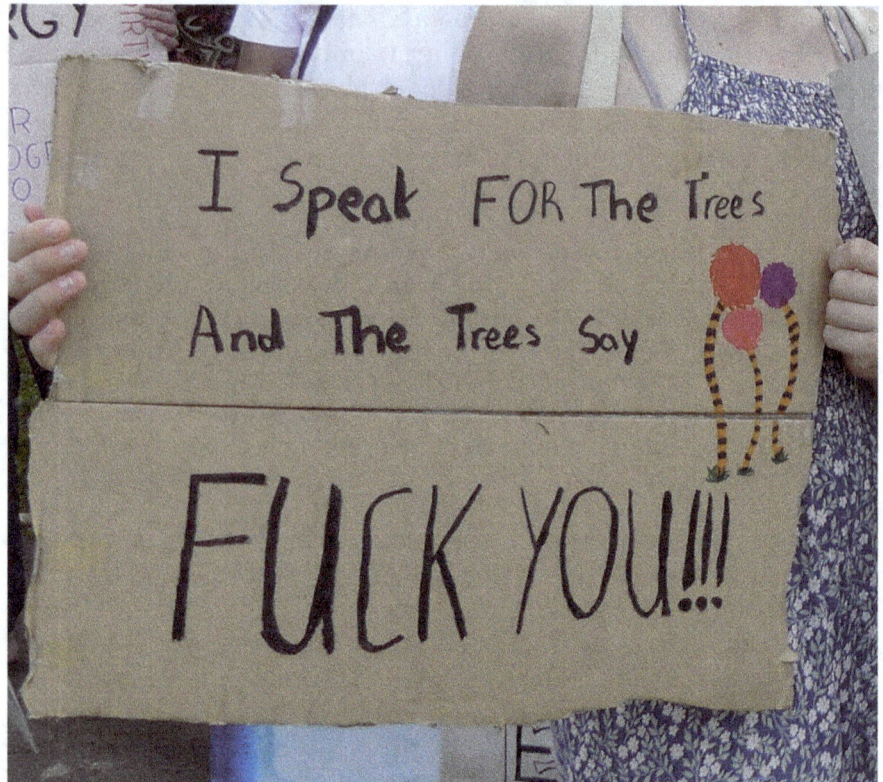

*Figure 7.3* A young person holds a cardboard sign: 'I Speak FOR The Trees And The Trees Say FUCK YOU!!!)", 21 May 2020, Sydney School Strike 4 Climate rally. Creative Commons 2.0 by School Strike 4 Climate. Original image cropped.

measures; the assertedly autonomous individual becomes impervious to the porous boundaries between bodies in the relationality of aerosol-borne viral transmission. Conspiracies that proclaim that climate change is a hoax in turn weaken political will for urgent action in response to a rapidly warming world. Such conspiracies bolster the boundaries between bodies and proliferate patterns of capitalist consumption.

But there may be other ways to conspire – to breathe together and form different tactics as we[11] affect and are affected by these changing climates. Breath ephemerally materialises at the interface of body and world (Oxley and Russell 2020: 3). As bodies breathe, they are part of constant metabolic corporeal processes where human and more-than-human intermix and transmute one another (Allen 2020: 79). Breath is invisible yet essential for ongoing sentient life – and speech – and listening and relating to human and more-than-human others. One cannot communicate – 'have a voice' – if there is no breath – whether that communication is through speaking, writing and myriad more-than-linguistic modes of communication.

Breathing together – while inherently shared, and necessary for living and speaking – is distinctly experienced; breathing together has never been easy, and is more dangerous for some than for others. To con-spire, according to Tim Choy, is to 'commit to breathing together from and in an unequally shared milieu, an unevenly constituted planetary medium for respiration' (2021: 249). Sefanit Habtom and Megan Scribe (2020), writing about the respiratory effects of COVID-19 that are disproportionately felt in Black, Indigenous and Black-Indigenous communities, amidst histories and continuities of respiratory violence, offer 'breathing together' as a more intimate alternative to the notion of Black-Indigenous 'coalitions'. In militarised, industrialised capitalist states, atmospheres of antiblackness (Sharpe 2016) and 'settler atmospherics' (Simmons 2017) make it difficult or impossible for some bodies to breathe, both 'literally and figuratively' (Habtom and Scribe 2020: para. 18). When it is difficult or impossible to breathe, it is also difficult – but not impossible – to speak, to listen, and to form new ways of relating.

To breathe together is to apprehend that we are not atomised individuals. The ontological separation of individual humans from each other and from the world is embedded in English grammar, where nouns are distinct from verbs as discrete units. Miranda Luiz (2020) explains Sylvia Wynter's critique of this grammar with the example: '*I am distinct from this tree next to me; the action of me breathing carbon dioxide into this tree* is distinct from either thing' (156, Luiz's emphasis). In its working paper for UNESCO, the Common Worlds Research Collective (2020) argues that education is implicated in perpetuating the Cartesian dualistic notion that humans are separate from the earth and can act upon it; this ontological dualism has perpetuated extractivist and exploitative modes of living that have destroyed human relations and are destroying the earth. I have wondered whether the concept of student voice and agency may also be complicit in perpetuating the pedagogical production of sovereign individuals with 'rights' and autonomous 'agency' who evaluate each other in judgement and consume education as if they are set apart from everything and everyone who teaches and learns with them. But to breathe together – and, consequently, to speak together, to be in dialogue with one another – is beyond the human.

It is a well-worn phrase that forests and marine microbes are the 'lungs of the earth' – absorbing carbon dioxide and releasing oxygen via photosynthesis. Natasha Myers argues that this phrase is an understatement – forests and marine microbes 'literally breathe us into being':

> ... communities of photosynthetic creatures [. . .] know how to compose liveable, breathable, nourishing worlds. As they exhale, they compose the atmosphere; as they decompose, they matter the compost and feed the soil. Holding the earth down and the sky up, they sing in nearly audible ultrasonic frequencies as they transpire, moving massive volumes of water from the depths of the earth up to the highest clouds. They cleanse the waters and nourish all other life. (Myers 2021: para. 15)

For feminist philosopher Luce Irigaray, breath connects us to an ontology of 'vegetal being' (Irigaray and Marder 2016); to attend and attune to breath is a feminist practice of bodily respect for respiring vegetal life, skies and atmospheres. What would it do, for pedagogical relations, to collectively attune and attend to how all bodies – human and non-human – are entwined in each other's ongoing breath – 'not just as consumers who have rights to an "ecosystem service"' but as 'co-producers of local and global transcorporeal respiratory relations' (Verlie 2022b: 19)?

Breathing together is not always harmonious, nor does breathing together bring consensus, nor is the politics and process of breathing together easily grasped. The challenges or impossibilities of breath are differentially distributed across and between forms of life, necessitating that we inquire after the differing conditions of breath's 'uneven manifestation and movement' (Choy 2016: paras. 4, 7). Inquiring after differing conditions for breathing (and relatedly, for speaking and acting) entails troubling established common sense – that is, what is taken for granted about breath and speech and relationality (see Chapters 3 and 4). Indeed, when breath (and, relatedly, speech) is dis-ordered or interrupted, the contingency of and conditions for this common sense are made explicit. In such moments of interruption, there is the possibility of what citizen of the Moapa Band of Southern Paiutes scholar Kristen Simmons (2017) describes as 'becoming-open in an atmosphere of violence' (para. 16). This becoming-open is a 'porous relationality' that Simmons describes as 'a site of potential, exposure, and entanglement all at once', where we attune 'to how others (cannot) breathe' and 'we develop capacities to feel one another otherwise' (para. 16).

To return to education, and the pedagogical relation, this becoming-open in processes of conspiring is an attunement to how those we teach and learn with can or cannot breathe, and can breathe but can or cannot, or refuse not, to speak. To conspire is to attune to overlaps, but also the potential dissonances and diverging metaphysics and ontologies of breath between bodies – where air, spirit, breath, soul and knowledge are intrisically connected – that are sacred but not necessarily sharable (Bawaka Country et al. 2020; Simpson 2014; Tuck and Yang 2014b). Differences are not ignored, nor are bodies essentialised nor compelled to speak or become like the imagined ideal; difference becomes potentiality to affect and be affected. To conspire is to interrogate the difficulties and impossibilities of expression in schools – whether in speech, or in other modes of communication – since any form of pedagogical communication is inextricable from breath. To conspire is to not compel another to breathe or speak a certain way, but to value moments of refusal that affirm life-otherwise. To conspire is to attend to the interval between the inhale and exhale – and the opacity of what is happening in these suspended micromoments – the im/possibilities of understanding (that is, grasping). The suspended micromoment is never an empty void (Barad 2018) – but is full, teeming, desire-seeking-connection. To conspire, perhaps, is to seek to be response-able to gasping, without grasping.

Breathing together is not one party 'empowering' the other party. It is not one party 'partnering' with the other party. To breathe together is beyond our institutional roles and positions (students, teachers, researchers), and even beyond our humanness – though these necessarily shape our sense of the capacity to breathe. It entails attention and attunement 'to our mortal entanglements and vulnerabilities with other species, no matter how small' (Taylor and Pacini-Ketchabaw 2015: 507). To conspire is to work to compound the capacities of all parties to breath-speak-listen-relate-act-live together – yielding to one another's needs. It is to inquire, collectively, into 'the capacities of the parties-in-relation needed for the relationship to continue to keep functioning' as a 'mutually enabling system of relations' (Verlie 2022a: 311). Not the student who becomes more satisfied at school, while the teacher is left exhausted; not the teacher who extracts a student's voice and governs them better in the process; not the school which relentlessly drives students and teachers to produce and consume more and more data, in order to divide these data up, in order to evaluate and judge what is happening.

## TOWARDS RESPAIR

The issue with reforms is that they do not trouble founding logics and received common sense. In the case of education, reforms keep the colonialist and capitalist extractivist purposes of education, and its expectations of endless growth, intact. Reforms may be infused with a cruel optimism (Berlant 2011) that promises transformation but can progressively deplete the capacities of bodies to act – though not uniformly. In the face of historical injustices that continue, the institutional invitation to 'have a voice' may not confront and dismantle the logics that keep present inequalities in place. The reform invitation to 'have a voice' may be framed by the school in terms of surface issues (for example, perceptions of student 'disengagement' or 'behaviour' issues in a school) rather than addressing the reasons why students may not be 'engaging' with schooling (including how schools may subjectificate and alienate students, parents and communities), and the cascading demands on teachers that 'erode' their capacities to listen. Students may refuse the terms of educational reform through 'voice' – for example, refusing the terms of their recognition (for example, as a 'disengaged student') – or refuse to be part of processes that tinker at the edges of structures and practices that maintain White supremacy in schools (Welton and Harris 2022). Such refusals are expressions of strength and knowledge and can be profoundly educative if the institution is willing to listen and learn.

Student voice has troubled me – in its perplexing enactments and its affective movements. These troubling times compel me to, as Donna Haraway (2016) urges, stay with the trouble, rather than retreat from it (Alcoff: 17). I am not arguing that there shouldn't be advocacy or work for student voice. The work of this book has been, instead, to gesture towards a different kind of student voice – an apprehension of how voice works as a material force, respecting all of what voices (in their more-than-human entanglements and collective agencements of enunciation) are capable of and might do. I aspire – and I deliberately use this verb for its connotations of breath – for different pedagogical ontologies and relationalities that exceed atomised lives, exceed liberal humanism, exceed consensus-driven modes of understanding, and compound the capacities for breathing-speaking-listening-feeling-thinking-living for all entwined in the relation.

To stay with the trouble, and breathe together, entails sitting with violent histories, unsettled presents and unknown futures that we are inescapably complicit and entangled with. Across our various situated locations, we are tangled up in institutions and complicit with ongoing inequalities of access, resources and representation in education and with the earth – some of us more than others. How might we create atmospheres that are simultaneously troubling and regenerative? How might we attune to radical interdependencies across differences, since the past, as well as our individual and collective futures, are bound up with each other?

Towards the end of 2020, I learnt the word 'respair' – revivified at the end of the first year of the global COVID-19 pandemic. To 'respair' is to hope again after a period of despair. I like its etymological connection to respiration – to breathe again after the suspension of breath, and its close connection to despair – distinguishable only by one letter. Respair is sensed in the thick of trouble, in the micro-moments between breaths. Respair is sensed in the dense moments that hover in suspension when a body speaks – before the response. Respair might materialise behind our backs, in the moment when we breathe, together. When we breathe together – when we conspire to refuse reform – respair affects the atmospheres of schools and worlds. Conspiring, respairing, there may be the possibility of re/generating other different worlds, in common, between us.

## Notes

1. In the settler colonial context of Australia, a climate justice stance centres Indigenous sovereignty as 'the ancestral tie between the land [. . .] and the Aboriginal and Torres Strait Islander peoples who were born therefrom, remain attached thereto, and must one day return thither to be united with our ancestors' (The Uluru Statement 2021).
2. Student climate justice activism is, of course, just one example of student-led social movements. In recent years in Australia, students have been at the forefront of campaigning for holistic sex education, and have also been involved across a range of transgenerational social movements – including Black Lives Matter, for Indigenous sovereignty, LGBTQI+ rights and Marriage Equality, and rights for people with a disability.
3. The 2012 film begins in Thneedville, a walled city where all plants and trees are artificial and where the mayor's company sells bottled oxygen to the people of the city. A 12-year-old boy, Ted, seeks to find a 'real tree' (to impress a girl), and in the process meets the Once-ler, who tells him the story of what happened to the Trufulla trees. The Once-ler tells Ted about how he met the Lorax, the 'guardian of the

forest', who 'speaks for the trees'; according to the Once-ler, the Lorax emerged from the stump of the first tree that the Once-ler cut down for his own commercial gain. The Once-ler gives Ted the last Trufulla seed to plant to regrow the forest. By the end of the film, Ted has declared to the city that he 'speaks for the trees' and convinces the people of the urgency to plant the tree and 'start anew'. While it has been widely used as a text for environmental education, *The Lorax* has also been criticised for its anthropocentric redemptive narrative (Pleasants 2006).
4. Sara Ahmed discusses institutional walls in *Living a Feminist Life* (2017): 'walls, brick walls, institutional walls; those hardenings of histories into barriers in the present' (135).
5. I am grateful to Blanche Verlie for noticing this connection between RESP tokens and respair, and for her insightful comments on an earlier version of this chapter.
6. The concept of climate justice emerges from First Nations land and water rights, environmental justice and ecofeminist movements; climate justice foregrounds First Nations sovereignty and highlights the inequalities experienced between industrialised countries in the Global North and the Global South, gender injustices, environmental racisms and multi-species injustices (Jafry et al. 2018).
7. 'ScoMo' is a nickname commonly used for the (now former) Australian prime minister Scott Morrison.
8. Lauren Tynan (2021) writes: 'trawlwulwuy, tebrakunna sometimes do not use capitalisation' (12).
9. While this section focuses on the Ngarrindjeri concept of Yannarumi, there is a significant body of work recognising the legal subjectivity of more-than-human Rivers and living systems in particular jurisdictions (see Takacs 2021 for a detailed overview). Alongside this environmental jurisprudence, careful scholarly work has been done 'voicing Rivers as first person', composed from 'place-based knowing' and 'an Indigenous worldview, which understands a deep responsiveness within all things' (Martuwarra RiverOfLife et al. 2022: 423). These matters of 'voicing' the more-than-human are of profound significance in reconceptualising voice beyond the human subject.
10. These reported responses come only from official spokespeople and from the principals of independent schools with greater autonomy to speak to the media. There are other stories to tell of how schools who 'officially' were not permitted to voice support for the student strikers found institutional cracks to support them, as well as how 'official' stances of support were differentially experienced across a school community.
11. I have avoided the first-person plural 'we' throughout this book, to make explicit which bodies and groups I am referring to. In this final

section, I use 'we' as a deliberate rhetorical tactic since all human bodies – across our distinctly differing embodied positionalities and agencements of enunciation – share in this collective, vital yet fragile process.

# Bibliography

ABC News [No author] (2019) 'Global climate strike sees "hundreds of thousands" of Australians rally across the country'. *ABC News*, 20 September.
Abdel-Fattah, Randa (2016) '"Lebanese Muslim": A Bourdieuian "capital" offense in an Australian coastal town'. *Journal of Intercultural Studies*, 37(4): 323–38.
Abdel-Fattah, Randa (2019) 'Countering violent extremism, governmentality and Australian Muslim youth as "becoming terrorist"'. *Journal of Sociology*, 56(3): 372–87.
Abdel-Fattah, Randa (2021) *Coming of Age in the War on Terror*. Sydney: NewSouth Publishing.
Ahmed, Sara (2004) *The Cultural Politics of Emotion*. Edinburgh: Edinburgh University Press.
Ahmed, Sara (2008) 'Open forum imaginary prohibitions: Some preliminary remarks on the founding gestures of the "new materialism"'. *European Journal of Women's Studies*, 15(1): 23–39.
Ahmed, Sara (2010) *The Promise of Happiness*. Durham, NC: Duke University Press.
Ahmed, Sara (2014) *Willful Subjects*. Durham, NC: Duke University Press.
Ahmed, Sara (2017) *Living a Feminist Life*. Durham, NC: Duke University Press.
Ahmed, Sara (2019) *What's the Use? On the Uses of Use*. Durham, NC: Duke University Press.
Alagraa, Bedour (2018) 'Homo narrans and the science of the word: Toward a Caribbean radical imagination'. *Critical Ethnic Studies*, 4(2): 164–81.
Alaimo, Stacey and Hekman, Susan, eds (2008) *Material Feminisms*. Bloomington: Indiana University Press.
Alanen, Leena and Mayall, Berry, eds (2001) *Conceptualising Child–Adult Relations*. London: Routledge.
Albrecht-Crane, Christa and Slack, Jennifer Daryl (2007) 'Toward a pedagogy of affect', in A. Hickey-Moody and P. Malins (eds), *Deleuzian Encounters: Studies in Contemporary Social Issues*. Basingstoke: Palgrave Macmillan, pp. 99–110.
Alcoff, Linda (1991) 'The problem of speaking for others'. *Cultural Critique*, 20: 5–32.

# Bibliography

Aldridge, Jill M., Fraser, Barry J., Fozdar, Farida, Ala'i, Kate, Earnest, Jaya and Afari, Ernest (2015) 'Students' perceptions of school climate as determinants of wellbeing, resilience and identity'. *Improving Schools*. DOI: 10.1177/1365480215612616.

Allan, David and Duckworth, Vicky (2018) 'Voices of disaffection: Disengaged and disruptive youths or agents of change and self-empowerment?' *British Journal of Special Education*, 45(1): 43–60.

Allen, Irma Kinga (2020) 'Thinking with a feminist political ecology of air-and-breathing-bodies'. *Body & Society*, 26(2): 79–105.

Alvermann, Donna E. (2000) 'Researching libraries, literacies, and lives: A rhizoanalysis', in E. A. St. Pierre and W. Pillow (eds), *Working the Ruins: Feminist Poststructural Theory and Methods in Education*. London: Routledge, pp. 114–29.

Aly, Anne and Green, Lelia (2010) 'Fear, anxiety and the state of terror'. *Studies in Conflict & Terrorism*, 33(3): 268–81.

Anderson, Ben (2009) 'Affective atmospheres'. *Emotion, Space and Society*, 2(2): 77–81.

Anderson, Donnah L. and Graham, Anne P. (2016) 'Improving student wellbeing: Having a say at school'. *School Effectiveness and School Improvement*, 27(3): 348–66.

Anyon, Jean (1980) 'Social class and the hidden curriculum of work'. *Journal of Education*, 162(1): 67–92.

Appadurai, Arjun (1988) 'Introduction: Place and voice in anthropological theory'. *Cultural Anthropology*, 3(1): 16–20.

Apple, Michael (1979) *Ideology and Curriculum*. Boston, MA: Routledge & Kegan Paul.

Arnot, Madeline and Reay, Diane (2004) 'The social dynamics of classroom learning', in M. Arnot, D. McIntyre, D. Pedder and D. Reay (eds), *Consultation in the Classroom: Developing Dialogue about Teaching and Learning*. Cambridge: Pearson, pp. 42–84.

Arnot, Madeleine and Reay, Diane (2007) 'A sociology of pedagogic voice: Power, inequality and pupil consultation'. *Discourse: Studies in the Cultural Politics of Education*, 28(3): 311–25.

Associated Press/Reuters (2019) 'Greta Thunberg doesn't want to hear how inspiring she is – she wants climate action'. *ABC News*, 18 September. Available at: https://www.abc.net.au/news/2019-09-18/greta-thunberg-meets-barack-obama-climate-change-action/11523504 (accessed 25 August 2022).

Australian Association for Research in Education (2014) *AARE 2013: Ian Buchanan and Taylor Webb*. Available at: https://www.youtube.com/watch?v=L8Bvd-Ob6SU (accessed 25 August 2022).

Australian Curriculum Assessment and Reporting Authority (ACARA) (2021) *My School*. Available at: https://www.myschool.edu.au (accessed 25 August 2022).

Australian Government, NSW Government, Association of Independent Schools NSW and NSW Catholic Education Commission (October 2010) *NSW Smarter Schools National Partnerships Implementation Plan: Improving Teacher Quality, Literacy and Numeracy, Low Socioeconomic Status School Communities*. Available at: file:///C:/Users/mayes/Downloads/nsw_summary_implementation_plan%20(1).pdf (accessed 15 July 2021).

Australian Institute for Teaching and School Leadership (AITSL) (n.d.) *Spotlight: Diversity in School Leadership*. Available at: https://www.aitsl.edu.au/docs/default-source/research-evidence/spotlight/spotlight-diversity-in-school-leadership.pdf?sfvrsn=93effa3c_2 (accessed 25 August 2022).

Ball, Stephen and Collet-Sabé, Jordi (2021) 'Against school: An epistemological critique'. *Discourse: Studies in the Cultural Politics of Education*. DOI: 10.1080/01596306.2021.1947780.

Ball, Stephen J. (2003) 'The teacher's soul and the terrors of performativity'. *Journal of Educational Policy*, 18: 215–28.

Ball, Stephen J., Maguire, Meg and Braun, Annette (2012) *How Schools Do Policy: Policy Enactments in Secondary Schools*. Abingdon: Routledge.

Barad, Karen (2007) *Meeting the Universe Halfway: Quantum Physics and the Entanglement of Matter and Meaning*. Durham, NC: Duke University Press.

Barad, Karen (2014) 'Diffracting diffraction: Cutting together-apart'. *Parallax*, 20(3): 168–87.

Barad, Karen (2018) 'Troubling time/s and ecologies of nothingness: Re-turning, re-membering, and facing the incalculable'. *new formations: a journal of culture/theory/politics*, 92: 56–86.

Barnes, D., Britton, James, Rosen, H. and LATE (1969) *Language, the Learner and the School*. Harmondsworth: Penguin.

Baroutsis, Aspa, McGregor, Glenda and Mills, Martin (2016) 'Pedagogic voice: Student voice in teaching and engagement pedagogies'. *Pedagogy, Culture & Society*, 24(1): 123–40.

Barthes, Roland (1974) 'From speech to writing', in Roland Barthes (ed.), *The Grain of the Voice: Interviews 1962–1980*. London: Jonathan Cape, pp. 3–7.

Barthes, Roland (1977/1984) 'The death of the author', in S. Heath (ed.), *Image, Music, Text*. London: Flamingo, pp. 142–8.

Baugh, Bruce (2016) 'The open society and the democracy to come: Bergson, Deleuze and Guattari'. *Deleuze Studies*, 10(3): 352–66.

Bawaka Country, Wright, Sarah, Suchet-Pearson, Sandie, Lloyd, Kate, Burarrwanga, Laklak, Ganambarr, Ritjillili, Ganambarr-Stubbs, Merrkiyawuy, Ganambarr, Banbapuy and Maymuru, Djawundil (2020) 'Gathering of the Clouds: Attending to Indigenous understandings of time and climate through songspirals'. *Geoforum*, 108: 295–304.

# Bibliography

Beaini, Adella, Gelli, Campbell, Krusche, Derrick and Barr, Eliza (2019) 'Albanese's office barged during kids' climate strike'. *Daily Telegraph*, 3 May.

Bergmark, Ulrika and Kostenius, Catrine (2009) '"Listen to me when I have something to say": Students' participation in research for sustainable school improvement'. *Improving Schools*, 12(3): 249–60.

Berlant, Lauren (2005) 'The epistemology of state emotion', in Austin Sarat (ed.), *Dissent in Dangerous Times*. Ann Arbor: University of Michigan Press, pp. 46–78.

Berlant, Lauren (2011) *Cruel Optimism*. Durham, NC: Duke University Press.

Berryman, Mere and Eley, Elizabeth (2018) 'Gathering and listening to the voices of Māori youth: What are the system responses?', in Roseanna Bourke and Judith Loveridge (eds), *Radical Collegiality Through Student Voice: Educational Experience, Policy and Practice*. Dordrecht: Springer, pp. 103–26.

Bertrand, Melanie (2016) '"I was very impressed": Responses of surprise to students of color engaged in Youth Participatory Action Research'. *Urban Education*, 54(9): 1370–97.

Bertrand, Melanie and Marsh, Julie (2021) 'How data-driven reform can drive deficit thinking'. *Phi Delta Kappan*, 102(8): 35–9.

Bessant, Judith (2021a) *Making-up People: Youth, Truth and Politics*. London: Routledge.

Bessant, Judith (2021b) 'Representations of young people and neoliberal developmentalism in the Global South', in Sharlene Swartz, Adam Cooper, Clarence M. Batan and Laura K. Causa (eds), *The Oxford Handbook of Global South Youth Studies*. Oxford: Oxford University Press, pp. 1–23.

Bhattacharya, Kakali (2021) 'Rejecting labels and colonization: In exile from post-qualitative approaches'. *Qualitative Inquiry*, 27(2): 179–84.

Biddle, Catharine and Hufnagel, Elizabeth (2019) 'Navigating the "danger zone": Tone policing and the bounding of civility in the practice of student voice'. *American Journal of Education*, 125(4): 487–520.

Biesta, Gert (2010) *Good Education in an Age of Measurement: Ethics, Politics, Democracy*. Boulder, CO: Paradigm Publishers.

Bignall, Simone (2014) '"Every existence is an event': Deleuze, Dewey, and Democracy', in: S. Bignall, S. Bowden and P. Patton ed., *Deleuze and Pragmatism*, London & New York: Routledge, pp. 105–123.

Bignall, Simone and Patton, Paul (2010) 'Deleuze and the postcolonial: Conversations, Negotiations, Mediations', in S. Bignall and P. Patton (ed.), *Deleuze and the Postcolonial*. Edinburgh: Edinburgh University Press, pp. 1–19.

Bignall, Simone and Rigney, Daryle (2019) 'Indigeneity, posthumanism and nomad thought: Transforming colonial ecologies', in Simone Bignall and

Rosi Braidotti (ed.), *Posthuman Ecologies: Complexity and Process after Deleuze*. New York: Rowman & Littlefield, pp. 159–81.

Bignall, Simone, Hemming, Steve and Rigney, Daryle (2016) 'Three ecosophies for the Anthropocene: Environmental governance, continental post-humanism and Indigenous expressivism'. *Deleuze Studies*, 10(4): 455–78.

Birch, Tony (2018) '"On what terms can we speak?" Refusal, resurgence and climate justice'. *Coolabah*, 24/25: 2–16.

Bishop, Russell (2011) 'Making it possible for minoritized students to take on student leadership roles'. *Leading and Managing*, 17(2): 110–21.

Black, Rosalyn (2012) 'Educating the reflexive citizen: Making a difference or entrenching difference?' Unpublished doctoral thesis, University of Melbourne.

Black, Rosalyn and Mayes, Eve (2020) 'Feeling voice: The emotional politics of "student voice" for teachers'. *British Educational Research Journal*, 46(5): 1064–80.

Bodkin-Andrews, Gawaian and Carlson, Bronwyn (2016) 'The legacy of racism and Indigenous Australian identity within education'. *Race Ethnicity and Education*, 19(4): 784–807.

Boler, Megan (1999) *Feeling Power: Emotions and Education*. New York: Routledge.

Bolt, Andrew (2018) 'Less marching, more learning'. *Herald Sun*, 3 December.

Borchers Arriagada, Nicolas, Palmer, Andrew J., Bowman, David M. J. S., Morgan, Geoffrey G., Jalaludin, Bin B. and Johnston, Fay H. (2020) 'Unprecedented smoke-related health burden associated with the 2019–20 bushfires in eastern Australia'. *Medical Journal of Australia*, 213(6): 282–3.

Bourdieu, Pierre and Passeron, Jean-Claude (1977) *Reproduction in Education, Society and Culture* (R. Nice, Trans.), London: SAGE.

Bourke, Roseanna and Loveridge, Judith (2018) 'Using student voice to challenge understandings of educational research, policy and practice', in Roseanna Bourke and Judith Loveridge (eds), *Radical Collegiality through Student Voice: Educational Experience, Policy and Practice*. Dordrecht: Springer, pp. 1–16.

Boutang, Pierre-André (1996) L'Abécédaire de Gilles Deleuze, avec Claire Parnet [Gilles Deleuze's ABC Primer, with Claire Parnet]. Paris: La Femis & Sodaperaga Productions.

Bowlby, John (1982) *Attachment and Loss*. New York: Basic Books.

Bowman, Benjamin (2020) '"They don't quite understand the importance of what we're doing today": The young people's climate strikes as subaltern activism'. *Sustainable Earth*, 3(1): 16.

Brady, Alison M. (2016) 'The regime of self-evaluation: Self-conception for teachers and schools'. *British Journal of Educational Studies*, 64(4): 523–41.

# Bibliography

Bragg, Sara (2001) 'Taking a joke: Learning from the voices we don't want to hear'. *Forum*, 43(2): 70–3.

Bragg, Sara (2007) '"Student voice" and governmentality: The production of enterprising subjects?' *Discourse: Studies in the Cultural Politics of Education*, 28(3): 343–58.

Bragg, Sara (2021) 'Student voice in education'. *Journal of the British Academy*, 8(s4): 41–51.

Bragg, Sara and Fielding, Michael (2005) '"It's an equal thing . . . It's about achieving together": Student voices and the possibility of a radical collegiality', in Hilary Street and Julie Temperley (eds), *Improving Schools Through Collaborative Enquiry*. London: Continuum, pp. 105–35.

Bragg, Sara and Manchester, Helen (2011) *Creativity, School Ethos and the Creative Partnerships Programme: Final Report of the Project: Evaluation of the Nature and Impact of the Creative Partnershps Programme on School Ethos, 2009–10*. Available at: https://www.creativitycultureeducation.org/wp-content/uploads/2018/10/may-2011-final-report-ou-creativity-school-ethos-and-creative-partnerships-282.pdf (accessed 25 August 2022).

Bragg, Sara and Manchester, Helen (2012) 'Pedagogies of student voice [Pedagogías de la voz del alumnado]'. *Revista de Educación*, Special Issue on Student Voice 359(September–December): 143–63.

Braidotti, Rosi (1994) *Nomadic Subjects: Embodiment and Sexual Difference in Contemporary Feminist Theory*. New York: Columbia University Press.

Braidotti, Rosi (2002), *Metamorphoses: Towards a Materialist Theory of Becoming*. Cambridge: Polity Press.

Braidotti, Rosi (2013) *The Posthuman*. Cambridge: Polity Press.

Braidotti, Rosi (2019) *Posthuman Knowledge*. Cambridge: Polity Press.

Brasof, Marc and Mansfield, Katherine (2018) 'Student voice and school leadership: Introduction'. *Journal of Ethical Educational Leadership*, Special Issue 1: 5–8.

Brasof, Marc and Spector, Ann (2016) 'Teach students about civics through schoolwide governance'. *Kappan Magazine*, 97(7): 63–8.

Brennan, Marie, Mayes, Eve and Zipin, Lew (2021) 'The contemporary challenge of activism as curriculum work'. *Journal of Educational Administration and History*, 54(3): 1–15. DOI: 10.1080/00220620.2020.1866508.

Brennan, Teresa (2004) *The Transmission of Affect*. London: Continuum.

Bright, David (2020) *Exploring Deleuze's Philosophy of Difference: Applications for Critical Qualitative Research*. Gorham, ME: Myers Education Press.

Bron, Jeroen and Veugelers, Wiel (2014) 'Why we need to involve our students in curriculum design: Five arguments for student voice'. *Curriculum and Teaching Dialogue*, 16(1&2): 125–39.

Brown, Martin, McNamara, Gerry, O'Brien, Shivaun, Skerritt, Craig and

O'Hara, Joe (2020) 'Policy and practice: Including parents and students in school self-evaluation'. *Irish Educational Studies*, 39(4): 511–34.

Buchanan, Ian (2013) 'The little Hans assemblage'. *Visual Arts Research*, 39(76): 9–17.

Buchanan, Ian (2014) 'Schizoanalysis and the pedagogy of the oppressed', in Matthew Carlin and Jason Wallin (eds), *Deleuze and Guattari, Politics and Education: For a People-Yet-to-Come*. New York: Bloomsbury Academic, pp. 1–14.

Buchanan, Ian (2021) *Assemblage Theory and Method*. London: Bloomsbury Academic.

Burbules, Nicholas C. (2004) 'Introduction', in Megan Boler (ed.), *Democratic Dialogue in Education: Troubling Speech, Disturbing Silence*. New York: Peter Lang, pp. xiii–xxxii.

Burman, Erica (1994) *Deconstructing Developmental Psychology*. New York: Routledge & Kegan Paul.

Butler, Judith (1997) *Excitable Speech: A Politics of the Performative*. London: Routledge.

Butler, Judith (2005) *Giving an Account of Oneself*. New York: Fordham University Press.

Byrd, Jodi (2011) *The Transit of Empire: Indigenous Critiques of Colonialism*. Minneapolis: University of Minnesota Press.

Cammarota, Julio and Fine, Michelle (2008) 'Youth Participatory Action Research: A pedagogy for transformational resistance', in Julio Cammarota and Michelle Fine (eds), *Youth Participatory Action Research in Motion*. New York: Taylor & Francis, pp. 1–11.

Carlin, Matthew and Wallin, Jason (2014) *Deleuze and Guattari, Politics and Education: For a People-Yet-to-Come*. London: Bloomsbury.

Charteris, Jennifer (2016) 'Dialogic feedback as divergent assessment for learning: An ecological approach to teacher professional development'. *Critical Studies in Education*, 57(3): 277–95.

Charteris, Jennifer and Smardon, Dianne (2019a) 'The politics of student voice: Unravelling the multiple discourses articulated in schools'. *Cambridge Journal of Education*, 49(1): 93–110.

Charteris, Jennifer and Smardon, Dianne (2019b) 'Student voice in learning: Instrumentalism and tokenism or opportunity for altering the status and positioning of students?' *Pedagogy, Culture & Society*, 27(2): 305–23.

Chomsky, Noam (1965) *Aspects of the Theory of Syntax*. Cambridge, MA: MIT Press.

Choy, Timothy K. (2016) *Distribution*. (Post in *Society for Cultural Anthropology: Theorizing the Contemporary*). Available at: https://culanth.org/fieldsights/distribution (accessed 25 August 2022).

Choy, Timothy K. (2020) 'A commentary: Breathing together now'. *Engaging Science, Technology, and Society*, 6: 586–90.

Choy, Tim (2021) 'Externality, breathers, conspiracy: Forms for atmospheric reckoning', in Dimitris Papadopoulos, María Puig de la Bellacasa and Natasha Myers (eds), *Reactivating Elements: Chemisty, Ecology, Practice*. Durham, NC: Duke University Press, pp. 231–56.

Chrysanthos, Natassia and Baker, Jordan (2019) 'Top schools won't punish pupils on strike'. *Sydney Morning Herald*, 19 September.

Clay, Kevin L. and Turner, David C. (2021) '"Maybe you should try it this way instead": Youth activism amid managerialist subterfuge'. *American Educational Research Journal*, 58(2): 386–419.

Clough, Patricia Ticineto and Halley, J., eds (2010) *The Affective Turn: Theorizing the Social*. Durham, NC: Duke University Press.

Cole, David R. (2013) 'Affective literacies: Deleuze, discipline and power', in Inna Semetsky and Diana Masny (eds), *Deleuze and Education*. Edinburgh: Edinburgh University Press, pp. 94–111.

Cole, David R. (2019) 'Analysing the matter flows in schools using Deleuze's method'. *Studies in Philosophy and Education*, 38(3): 229–40.

Cole, David R. and Bradley, Joff P. N., eds (2018a) *Principles of Transversality in Globalization and Education*. Dordrecht: Springer.

Cole, David R. and Bradley, Joff P. N. (2018b) 'Principles of transversality in globalisation and education', in David R. Cole and Joff P. N Bradley (eds), *Principles of Transversality in Globalization and Education*. Dordrecht: Springer, pp. 1–15.

Colebrook, Claire (2010) 'Woolf, Virginia', in Adrian Parr (ed.), *The Deleuze Dictionary*, rev. edn. Edinburgh: Edinburgh University Press, pp. 308–9.

Colebrook, Claire (2012) 'Power', in Adrian Parr (ed.), *The Deleuze Dictionary*, rev. edn. Edinburgh: Edinburgh University Press, pp. 215–16.

Colebrook, Claire (2020) 'Extinction, deterritorialisation and end times: Peak Deleuze'. *Deleuze and Guattari Studies*, 14(3): 327–48.

Coleman, Rebecca and Ringrose, Jessica (2013) 'Introduction: Deleuze and research methodologies', in Rebecca Coleman and Jessica Ringrose (eds), *Deleuze and Research Methodologies*. Edinburgh: Edinburgh University Press, pp. 1–22.

Coll, Leanne, Ollis, Deb and O'Keefe, Briony (2019) 'Rebel becomings: Queer(y)ing school spaces with young people', in Jón I. Kjaran and Helen Sauntson (eds), *Schools as Queer Transformative Spaces: Global Narratives on Sexualities and Genders*. London: Routledge, pp. 54–69.

Collins, Antonette and Coleman, Oscar (2019) 'Climate change protest attendance encouraged by some Sydney schools'. *ABC News*, 15 March.

Collins, Patricia Hill (2000) *Black Feminist Thought: Knowledge, Consciousness and the Politics of Empowerment*. London: Routledge.

Collins, Patricia Hill and Bilge, Sirma (2016) *Intersectionality*. Cambridge: Polity Press.

Common Worlds Research Collective (2020) 'Learning to Become *With* the World: Education for Future Survival'. *UNESCO Education Research and Foresight Working Papers*, 28. Available at: https://unesdoc.unesco.org/ark:/48223/pf0000374032 (accessed 25 August 2022).

Commonwealth of Australia (2015) *Preventing Violent Extremism and Radicalisation in Australia*. Available at: https://www.livingsafetogether.gov.au/Documents/preventing-violent-extremism-and-radicalisation-in-australia.PDF (accessed 25 August 2022).

Commonwealth of Australia (2020a) 'Lessons to be learned in relation to the Australian bushfire season 2019–20: Introduction and overview of the 2019–20 bushfire season'. Available at: https://www.aph.gov.au/Parliamentary_Business/Committees/Senate/Finance_and_Public_Administration/Bushfirerecovery/Interim_Report/section?id=committees%2Freportsen%2F024518%2F73522#footnote8target (accessed 25 August 2022).

Commonwealth of Australia (2020b) *Living Safe Together*. Available at: https://www.livingsafetogether.gov.au/ (accessed 25 August 2022).

Conio, Andrew (2015a) 'Introduction', in Andrew Conio (ed.), *Occupy: A People Yet to Come*. London: Open Humanities Press, pp. 22–66.

Conio, Andrew, ed. (2015b) *Occupy: A People Yet to Come*. London: Open Humanities Press.

Cook, Henrietta (2017) Students to help hire principals under school council overhaul. *The Age*, 11 October. Available at: https://www.theage.com.au/national/victoria/students-to-help-hire-principals-under-school-council-overhaul-20171011-gyyrx4.html (accessed 25 August 2022).

Cook-Sather, Alison (2006) 'Sound, presence, and power: "Student voice" in educational research and reform'. *Curriculum Inquiry*, 36(4): 360–90.

Cook-Sather, Alison (2007) 'Resisting the impositional potential of student voice work: Lessons from liberatory educational research from poststructuralist feminist critiques of critical pedagogy'. *Discourse: Studies in the Cultural Politics of Education*, 28(3): 389–403.

Cook-Sather, Alison (2020) 'Student voice across contexts: Fostering student agency in today's schools'. *Theory into Practice*, 59(2): 182–91.

Cooke, Bill and Kothari, Uma, eds (2001) *Participation: The New Tyranny?* London: Zed Books.

Coole, Diana and Frost, Samantha, eds (2010) *New Materialisms: Ontology, Agency, and Politics*. Durham, NC: Duke University Press.

Coppock, Vicki (2014) '"Can you spot a terrorist in your classroom?" Problematising the recruitment of schools to the "War on Terror" in the United Kingdom'. *Global Studies of Childhood*, 4(2): 115–25.

Council of Australian Governments (COAG) (2012) *National Partnership Agreement on Low Socioeconomic Status School Communities*. Available at: https://www.federalfinancialrelations.gov.au/content/npa/education/national-partnership/past/Low_SES_NP.pdf (accessed 15 July 2021).

Cox, Sue and Robinson-Pant, Anna (2006) 'Enhancing participation in primary school and class councils through visual communication'. *Cambridge Journal of Education*, 36(4): 515–32.

## Bibliography

Cox, Sue and Robinson-Pant, Anna (2008) 'Power, participation and decision making in the primary classroom: Children as action researchers'. *Educational Action Research*, 16(4): 457–68.

Crenshaw, Kimberlé (1991) 'Mapping the margins: Intersectionality, identity politics and violence against women of color'. *Stanford Law Review*, 43(6): 1241–99.

Cudworth, Erika and Hobden, Stephen (2015) 'Liberation for straw dogs? Old materialism, new materialism, and the challenge of an emancipatory posthumanism'. *Globalizations*, 12(1): 134–48.

da Silva, Denise Ferreira (2015) 'Before *Man*: Sylvia Wynter's rewriting of the modern episteme', in Katherine McKittrick (ed.), *Sylvia Wynter: On Being Human as Praxis*. Durham, NC: Duke University Press, pp. 90–105.

Davies, Bronwyn (2014) 'Reading anger in early childhood intra-actions: A diffractive analysis'. *Qualitative Inquiry*, 20(6): 734–41.

Davies, Bronwyn and Gannon, Susanne, eds (2009) *Pedagogical Encounters*. New York: Peter Lang.

Davis, C. B. (1998) 'Reading the ventriloquist's lips: The performance genre behind the metaphor'. *The Drama Review*, 42(4): 133–56.

de Freitas, Elizabeth (2012) 'The classroom as rhizome: New strategies for diagramming knotted interactions'. *Qualitative Inquiry*, 18(7): 557–70.

de Freitas, Elizabeth (2017) 'Karen Barad's quantum ontology and posthuman ethics: Rethinking the concept of relationality'. *Qualitative Inquiry*, 23(9): 741–8.

de Freitas, Elizabeth and Curinga, Matthew X. (2015) 'New materialist approaches to the study of language and identity: Assembling the posthuman subject'. *Curriculum Inquiry*, 45(3): 249–65.

de Moor, Joost, Uba, Katrin, Wahlström, Mattias, Wennerhag, Magnus and De Vydt, Michiel (2020) *Protest for a Future II: Composition, Mobilization and Motives of the Participants in Fridays For Future Climate Protests on 20–27 September, 2019, in 19 Cities Around the World*. Available at: https://osf.io/3hcxs/download (accessed 25 August 2022).

Dean, Mitchell and Zamora, Daniel (2021) 'Today, the self is the battlefield of politics. Blame Michel Foucault'. *The Guardian*, 15 June. Available at: https://www.theguardian.com/commentisfree/2021/jun/15/michel-foucault-self-individual-politics (accessed 25 August 2022).

Deleuze, Gilles (1953/1991) *Empiricism and Subjectivity*, trans. Constantin V. Boundas. New York: Columbia University Press.

Deleuze, Gilles (1962/1983) *Nietzsche and Philosophy*, trans. Hugh Tomlinson. New York: Columbia University Press.

Deleuze, Gilles (1964/2008) *Proust and Signs*, trans. Richard Howard. London: Continuum.

Deleuze, Gilles (1968/1994) *Difference and Repetition*, trans. Paul Patton. New York: Columbia University Press.

Deleuze, Gilles (1969/2013) *The Logic of Sense*, trans. Mark Lester and Charles Stivale. London: Bloomsbury.
Deleuze, Gilles (1988) *Spinoza: Practical Philosophy*, trans. Robert Hurley. San Francisco: City Lights Books.
Deleuze, Gilles (1992a) *Expressionism in Philosophy: Spinoza*. trans. Martin Joughin. New York: Zone Books.
Deleuze, Gilles (1992b) 'Postscript on the societies of control'. *October*, 59: 3–7.
Deleuze, Gilles (1994) 'Desire and pleasure'. *Magazine littéraire* (trans. McMahon, M.). 59–65.
Deleuze, Gilles (1995) *Negotiations: 1972–1990*, trans. Martin Joughin. New York: Columbia University Press.
Deleuze, Gilles (1997) *Essays Critical and Clinical*, trans. Daniel W. Smith and Michael A. Greco. Minneapolis: University of Minnesota Press.
Deleuze, Gilles (1999/1986) *Foucault*, trans. Seán Hand. London: Continuum.
Deleuze, Gilles (2004) *Desert Islands and Other Texts: 1953–1974, Gilles Deleuze*, trans. Michael Taormina. Los Angeles: Semiotext(e).
Deleuze, Gilles (2007) *Two Regimes of Madness: Texts and Interviews 1975–1995*, trans. Ames Hodges and Michael Taormina. New York: Semiotext(e).
Deleuze, Gilles and Foucault, Michel (1977) 'Intellectuals and power', in Donald Bouchard (ed.), *Language, Counter-Memory, Practice*. Ithaca, NY: Cornell University Press, pp. 205–17.
Deleuze, Gilles and Guattari, Félix (1980/1987) *A Thousand Plateaus: Capitalism and Schizophrenia*, trans. Brian Massumi. Minneapolis: University of Minnesota Press.
Deleuze, Gilles and Guattari, Félix (1983) *Anti-Oedipus: Capitalism and Schizophrenia*, trans. Robert Hurley, Mark Seem and Helen R. Lane. Minnesota: University of Minnesota Press.
Deleuze, Gilles and Guattari, Félix (1994/2009) *What is Philosophy?*, trans. Hugh Tomlinson and Graham Burchill. London: Verso.
Deleuze, Gilles and Guattari, Félix (2006) *Kafka: Toward a Minor Literature*, trans. Dana Polan. Minneapolis: University of Minnesota Press.
Deleuze, Gilles and Parnet, Claire (2006/1977) *Dialogues II*, trans. Hugh Tomlinson and Barbara Habberjam. London: Continuum.
Dernikos, Bessie P., Ferguson, Daniel E. and Siegel, Marjorie (2019) 'The possibilities for "humanizing" posthumanist inquiries: An intra-active conversation'. *Cultural Studies ↔ Critical Methodologies*, 20(5): 434–47.
Dernikos, Bessie P., Lesko, Nancy, McCall, Stephanie D. and Niccolini, Alyssa D. (2020) 'Feeling education', in Bessie P. Dernikos, Nancy Lesko, Stephanie D. McCall and Alyssa D. Niccolini (eds), *Mapping the Affective Turn in Education: Theory, Research, and Pedagogies*. New York: Routledge, pp. 3–27.

# Bibliography

Derrida, Jacques (1967/1973), *Speech and Phenomena and Other Essays on Husserl's Theory of Signs*, trans. David B. Allison. Evanston, IL: Northwestern University Press.

Dewey, John (1937) 'Democracy and educational administration', in Jo A. Boydston (ed.), *John Dewey: The Later Works, 1925–1953*. Carbondale, IL: South Illinois University Press, pp. 217–25.

Dolphijn, Rick and van der Tuin, Iris (2012) *New Materialism: Interviews & Cartographies*. Ann Arbor, MI: Open Humanities Press.

Dosse, Francois (2007/2010) *Gilles Deleuze & Félix Guattari: Intersecting lives*, trans. Deborah Glassman. New York: Columbia University Press.

Dunlop, Lynda, Atkinson, Lucy, Stubbs, Joshua E. and Turkenburg-van Diepen, Maria (2021) 'The role of schools and teachers in nurturing and responding to climate crisis activism'. *Children's Geographies*, 19(3): 291–9. DOI: 10.1080/14733285.2020.1828827.

Ellsworth, Elizabeth (1989) 'Why doesn't this feel empowering? Working through the repressive myths of critical pedagogy'. *Harvard Educational Review*, 59(3): 297–324.

Evans, Brad (2013) 'Fascism and the bio-political', in Brad Evans and Julian Reid (eds), *Deleuze & Fascism: Security: War: Aesthetics*, London: Routledge, pp. 42–63.

Evelyn, Kenya (2020) '"Like I wasn't there": Climate activist Vanessa Nakate on being erased from a movement'. *The Guardian*, 29 January.

Fielding, Michael (1999a) 'Radical collegiality: Affirming teaching as an inclusive professional practice'. *Australian Educational Researcher*, 26(2): 1–34.

Fielding, Michael (1999b) 'Target setting, policy pathology and student perspectives: Learning to labour in new times'. *Cambridge Journal of Education*, 29(2): 277–87.

Fielding, Michael (2001) 'Students as radical agents of change'. *Journal of Educational Change*, 2: 123–41.

Fielding, Michael (2004) 'Transformative approaches to student voice: Theoretical underpinnings, recalcitrant realities'. *British Educational Research Journal*, 30(2): 295–311.

Fielding, Michael (2005) 'Alex Bloom, pioneer of radical state education'. *Forum*, 47(2): 119–34.

Fielding, Michael (2006) 'Leadership, radical student engagement and the necessity of person-centred education'. *International Journal of Leadership in Education*, 9(4): 299–313.

Fielding, Michael (2007) 'Beyond "voice": New roles, relations and contexts in researching with young people'. *Discourse: Studies in the Cultural Politics of Education*, 28(3): 301–10.

Fielding, Michael (2011) 'Student voice and the possibility of radical democratic education: Re-narrating forgotten histories, developing alternative futures', in Gerry Czerniawski and Warren Kidd (eds), *The Student Voice*

*Handbook: Bridging the Academic/Practitioner Divide*. Bingley: Emerald Publishing, pp. 3–17.

Fielding, Michael and Bragg, Sara (2003) *Students as Researchers: Making a Difference*. London: Pearson.

Fielding, Michael and Moss, Peter (2011) *Radical Education and the Common School: A Democratic Alternative*. London: Routledge.

Fine, Michelle (1991) *Framing Dropouts: Notes on the Politics of an Urban Public High School*. Albany: State University of New York Press.

Fine, Michelle and Torre, María Elena (2004) 'Re-membering exclusions: Participatory action research in public institutions'. *Qualitative Research in Psychology*, 1(1): 15–37.

Fine, Michelle, Torre, Maria Elena, Burns, April and Payne, Yasser A. (2007) 'Youth research/participatory methods for reform', in D. Thiessen and A. Cook-Sather (eds), *International Handbook of Student Experience in Elementary and Secondary School*. Dordrecht: Springer, pp. 805–29.

Finefter-Rosenbluh, Ilana, Ryan, Tracii and Barnes, Melissa (2021) 'The impact of student perception surveys on teachers' practice: Teacher resistance and struggle in student voice-based assessment initiatives of effective teaching'. *Teaching and Teacher Education*, 106: 103436.

Finneran, Rachel, Mayes, Eve and Black, Rosalyn (2021) 'Pride and privilege: The affective dissonance of student voice'. *Pedagogy, Culture & Society*. DOI: 10.1080/14681366.2021.1876158. 1–16.

Flutter, Julia (2007) 'Teacher development and pupil voice'. *The Curriculum Journal*, 18(3): 343–54.

Fogarty, William, Bulloch, Hannah, McDonnell, Siobhan and Davis, Michael (2018) *Deficit Discourse and Indigenous Health: How Narrative Framings of Aboriginal and Torres Strait Islander People are Reproduced in Policy*. Melbourne: The Lowitja Institute.

Ford, Alison and Norgaard, Kari M. (2020) 'Whose everyday climate cultures? Environmental subjectivities and invisibility in climate change discourse'. *Climatic Change*, 163(1): 43–62. DOI: 10.1007/s10584-019-02632-1.

Foucault, Michel (1972) *The Archaeology of Knowledge and the Discourse on Language*, trans A.M. Sheridan Smith. New York: Pantheon.

Foucault, Michel (1976/1990) *The History of Sexuality, Vol. 1: The Will to Knowledge*, trans. Robert Hurley. London: Penguin.

Foucault, Michel (1977) Preface. In Gilles Deleuze and Félix Guattari, *Anti-Oedipus*, trans. Robert Hurley, Mark Seem and Helen R. Lane. New York: Penguin, pp. xi–xiv.

Foucault, Michel (1980) *Power/Knowledge: Selected Interviews and Other Writings by Michel Foucault 1972–1977*, trans. Colin Gordon, Leo Marshall, John Mapham and Kate Soper. New York: Pantheon.

Foucault, Michel (1983) 'On the genealogy of ethics: An overview of work in progress', in Hubert L. Dreyfus and Paul Rabinow (eds), *Michel Foucault: Beyond Structuralism and Hermeneutics*. Chicago: University of Chicago Press, pp. 229–52.

Foucault, Michel (1991) *Discipline and Punish: The Birth of the Prison*, trans. Alan Sheridan. London: Penguin.

Foucault, Michel (1992) *The Use of Pleasure: The History of Sexuality, Vol. 2*, trans. Robert Hurley. London: Penguin.

Foucault, Michel (2007) *Security, Territory, Population: Lectures at the Collège de France, 1978–79*, trans. Graham Burchell. New York: Palgrave Macmillan.

Foucault, Michel (2010) *The Birth of Biopolitics. Lectures at the Collège de France 1978–1979*, trans. Graham Burchell. Basingstoke: Palgrave Macmillan.

Francis, Becky, Taylor, Becky and Tereshchenko, Antonina (2020) *Reassessing 'Ability' Grouping: Improving Practice for Equity and Attainment*. Abingdon: Routledge.

Freire, Paolo (1970) *Pedagogy of the Oppressed*, trans. Myra B. Ramos. New York: Herder & Herder.

Freire, Paolo (1996) 'Reading the world and reading the word: An interview with Paolo Freire', in William Hare and John P. Portelli (eds), *Philosophy of Education: Introductory Readings*. Calgary: Detselig, pp. 145–52.

Freire, Paolo and Macedo, Donaldo (1987) *Literacy: Reading the World and the World*. Westport, CT: Bergin & Garvey.

Freud, Sigmund (1925/1968) 'Preface to Aichhorn's "Wayward Youth"', in James Strachey, Anna Freud, Alix Strachey and Alan Tyson (eds), *The Standard Edition of the Complete Psychological Works of Sigmund Freud*. London: Hogarth Press and Institute for Psychoanalysis, pp. 273–5.

Furlong, John (1991) 'Disaffected pupils: Reconstructing the sociological perspective'. *British Journal of Sociology of Education*, 12(3): 293–307.

Fuss, Diana (1990) *Essentially Speaking: Feminism, Nature and Difference*. London: Routledge.

Genosko, Gary (2009) *Félix Guattari: A Critical Introduction*. Northhampton: Pluto Press.

Gerrard, Jessica (2014) *Radical Childhoods: Schooling and the Struggle for Social Change*, Manchester: Manchester University Press.

Gerrard, Jessica and Savage, Glenn C. (2021) 'The governing parent-citizen: Dividing and valorising parent labour through school governance'. *Journal of Education Policy*. DOI: 10.1080/02680939.2021.1877357. 1–19.

Gerrard, Jessica, Rudolph, Sophie and Sriprakash, Arathi (2016) 'The politics of post-qualitative inquiry: History and power'. *Qualitative Inquiry*. DOI: 10.1177/1077800416672694. 1077800416672694.

Gillett-Swan, Jenna K. and Sargeant, Jonathon (2019) 'Perils of perspective: Identifying adult confidence in the child's capacity, autonomy, power and agency (CAPA) in readiness for voice-inclusive practice'. *Journal of Educational Change*, 20(3): 399–421.

Gillies, Val (2011) 'Social and emotional pedagogies: Critiquing the new orthodoxy of emotion in classroom behaviour management'. *British Journal of Sociology of Education*, 32(2): 185–202.

Giroux, Henry (1983) *Theory and Resistance: A Pedagogy for the Opposition*. South Hadley, MA: Bergin & Garvey.

Glissant, Édouard (1990/1997) *Poetics of Relation*, trans. Betsy Wing. Ann Arbor: University of Michigan Press.

Gómez-Barris, Macarena (2017) *The Extractive Zone: Social Ecologies and Decolonial Perspectives*. Durham, NC: Duke University Press.

Goodchild, Philip (1996) *Deleuze and Guattari: An Introduction to the Politics of Desire*. Thousand Oaks, CA: Sage.

Goodley, Dan (2007) 'Towards socially just pedagogies: Deleuzoguattarian critical disability studies'. *International Journal of Inclusive Education*, 11(3): 317–34.

Gore, Jennifer M. (1993) *The Struggle for Pedagogies: Critical and Feminist Discourses as Regimes of Truth*. New York: Routledge.

Gough, Annette and Gough, Noel (2017) 'Beyond cyborg subjectivities: Becoming-posthumanist educational researchers'. *Educational Philosophy and Theory*, 49(11): 1112–24.

Gough, Noel (2004) 'RhizomANTically Becoming-Cyborg: Performing posthuman pedagogies'. *Educational Philosophy and Theory*, 36(3): 253–65.

Graham, Anne, Powell, Mary Ann and Truscott, Julia (2016) 'Facilitating student well-being: Relationships do matter'. *Educational Research*, 58(4): 366–83.

Graham, Anne, Anderson, Donnah, Truscott, Julia, Simmons, Catharine, Thomas, Nigel Patrick, Cashmore, Judy and Bessell, Sharon (2022) 'Exploring the associations between student participation, wellbeing and recognition at school'. *Cambridge Journal of Education*. DOI: 10.1080/0305764X.2022.2031886. 1–20.

Graham, Archie (2012) 'Revisiting school ethos: The student voice'. *School Leadership & Management*, 32(4): 34–54.

Gregg, Melissa and Seigworth, Gregory J., eds (2010) *The Affect Theory Reader*. Durham, NC: Duke University Press.

Gregory, Helen (2019) 'Students ask adults to vote for the climate'. *Newcastle Herald*, 4 May.

Grisham, Therese (1991) 'Linguistics as an indiscipline: Deleuze and Guattari's pragmatics'. *SubStance*, 20(3): 36–54.

Groundwater-Smith, Susan and Mockler, Susan (2019) 'Student voice work as an educative practice', in Ilene R. Berson, Michael J. Berson and Colette Gray (eds), *Participatory Methodologies to Elevate Children's Voice and Agency*. Charlotte, NC: Information Age Publishing, pp. 25–46.

Groundwater-Smith, Susan, Mayes, Eve and Arya-Pinatyh, Kadek (2014)

## Bibliography

'A bridge over troubling waters in education: The complexity of a students as co-researchers project'. *Curriculum Matters*, 10: 213–31.

Guattari, Félix (1985/1996) 'Institutional schizo-analysis', in Sylvere Lotringer (ed.), *Soft Subversions: Texts and Interviews 1977–1985*, trans. Chet Weiner and Emily Wittman. New York: Semiotext(e), pp. 268–77.

Guattari, Félix (1989/2013) *Schizoanalytic Cartographies*, trans. Andrew Goffey. London: Bloomsbury.

Guattari, Félix (1995) *Chaosmosis: An Ethico-Aesthetic Paradigm*, trans. Paul Bains and Julian Pefanis. Bloomington: Indiana University Press.

Guattari, Félix (2000) *The Three Ecologies*, trans. Ian Pindar and Paul Sutton. London: Athlone Press.

Guattari, Félix (2011) *Lignes de Fuite: Pour un Autre Mode de Possible*. La Tour d'Aigues, France: Aube.

Guattari, Félix (2015) *Psychoanalysis and Transversality: Texts and Interviews 1955–1971*, trans. Ames Hodges. South Pasadena, CA: Semiotext(e).

Guattari, Félix and Rolnik, Suely (1982/2008) *Molecular Revolution in Brazil*, trans. Karel Clapshow and Brian Holmes. Los Angeles: Semiotext(e).

Haberman, M. (1991/2010) 'The pedagogy of poverty versus good teaching'. *Phi Delta Kappan*, 92(2): 81–7.

Habermas, Jürgen (1984) *Theory of Communicative Action*. Boston, MA: Beacon Press.

Habtom, Sefanit and Scribe, Megan (2020) *To Breathe Together: Co-Conspirators For Decolonial Futures*. Yellowhead Institute. Available at: https://yellowheadinstitute.org/2020/06/02/to-breathe-together/ (accessed 25 August 2022).

Hackett, Abigail, MacLure, Maggie and McMahon, Sarah (2021) 'Reconceptualising early language development: Matter, sensation and the more-than-human'. *Discourse: Studies in the Cultural Politics of Education*, 42(6): 913–29.

Hadfield, Mark and Haw, Kaye (2001) '"Voice", young people and action research'. *Educational Action Research*, 9(3): 485–99.

Hall, G. Stanley (1904) *Adolescence*. Englewood Cliffs, NJ: Prentice Hall.

Hall, Valerie (2017) 'A tale of two narratives: Student voice – what lies before us?' *Oxford Review of Education*, 43(2): 180–93.

Haraway, Donna (1988) 'Situated knowledges: The science question in feminism and the privilege of partial perspective'. *Feminist Studies*, 14(3): 575–99.

Haraway, Donna (1991) *Simians, Cyborgs, and Women: The Reinvention of Nature*. New York: Routledge.

Haraway, Donna (2016) *Staying with the Trouble*. Durham, NC: Duke University Press.

Harding, Sandra (1987) 'Introduction: Is there a feminist method?', in

S. Harding (ed.), *Feminism and Methodology*. Bloomington: Indiana University Press, pp. 1–14.

Harding, Sandra (2004) 'Introduction: Standpoint theory as a site of political, philosophic, and scientific debate', in S. Harding (ed.), *The Feminist Standpoint Theory Reader: Intellectual and Political Controversies*. London: Routledge, pp. 1–20.

Hardt, Michael and Negri, Antonio (2000) *Empire*. Cambridge, MA: Harvard University Press.

Hardt, Michael and Negri, Antonio (2004) *Multitude: War and Democracy in the Age of Empire*. Cambridge, MA: Harvard University Press.

Hardt, Michael and Negri, Antonio (2009) *Commonwealth*. Cambridge, MA: Harvard University Press.

Harney, Stefano and Moten, Fred (2013) *The Undercommons: Fugitive Planning and Black Study*. Wivenhoe, NY: Minor Compositions.

Hartsock, Nancy C. M. (1983/2016) 'The feminist standpoint: Developing the ground for a specifically feminist historical materialism', in Carole R. McCann and Seung-Kyung Kim (eds), *Feminist Theory Reader: Local and Global Perspectives*, 4th edn. London: Routledge, pp. 368–83.

Harvey, David (2005) *A Brief History of Neoliberalism*. Oxford: Oxford University Press.

Harwood, Valerie (2006) *Diagnosing Disorderly Children: A Critique of Behaviour Disorder Discourses*. Oxford: Routledge.

Harwood, Valerie and Allan, Julie (2014) *Psychopathology at School: Theorizing Mental Disorders in Education*. New York: Routledge.

Hazelhurst Regional Gallery and Arts Centre (2013a) *Art Magic with Hiromi Tango*. Available at: https://www.youtube.com/watch?v=Qsf8yC_SEug (accessed 25 August 2022).

Hazelhurst Regional Gallery and Arts Centre (2013b) Art Magic Education Package.

Hein, Serge F. (2016) 'The new materialism in qualitative inquiry: How compatible are the philosophies of Barad and Deleuze?' *Cultural Studies ↔ Critical Methodologies*, 16(2): 132–40. DOI: 10.1177/1532708616634732.

Hemming, Steve, Rigney, Daryle, Hartman, Tim, Rigney, Clyde Jnr, Rigney, Grant and Sutherland, Lachlan (2015) 'Ngarrindjeri Speaking as Country: Innovations in Indigenous Engagement in Water'. 18th International River Symposium. Brisbane.

Hemming, Steve, Rigney, Daryle, Bignall, Simone, Berg, Shaun and Rigney, Grant (2019) 'Indigenous nation building for environmental futures: Murrundi flows through Ngarrindjeri country'. *Australasian Journal of Environmental Management*, 26(3): 216–35.

Her Majesty's Government (2011) *Prevent Strategy*. Available at: https://www.gov.uk/government/uploads/system/uploads/attachment_data/file/97976/prevent-strategy-review.pdf (accessed 25 August 2022).

# Bibliography

Her Majesty's Government (2012) *Channel: Protecting vulnerable young people from being drawn into terrorism*. Available at: file:///C:/Users/mayes/Downloads/1626411625_Ingleby_Manor_School_Document.pdf (accessed 16 July 2021).

Hickey-Moody, Anna (2007a) 'Intellectual disability, sensation and thinking through affect', in Anna Hickey-Moody and Peta Malins (eds), *Deleuzian Encounters: Studies in Contemporary Social Issues*. Basingstoke: Palgrave Macmillan, pp. 79–98.

Hickey-Moody, Anna (2007b) *Unimaginable Bodies: Intellectual Disability, Performance and Becomings*. Rotterdam: Sense Publishers.

Hickey-Moody, Anna, Knight, Linda and Florence, Eloise (2021) *Childhood, Citizenship, and the Anthropocene*. London and New York: Rowman & Littlefield.

Higgins, Isabella (2021) 'The destruction of a mighty fiddleback in Victoria sparks a common conundrum for Aboriginal Australians'. *ABC News*, 1 November.

Ho, Christina (2015) '"People like us": School choice, multiculturalism and segregation in Sydney'. *Australian Review of Public Affairs*. Available at: http://www.australianreview.net/digest/2015/08/ho.html (accessed 25 August 2022).

Hogarth, Melitta (2018) 'Talkin' bout a revolution: The call for transformation and reform in Indigenous education'. *The Australian Educational Researcher*, 45(5): 663–74.

Holdsworth, Roger (2000) 'What is this about a "whole-school approach"?', in Roger Holdsworth (ed.), *Discovering Democracy in Action: Learning from School Practice*. Melbourne: Australian Youth Research Centre and Commonwealth of Australia.

Holland, Eugene W. (2003) 'Representation and misrepresentation in postcolonial literature and theory'. *Research in African Literatures*, 34(1): 159–73.

Holmberg, Arita and Alvinius, Aida (2019) 'Children's protest in relation to the climate emergency: A qualitative study on a new form of resistance promoting political and social change'. *Childhood*, 27(1): 78–92.

Honan, Eileen (2007) 'Writing a rhizome: An (im)plausible methodology'. *International Journal of Qualitative Studies in Education*, 20(5): 531–46.

Honneth, Axel and Joas, J., eds (1991) *Communicative Action: Essays on Jürgen Habermas's The Theory of Communicative Action*. Cambridge: Polity Press.

hooks, bell (1990) *Yearning: Race, Gender, and Cultural Politics*. Boston, MA: South End Press.

Howell, William G., ed. (2005) *Besieged: School Boards and the Future of Education Politics*. Washington, DC: Brookings Institution Press.

Hynes, Maria (2013) 'Reconceptualizing resistance: Sociology and the affective dimension of resistance'. *British Journal of Sociology*, 64(4): 559–77.

Ibrahim, Awad (2014) *The Rhizome of Blackness: A Critical Ethnography of Hip-Hop Culture, Language, Identity and the Politics of Becoming.* New York: Peter Lang.
Ibrahim, Awad (2015) 'Body without organs: Notes on Deleuze & Guattari, critical race theory and the socius of anti-racism'. *Journal of Multilingual and Multicultural Development,* 36(1): 13–26.
Irigaray, Luce and Marder, Michael (2016) *Through Vegetal Being: Two Philosophical Perspectives.* New York: Columbia University Press.
Issa, Antoun (2021) 'Demographic clones: Time to shift power away from white privileged men in Australian politics'. *The Guardian,* 18 March.
Jackson, Alecia Youngblood (2003) 'Rhizovocality'. *Qualitative Studies in Education,* 16(5): 693–710.
Jackson, Alecia Youngblood and Mazzei, Lisa A., eds (2009) *Voice in Qualitative Inquiry: Challenging Conventional, Interpretive and Critical Conceptions in Qualitative Research.* London: Routledge.
Jackson, Alecia Youngblood and Mazzei, Lisa A. (2012) *Thinking with Theory in Qualitative Research.* Abingdon: Routledge.
Jackson, Alecia Youngblood and Mazzei, Lisa A. (2013) 'Plugging one text into another: Thinking with theory in qualitative research'. *Qualitative Inquiry,* 19(4): 261–71.
Jackson, Zakiyyah Iman (2015) 'Outer worlds: The persistence of race in movement "beyond the human"'. *GLQ: A Journal of Lesbian and Gay Studies,* 21(2–3): 215–18.
Jafry, Tahseen, Mikulewicz, Michael and Helwig, Karin (2018) 'Introduction: Justice in the era of climate change', in Tahseen Jafry (ed.), *Routledge Handbook of Climate Justice.* London: Routledge, pp. 1–9.
Jaggar, Alison (1989) 'Love and knowledge: Emotion in feminist epistemology', in Alison Jaggar and Susan Bordo (eds), *Gender/Body/Knowledge.* New Brunswick: Rutgers University Press.
James, Allison and Prout, Alan (1990) *Constructing and Reconstructing Childhood.* Basingstoke: Falmer Press.
Johnston, Olivia, Wildy, Helen and Shand, Jennifer (2021) 'Projecting student voice by constructing grounded theory'. *The Australian Educational Researcher,* 48(3): 543–64.
Jones, Charlotte A. and Davison, Aidan (2021) 'Disempowering emotions: The role of educational experiences in social responses to climate change'. *Geoforum,* 118: 190–200.
Kafka, Franz (1915/1992) *Metamorphosis and Other Stories,* trans. Malcolm Pasley. London: Penguin.
Kahne, Joseph, Bowyer, Benjamin, Marshall, Jessica and Hodgin, Erica (2022) 'Is responsiveness to student voice related to academic outcomes? Strengthening the rationale for student voice in school reform'. *American Journal of Education.* DOI: 10.1086/719121.
Kane, Ruth G. and Chimwayange, Chris (2013) 'Teacher action research

and student voice: Making sense of learning in secondary school'. *Action Research*, 12(1): 52–77.
Keddie, Amanda (2015) 'Student voice and teacher accountability: Possibilities and problematics'. *Pedagogy, Culture & Society*, 23(2): 225–44.
Keddie, Amanda (2021) 'The difficulties of "action" in Youth Participatory Action Research: Schoolifying YPAR in two elite settings'. *Discourse: Studies in the Cultural Politics of Education*, 42(3): 381–93.
Keeling, Kara (2019) *Queer Times, Black Futures*. New York: NYU Press.
King, Tiffany Lethabo (2017) 'Humans involved: Lurking in the lines of posthumanist flight'. *Critical Ethnic Studies*, 3(1): 162–85.
Kleist, Heinrich Von (1972) 'On the marionette theatre'. *The Drama Review*, 16(3): 22–6.
Knight, Linda (2009) 'Desire and rhizome: Affective literacies in early childhood', in Diana Masny and David R. Cole (eds), *Multiple Literacies Theory: A Deleuzian Perspective*. Rotterdam: Sense Publishers, pp. 51–62.
Knight, Linda (2016) 'Playgrounds as sites of radical encounters: Mapping material, spatial, and pedagogical collisions', in Nathan Snaza, Debbie Sonu, Sarah E. Truman and Zofia Zaliwska (eds), *Pedagogical Matters: New Materialisms and Curriculum Studies*. New York: Peter Lang, pp. 13–28.
Kraftl, Peter (2013) 'Beyond "voice", beyond "agency", beyond "politics"? Hybrid childhoods and some critical reflections on children's emotional geographies'. *Emotion, Space and Society*, 9: 13–23.
Kraftl, Peter (2020) *After Childhood: Re-thinking Environment, Materiality and Media in Children's Lives*. London: Routledge.
Kundnani, Arun (2012) 'Radicalisation: The journey of a concept'. *Race & Class*, 54(2): 3–25.
Kuntz, Aaron M. (2021) 'Materially just: Virtuous methodology in fascist times'. *International Review of Qualitative Research*. DOI: 10.1177/19408447211012651. 19408447211012651.
Kuntz, Aaron M. and Presnall, Marni M. (2012) 'Wandering the tactical: From interview to intraview'. *Qualitative Inquiry*, 18(9): 732–44.
Land, Clare (2015) *Decolonizing Solidarity: Dilemmas and Directions for Supporters of Indigenous Struggles*. London: Zed Books.
Lasczik, Alexandra and Cutter-Mackenzie-Knowles, Amy (2022) 'Who can speak for the Earth? Working the socioecological touchstones of the Anthropocene, the posthuman and common worlds through the creative milieux of speculative fiction', in Alexandra Lasczik and Amy Cutter-Mackenzie-Knowles (eds), *Arts-Based Thought Experiments for a Posthuman Earth: A Touchstones Companion*. Leiden: Brill, pp. 6–16.
Lather, Patti (1986) 'Issues of validity in openly ideological research: Between a rock and a soft place'. *Interchange*, 17(4): 63–84.

Latour, Bruno (2005) *Reassembling the Social: An Introduction to Actor-Network Theory*. Oxford: Oxford University Press.
Laville, Sandra and Watts, Jonathan (2019) 'Across the globe, millions join biggest climate protest ever'. *The Guardian*, 21 September.
Leafgren, Sheri L. (2009) *Reuben's Fall: A Rhizomatic Analysis of Disobedience in Kindergarten*. Walnut Creek, CA: Left Coast Press.
Leboiron, Max (2021) *Pollution is Colonialism*. London: Duke University Press.
Lecercle, Jean-Jacques (2002) *Deleuze and Language*. Basingstoke: Palgrave Macmillan.
Lenz Taguchi, Hillevi and Palmer, Anna (2014) 'Reading a Deleuzio-Guattarian cartography of young girls' "school-related" ill-/well-being'. *Qualitative Inquiry*, 20(6): 764–71.
Lesko, Nancy (2012) *Act Your Age! A Cultural Construction of Adolescence*. New York: Routledge.
Lévi-Strauss, Claude (1973/2009) *Structural Anthropology*, trans. Claire Jacobson and Brooke Grundfest Schoepf. New York: Basic Books.
Lewis, Abigail (2019) *The Way In: Representation in the Australian Parliament*. Report. Available at: https://percapita.org.au/wp-content/uploads/2019/01/The-Way-In-Representation-in-the-Australian-Parliament-2.pdf (accessed 26 August 2022).
Lewis, Steven and Holloway, Jessica (2019) 'Datafying the teaching "profession": Remaking the professional teacher in the image of data'. *Cambridge Journal of Education*, 49(1): 35–51.
Liddiard, Kirsty, Runswick-Cole, Katherine, Goodley, Dan, Whitney, Sally, Vogelmann, Emma and Watts, Lucy (2019) '"I was excited by the idea of a project that focuses on those unasked questions": Co-producing disability research with disabled young people'. *Children & Society*, 33(2): 154–67.
Lingard, Bob, Sellar, Sam and Lewis, Steven (2017) 'Accountabilities in schools and school systems'. *Oxford Research Encyclopedia of Education*, pp. 1–27. DOI: 10.1093/acrefore/9780190264093.013.74.
Lister, Ruth (2007) 'Why citizenship: Where, when and how children?' *Theoretical Inquiries in Law*, 8(2): 693–718.
Lloyd, Genevieve (1984) *Man of Reason: 'Male' and 'Female' in Western Philosophy*. Minneapolis: University of Minnesota Press.
Lobo, Michele, Bedford, Laura, Bellingham, Robin Ann, Davies, Kim, Halafoff, Anna, Mayes, Eve, Sutton, Bronwyn, Walsh, Aileen Marwung, Stein, Sharon and Lucas, Chloe (2021) 'Earth unbound: Climate change, activism and justice'. *Educational Philosophy and Theory*, pp. 1–20. DOI: 10.1080/00131857.2020.1866541.
López López, Ligia (Licho) (2017) *The Making of Indigeneity, Curriculum History, and the Limits of Diversity*. London: Routledge.

## Bibliography

López López, Ligia (Licho) (2019) 'Refusing making'. *Journal of Curriculum and Pedagogy*, 16(2): 161–74.

Low, Remy (2016) 'Making up the Ummah: The rhetoric of ISIS as public pedagogy'. *Review of Education, Pedagogy, and Cultural Studies*, 38(4): 297–316.

Low, Remy, Mockler, Nicole, Mayes, Eve, Proctor, Helen and Groundwater-Smith, Susan (2016) 'Religion, radicalisation and critical education'. Unpublished research proposal: University of Sydney.

Low, Remy, Mayes, Eve and Proctor, Helen (2019) 'Tracing the radical, the migrant, and the secular in the history of Australian schooling: Contrapuntal historiographies'. *History of Education Review*, 48(2): 137–41.

Lugones, M. C. and Spelman, Elizabeth V. (1983/2000) 'Have we got a theory for you! Feminist theory, cultural imperialism, and the demand for "the woman's voice"'. *Women's Studies International Forum*, 6(6): 573–81.

Luiselli, James K., Putnam, Robert F., Handler, Marcie W. and Feinberg, Adam B. (2005) 'Whole-school positive behaviour support: Effects on student discipline problems and academic performance'. *Educational Psychology*, 25(2–3): 183–98.

Luiz, Miranda (2020) 'A poetics of reimagining: The radical epistemologies of Wynter and Glissant'. *The CLR James Journal*, 26(1–2): 155–61.

Luke, Carmen and Gore, Jennifer M., eds (1992) *Feminisms and Critical Pedagogy*. New York: Routledge.

Lundy, Laura (2007) '"Voice" is not enough: Conceptualising Article 12 of the United Nation Convention on the Rights of the Child'. *British Educational Research Journal*, 33(6): 927–42.

MacLure, Maggie, Holmes, Rachel, MacRae, Christina and Jones, Liz (2010) 'Animating classroom ethnography: Overcoming video-fear'. *International Journal of Qualitative Studies in Education*, 23(5): 543–56.

MacNeil, Angus J., Prater, Doris L. and Busch, Steve (2009) 'The effects of school culture and climate on student achievement'. *International Journal of Leadership in Education*, 12(1): 73–84.

Mager, Ursula and Nowak, Peter (2012) 'Effects of student participation in decision making at school. A systematic review and synthesis of empirical research'. *Educational Research Review*, 7: 38–61.

Mahomet, Amanda (2020) 'Return the Directions Tree!' Djab Wurrung Embassy, 5 November. Available at: https://dwembassy.com/return-the-directions-tree/ (accessed 26 August 2022).

Malone, Karen, Tesar, Marek and Arndt, Sonja (2020) *Theorising Posthuman Childhood Studies*. Dordrecht: Springer.

Manning, Erin (2007) *Politics of Touch: Sense, Movement, Sovereignty*. Minneapolis: University of Minnesota Press.

Manning, Erin (2013) *Always More Than One: Individuation's Dance*. Durham, NC: Duke University Press.

Manning, Erin (2016) *The Minor Gesture*. Durham, NC: Duke University Press.

Mannion, Greg (2007) 'Going spatial, going relational: Why "listening to children" and children's participation needs reframing'. *Discourse: Studies in the Cultural Politics of Education*, 28(3): 405–20.

Martuwarra RiverOfLife, Unamen Shipu Romain River, Poelina, Anne, Wooltorton, Sandra, Guimond, Laurie and Sioui Durand, Guy (2022) 'Hearing, voicing and healing: Rivers as culturally located and connected'. *River Research and Applications*, 38(3): 422–34. DOI: 10.1002/rra.3843.

Marx, Karl (1978) 'Theses on Feuerbach', in Robert C. Tucker (ed.), *The Marx-Engels Reader*, 2nd edn. New York: W. W. Norton, pp. 143–5.

Masny, Diana and Cole, David R., eds (2009) *Multiple Literacies Theory: A Deleuzian Perspective*. Rotterdam: Sense Publishers.

Massumi, Brian (1993a) 'Everywhere you want to be: Introduction to fear', in Brian Massumi (ed.), *The Politics of Everyday Fear*. Minneapolis: University of Minnesota Press, pp. 3–38.

Massumi, Brian (1993b) 'Preface', in Brian Massumi (ed.), *The Politics of Everyday Fear*. Minneapolis: University of Minnesota Press, pp. vii–x.

Massumi, Brian (2002) *Parables for the Virtual: Movement, Affect, Sensation*. Durham, NC: Duke University Press.

Massumi, Brian (2005) 'Fear (the spectrum said)'. *positions: east asia cultures critique*, 13(1): 31–48.

Massumi, Brian and McKim, Joel (2009) 'Micropolitics: Exploring ethico-aesthetics'. *Inflexions: A Journal for Research-Creation*, 3(Oct.): 1–20.

May, Todd (1989) 'Is post-structuralist political theory anarchist?' *Philosophy & Social Criticism*, 15(2): 167–82.

Mayes, Eve (2016a) 'The lines of the voice: An ethnography of the ambivalent affects of student voice'. Unpublished PhD thesis, University of Sydney.

Mayes, Eve (2016b) 'Shifting research methods with a becoming-child ontology: Co-theorising puppet production with high school students'. *Childhood*, 23(1): 105–22.

Mayes, Eve (2016c) *Student Representation on School Governance Councils*. Available at: https://gallery.mailchimp.com/f4c8b5faedc14e0a a5a5fe825/files/VicSRC_Students_and_school_governance_report_1312 16.compressed.pdf (accessed 26 August 2022).

Mayes, Eve (2018) 'The ontological plurality of digital voice: A schizoanalysis of Rate My Professors and Rate My Teachers', in David Cole and Joff P. N. Bradley (eds), *Principles of Transversality in Globalization and Education*. Dordrecht: Springer, pp. 195–210.

## Bibliography

Mayes, Eve (2019a) 'Radical reform and reforming radicals in Australian schooling'. *History of Education Review*, 48(2): 156–70.

Mayes, Eve (2019b) 'Student voice, desire and power with Deleuze and Guattari', in Michael A. Peters (ed.), *Springer Encyclopedia of Teacher Education – A Living Reference Work*. Dordrecht: Springer, pp. 1–6.

Mayes, Eve (2020a) 'Re-arranging the grammar of schooling: The affective force of "student voice"', in Kelsey C. Schmitz, Megan Cotnam-Kappel and Nichole E. Grant (eds), *Interrupting, Infiltrating, Investigating: Radical Youth Pedagogy in Education*. New York: DIO Press, pp. 103–16.

Mayes, Eve (2020b) 'Student voice in an age of "security"?' *Critical Studies in Education*, 61(3): 380–97.

Mayes, Eve (2020c) 'Student voice in school reform? Desiring simultaneous critique and affirmation'. *Discourse: Studies in the Cultural Politics of Education*, 41(3): 454–70.

Mayes, Eve (2021a) 'Bessant, J.: *Making-up People: Youth, Truth and Politics*'. *Journal of Applied Youth Studies*, 4(1): 83–8.

Mayes, Eve (2021b) 'Politics of solidarity in educational partnerships', in Michael A. Peters (ed.), *Encyclopedia of Teacher Education*. Singapore: Springer Singapore, pp. 1–5.

Mayes, Eve and Center, Evan (2022) 'Learning with student climate strikers' humour: Towards critical affective climate justice literacies'. *Environmental Education Research*, 1–19. DOI: 10.1080/13504622.2022.2067322.

Mayes, Eve and Hartup, Michael E. (2021) 'News coverage of the School Strike for Climate movement in Australia: The politics of representing young strikers' emotions'. *Journal of Youth Studies*, 25(7): 994–1016. DOI: 10.1080/13676261.2021.1929887.

Mayes, Eve and Hartup, Michael E. (2022) 'Passion as politics: An analysis of Australian newspaper reporting of institutional responses to the School Strikes for Climate', in Stewart Riddle, Amanda Heffernan and David Bright (eds), *New Perspectives on Education for Democracy*. London: Routledge, pp. 180–99.

Mayes, Eve and Holdsworth, Roger (2020) 'Learning from contemporary student activism: Towards a curriculum of fervent concern and critical hope'. *Curriculum Perspectives*, 40(1): 99–103.

Mayes, Eve and Howell, Angelique (2018) 'The (hidden) injuries of NAPLAN: Two standardised test events and the making of 'at risk' student subjects'. *International Journal of Inclusive Education*, 22(10): 1108–23.

Mayes, Eve and Kelly, Merinda (2022) 'Students researching "inequality": Perplexities and potentialities of arts-informed research methods for students as researchers', in Deborah Price, Belinda MacGill and Jenni Carter (eds), *Arts-based Practices with Young People at the Edge*. London: Palgrave Macmillan, pp. 59–86.

Mayes, Eve, Davis, Brooke, Towers, Isaac, The Steering Committee,

Arya-Pinatyh, Kadek and Groundwater-Smith, Susan (2013) 'Students researching curriculum development: Sharing our voices on education'. *Connect*, 204: 14–21.

Mayes, Eve, Breheny, Pinchy, Cantwell, Laura, Gilbert, Emma, Goh, Sarah, Grover, Vansh, Sadeghi, Roghayeh, Wilson, William and Holdsworth, Roger (2016a) 'Students on school councils: A collaborative study of student representation in Victorian school governance'. *Connect*, 222(Dec.): 3–10.

Mayes, Eve, Mitra, Dana L. and Serriere, Stephanie C. (2016b) 'Figured worlds of citizenship: Examining differences made in "making a difference" in an elementary school classroom'. *American Educational Research Journal*, 53(3): 605–58.

Mayes, Eve, Bakhshi, Shukria, Wasner, Victoria, Cook-Sather, Alison, Mohammad, Madina, Bishop, Daniel C., Groundwater-Smith, Susan, Prior, Megan, Nelson, Emily, McGregor, Jane, Carson, Karson, Webb, Rebecca, Flashman, Lily, McLaughlin, Colleen and Cowley, Emily (2017) 'What can a conception of power do? Theories and images of power in student voice work'. *International Journal of Student Voice*, 2(1).

Mayes, Eve, Finneran, Rachel and Black, Rosalyn (2019) 'The challenges of student voice in primary schools: Students "having a voice" and "speaking for" others'. *Australian Journal of Education*, 63(2): 157–72.

Mayes, Eve, Wolfe, Melissa Joy and Higham, Leanne (2020) 'Re/imagining school climate: Towards processual accounts of affective ecologies of schooling'. *Emotion, Space and Society*, 36: 100703.

Mayes, Eve, Black, Rosalyn and Finneran, Rachel (2021) 'The possibilities and problematics of student voice for teacher professional learning: Lessons from an evaluation study'. *Cambridge Journal of Education*, 51(2): 195–212.

Mazzei, Lisa A. (2003) 'Inhabited silences: In pursuit of a muffled subtext'. *Qualitative Inquiry*, 9(3): 355–68.

Mazzei, Lisa A. (2007) *Inhabited Silence in Qualitative Research: Putting Poststructural Theory to Work*. New York: Peter Lang.

Mazzei, Lisa A. (2008) 'Silence speaks: Whiteness revealed in the absence of voice'. *Teaching and Teacher Education*, 24(5): 1125–36.

Mazzei, Lisa A. (2016) 'Voice without a subject'. *Cultural Studies ↔ Critical Methodologies*, 16(2): 151–61.

Mazzei, Lisa A. (2020) 'Postqualitative inquiry: Or the necessity of theory'. *Qualitative Inquiry*, 27(2): 198–200.

Mazzei, Lisa A. and Jackson, Alecia Youngblood (2009) 'Introduction: The limit of voice', in Alecia Youngblood Jackson and Lisa A. Mazzei (eds), *Voice in Qualitative Inquiry: Challenging Conventional, Interpretive and Critical Conceptions in Qualitative Research*. London: Routledge, pp. 1–13.

Mazzei, Lisa A. and Jackson, Alecia Youngblood (2012) 'Complicating

voice in a refusal to "let participants speak for themselves"'. *Qualitative Inquiry*, 18(9): 745–51.
Mazzei, Lisa A. and Jackson, Alecia Y. (2017) 'Voice in the agentic assemblage'. *Educational Philosophy and Theory*, 49(11): 1090–8.
Mbembe, Achille (2018) *The Holberg Debate 2018*. Available at: https://holbergprisen.no/en/news/holberg-prize/professor-achille-mbembes-address-2018-holberg-debate (accessed 26 August 2022).
Mbembe, Achille (2020) 'The universal right to breathe'. *Critical Inquiry*, 47(S2): S58–S62.
McCarthy, Thomas A. (1978) *The Critical Theory of Jürgen Habermas*. Cambridge, MA: MIT Press.
McDermott, Mairi (2020a) *Mapping the Terrains of Student Voice Pedagogies: An Autoethnography*. New York: Peter Lang.
McDermott, Mairi (2020b) 'On what autoethnography did in a study on student voice pedagogies: A mapping of returns'. *The Qualitative Report*, 25(2): 347–58.
McGrath-Champ, Susan, Wilson, Rachel, Stacey, Meghan and Fitzgerald, Scott (2018) *Understanding Work in Schools: The Foundation for Teaching and Learning*. Available at: https://hdl.handle.net/2123/21926 (accessed 26 August 2022).
McGregor, Jane (2004) 'Spatiality and the place of the material in schools'. *Pedagogy, Culture & Society*, 12(3): 347–72.
McIntyre, Donald, Pedder, David and Rudduck, Jean (2005) 'Pupil voice: Comfortable and uncomfortable learnings for teachers'. *Research Papers in Education*, 20(2): 149–68.
Melville, Herman (1853/2014) *Bartleby, the Scrivener: A Story of Wall-Street*. New York: Open Road Integrated Media.
Mendes, Ana Barbosa and Hammett, Daniel (2020) 'The new tyranny of student participation? Student voice and the paradox of strategic-active student-citizens'. *Teaching in Higher Education*, 1–16. DOI: 10.1080/13562517.2020.1783227.
Mengue, Philippe (2005) 'The Absent people and the void of democracy'. *Contemporary Political Theory*, 4(4): 386–99.
Messiou, Kyriaki (2019) 'The missing voices: Students as a catalyst for promoting inclusive education'. *International Journal of Inclusive Education*, 23(7–8): 768–81.
Messiou, Kyriaki and Ainscow, Mel (2015) 'Responding to learner diversity: Student views as a catalyst for powerful teacher development?' *Teaching and Teacher Education*, 51: 246–55.
Milne, Ann (2020) 'Colouring in the white spaces: The Warrior-Researchers of Kia Aroha College'. *Curriculum Perspectives*, 40(1): 87–91.
Mitra, Dana L. (2004) 'The significance of students: Can increasing "student voice" in schools lead to gains in youth development?' *Teachers College Record*, 106(4): 651–88.

Mitra, Dana L. (2006) 'Youth as a bridge between home and school: Comparing student voice and parent involvement as strategies for change'. *Education and Urban Society*, 38(4): 455–80.

Mitra, Dana L. (2009) 'Strengthening student voice initiatives in high schools: An examination of the supports needed for school-based youth-adult partnerships'. *Youth and Society*, 40(3): 311–35.

Mocatta, Gabi, Mayes, Eve, Hess, Kristy and Hartup, Michael E. (2022) 'The trouble with "quiet advocacy": Local journalism and reporting climate change in rural and regional Australia'. *Media, Culture & Society*. DOI: 10.1177/01634437221104686.

Mockler, Nicole and Groundwater-Smith, Susan (2015) *Engaging with Student Voice in Research, Education and Community: Beyond Legitimation and Guardianship*. Dordrecht: Springer.

Mohammed, Ilyas (2021) 'Decolonising terrorism journals'. *Societies*, 11(1): 1–18.

Moreton-Robinson, Aileen (2000/2020) *Talkin' Up to the White Woman: Indigenous Women and Feminism*. St Lucia: University of Queensland Press.

Moreton-Robinson, Aileen (2015) *The White Possessive: Property, Power, and Indigenous Sovereignty*. Minneapolis: University of Minnesota Press.

Morgan, Bethan (2021) *Cambridge Student Voice Seminars*. Available at: https://cambridgestudentvoiceseminars.wordpress.com/ (accessed 26 August 2022).

Morsi, Yassir (2017) *Radical Skin, Moderate Masks*. Lanham, MD: Rowman & Littlefield.

Muijs, Daniel, Harris, Alma, Chapman, Christopher, Stoll, Louise and Russ, Jennifer (2004) 'Improving schools in socioeconomically disadvantaged areas – A review of research evidence'. *School Effectiveness and School Improvement*, 15(2): 149–75.

Mulcahy, Dianne (2012) 'Affective assemblages: Body matters in the pedagogic practices of contemporary school classrooms'. *Pedagogy, Culture & Society*, 20(1): 9–27.

Munns, Geoff and Sawyer, Wayne (2013) 'Student engagement: The research methodology and the theory', in G. Munns, W. Sawyer and B. Cole (eds), *Exemplary Teachers of Students in Poverty*. Abingdon: Routledge, pp. 14–32.

Murphie, Andrew (2001) 'Computers are not theatre: The machine in the ghost in Gilles Deleuze and Félix Guattari's thought', in G. Genosko (ed.), *Deleuze and Guattari: Critical Assessments of Leading Philosophers*. London: Routledge, pp. 1299–331.

Murphy, Damien (2017) 'Dylan Voller's violent past detailed at Don Dale royal commission'. *Sydney Morning Herald*, 20 April.

Murris, Karin (2016) *The Posthuman Child: Educational Transformation Through Philosophy with Picturebooks*. London: Routledge.

## Bibliography

Myers, Natasha (2019) 'From Edenic apocalpyse to gardens against Eden', in Kregg Hetherington (ed.), *Infrastructure, Environment, and Life in the Anthropocene*. Durham, NC: Duke University Press, pp. 115–48.

Myers, Natasha (2021) 'How to grow liveable worlds: Ten (not-so-easy) steps for life in the Planthroposcene' (blog post for ABC Religion and Ethics). Available at: https://www.abc.net.au/religion/natasha-myers-how-to-grow-liveable-worlds:-ten-not-so-easy-step/11906548 (accessed 26 August 2022).

Nakata, Martin (2007) *Disciplining the Savages, Savaging the Discipline*. Canberra, ACT: Aboriginal Studies Press.

Nakata, Sana (2015) *Childhood Citizenship, Governance and Policy: The Politics of Becoming Adult*. London: Routledge.

Neimanis, Astrida and Walker, Rachel Loewen (2014) 'Weathering: Climate change and the "thick time" of transcorporeality'. *Hypatia*, 29(3): 558–75.

Nelson, Emily (2015) 'Opening up to student voice: Supporting teacher learning through collaborative action research'. *Learning Landscapes*, 8(2): 285–99.

Nelson, Emily and Charteris, Jennifer (2020) 'Student voice research as a technology of reform in neoliberal times'. *Pedagogy, Culture & Society*, 1–18. DOI: 10.1080/14681366.2020.1713867.

Niccolini, Alyssa D. (2009) 'Mouthy students and the teacher's apple: Questions of orality and race in the urban public school', in Gail Boldt, Paula M. Salvio and Peter M. Taubman (eds), *Classroom Life in the Age of Accountability* [Occasional Paper Series]. New York: Bank Street College of Education, pp. 41–9.

Niccolini, Alyssa D., Zarabadi, Shiva and Ringrose, Jessica (2018) 'Spinning yarns: Affective kinshipping as posthuman pedagogy'. *Parallax*, 24(3): 324–43.

Noelle-Neumann, Elisabeth (1974) 'The spiral of silence: A theory of public opinion'. *Journal of Communication*, 24(2): 43–51.

Noonan, Andie (2018) 'Students strike'. *ABC News*, 30 November.

Nordstrom, Susan Naomi (2015) 'Not so innocent anymore: Making recording devices matter in qualitative interviews'. *Qualitative Inquiry*, 21(4): 388–401.

NSW Government: Education (n.d.) *School Communities Working Together: Management Guidelines for Department of Education Executive Staff*. Available at: https://education.nsw.gov.au/content/dam/main-education/en/home/inside-the-department/health-and-safety/media/documents/PROC004_SCWTGUIDELINES_v1.pdf (accessed 16 July 2021).

O'Donnell, Aislinn (2018) 'Contagious ideas: Vulnerability, epistemic injustice and counter-terrorism in education'. *Educational Philosophy and Theory*, 50(10): 981–97.

OECD (2012) *Equity and Quality in Education: Supporting Disadvantaged Students and Schools* Available at: http://www.oecd-ilibrary.org/education/equity-and-quality-in-education_9789264130852-en (accessed 16 July 2021).

Olmedo, Antonio and Wilkins, Andrew (2017) 'Governing through parents: A genealogical enquiry of education policy and the construction of neoliberal subjectivities in England'. *Discourse: Studies in the Cultural Politics of Education*, 38(4): 573–89.

Olsson, Liselott Mariett (2009) *Movement and Experimentation in Young Children's Learning: Deleuze and Guattari in Early Childhood Education*. Abingdon: Routledge.

Oxley, Rebecca and Russell, Andrew (2020) 'Interdisciplinary perspectives on breath, body and world'. *Body & Society*, 26(2): 3–29.

Ozga, Jenny (2015) 'Trust in numbers? Digital Education Governance and the inspection process'. *European Educational Research Journal*, 15(1): 69–81.

Page, Angela and Charteris, Jennifer (2021) 'Student evaluations of teaching and student cyberaggression: The impact of keyboard warriors in tertiary education'. *Journal of Education and Humanities*, 4(1): 96–123.

Parker, Michael (2019) 'Climate strike? Damn the year 11s'. *Sydney Morning Herald*, 12 October. https://www.smh.com.au/national/nsw/damn-these-year-11s-they-asked-me-to-support-the-climate-strike-20191007-p52ydq.html (accessed 26 August 2022).

Patton, Paul (2000) *Deleuze and the Political*. Abingdon: Routledge.

Patton, Paul (2008) 'Becoming-democratic', in Nicholas Thoburn and Ian Buchanan (eds), *Deleuze and Politics*. Edinburgh: Edinburgh University Press, pp. 178–95.

Pearce, Thomas C. and Wood, Bronwyn E (2019) 'Education for transformation: An evaluative framework to guide student voice work in schools'. *Critical Studies in Education*, 60(1): 113–30.

Pedersen, Helena and Pini, Barbara (2017) 'Educational epistemologies and methods in a more-than-human world'. *Educational Philosophy and Theory*, 49(11): 1051–4.

Perkins, Miki (2020) '"Devastated": Anger after "culturally significant" tree cut down at highway site'. *ABC News*, 26 October.

Perry-Hazan, Lotem (2021) 'Students' perceptions of their rights in school: A systematic review of the international literature'. *Review of Educational Research*, 91(6): 919–57.

Peters, Michael A. (2020) '"The fascism in our heads": Reich, Fromm, Foucault, Deleuze and Guattari – The social pathology of fascism in the 21st century'. *Educational Philosophy and Theory*, 1–9. DOI: 10.1080/00131857.2020.1727403.

Petersen, Eva Bendix (2018) '"Data found us": A critique of some new materialist tropes in educational research'. *Research in Education*, 101(1): 5–16.

Phelan, Peggy (1993) *Unmarked: The Politics of Performance*. New York: Routledge.

Phillips, Jay (2021) 'Foundations of teacher knowledge in Indigenous education', in Marnee Shay and Rhonda Oliver (eds), *Indigenous Education in Australia: Learning and Teaching for Deadly Futures*. Abingdon: Routledge, pp. 7–20.

Piaget, Jean (1977) *The Development of Thought: Equilibration of Cognitive Structures*, trans. Arnold Rosin. Oxford: Basil Blackwell.

Pleasants, Kathleen (2006) 'Does environmental education need a Thneed? Displacing The Lorax as environmental text'. *Canadian Journal of Environmental Education*, 11: 179–94.

Poelina, Anne, Wooltorton, Sandra, Blaise, Mindy, Aniere, Catrina Luz, Horwitz, Pierre, White, Peta J. and Muecke, Stephen (2022) 'Regeneration time: Ancient wisdom for planetary wellbeing'. *Australian Journal of Environmental Education*, 1–18. Epub ahead of print 2022/01/24. DOI: 10.1017/aee.2021.34.

Porter, Robert and Porter, Kerry-Ann (2003) 'Habermas and the pragmatics of communication: A Deleuze–Guattarian critique'. *Social Semiotics*, 13(2): 129–45.

Pratt, Hawley (1972) *The Lorax* (animated short). Produced by DePatie–Freleng Enterprises.

Puar, Jaspir K. (2007) *Terrorist Assemblages: Homonationalism in Queer Times*. Durham, NC: Duke University Press.

Puar, Jaspir K. (2012) '"I would rather be a cyborg than a goddess": Becoming-intersectional in assemblage theory'. *philoSOPHIA*, 2(1): 49–66.

Puar, Jasbir K. and Rai, A. (2002) 'Monster, terrorist, fag: The war on terrorism and the production of docile patriots'. *Social Text*, 20(3): 117–48.

Quaglia, Russ, Fox, Kristine, Lande, Lisa and Young, Deborah (2020) *The Power of Voice in Schools: Listening, Learning, and Leading Together*. Alexandria, VA: Association for Supervision & Curriculum Development (ASCD).

Quinn, Sarah and Owen, Susanne (2016) 'Digging deeper: Understanding the power of "student voice"'. *Australian Journal of Education*, 60(1): 60–72.

Raby, Rebecca (2014) 'Children's participation as neo-liberal governance'. *Discourse: Studies in the Cultural Politics of Education*, 35(1): 77–89.

Ranson, Stewart, Arnott, Margaret, McKeown, Penny, Martin, Jane and Smith, Penny (2005) 'The participation of volunteer citizens in school governance'. *Educational Review*, 57(3): 357–71.

Reich, Wilhelm (1946/1933) *The Mass Psychology of Fascism*. New York: Orgone Institute Press.

Renaud, Chris (2012) *The Lorax* (feature film). Universal Pictures.

Renold, E (2018) '"Feel what I feel": Making da(r)ta with teen girls for creative activisms on how sexual violence matters'. *Journal of Gender Studies*, 27(1): 37–55.

Renold, E and Ivinson, Gabrielle (2014) 'Horse-girl assemblages: Towards a post-human cartography of girls' desire in an ex-mining valleys community'. *Discourse: Studies in the Cultural Politics of Education*, 35(3): 361–76.

Renold, E and Ivinson, Gabrielle (2019) 'Anticipating the more-than: Working with prehension in artful interventions with young people in a post-industrial community'. *Futures*, 112: 102428.

Renold, E and Ringrose, Jessica (2008) 'Regulation and rupture: Mapping tween and teenage girls' resistance to the heterosexual matrix'. *Feminist Theory*, 9(3): 313–38.

Renold, E and Ringrose, Jessica (2019) 'JARing: Making phematerialist research practices matter'. *MAI: Feminism and Visual Culture*, Spring.

Rights Watch UK (2016) *Preventing Education? Human Rights and UK Counter-Terrorism Policy in Schools*. Available at: https://www.rightsandsecurity.org/assets/downloads/preventing-education-final-to-print-3.compressed-1_.pdf (accessed 26 August 2022).

Rigney, Daryle, Hemming, Steve, Bignall, Simone and Maher, Katie (2018) 'Ngarrindjeri Yannarumi: Educating for Transformation and Indigenous Nation (Re)building', in Elizabeth A. McKinley and Linda T. Smith (eds), *Handbook of Indigenous Education*. Singapore: Springer Singapore, pp. 1–26.

Rigney, Lester-Irabinna (1999) 'Internationalization of an Indigenous anticolonial cultural critique of research methodologies: A guide to Indigenist Research Methodology and its principles'. *Wicazo Sa Review*, 14(2): 109–21.

Ringrose, Jessica (2015) 'Schizo-feminist educational research cartographies'. *Deleuze Studies*, 9(3): 393–409.

Ringrose, Jessica and Renold, E (2011) 'Teen girls, working-class femininity and resistance: Retheorising fantasy and desire in educational contexts of heterosexualised violence'. *International Journal of Inclusive Education*, 16(4): 461–77.

Ringrose, Jessica and Renold, E (2014) '"F**k rape!": Exploring affective intensities in a feminist research assemblage'. *Qualitative Inquiry*, 20(6): 772–80.

Ringrose, Jessica and Zarabadi, Shiva (2018) 'Deleuzo-Guattarian decentering of the I/Eye: A conversation with Jessica Ringrose and Shiva Zarabadi', in Kathryn J. Strom, Tammy Mills and Alan Ovens (eds), *Decentering the Researcher in Intimate Scholarship: Critical Posthuman*

*Methodoloical Perspectives in Education*. Bingley: Emerald Publishing, pp. 207–17.

Ringrose, Jessica, Warfield, Katie and Zarabadi, Shiva, eds (2018) *Feminist Posthumanisms, New Materialisms and Education*. London: Routledge.

Robinson, Andrew and Tormey, Simon (2010) 'Living in smooth space: Deleuze, postcolonialism and the subaltern', in Simone Bignall and Paul Patton (eds), *Deleuze and the Postcolonial*. Edinburgh: Edinburgh University Press, pp. 20–40.

Robinson, Carol and Taylor, Carol (2007) 'Theorizing student voice: Values and perspectives'. *Improving Schools*, 10(1): 5–17.

Robinson, Carol and Taylor, Carol (2013) 'Student voice as a contested practice: Power and participation in two student voice projects'. *Improving Schools*, 16(1): 32–46.

Robinson, Janean and Smyth, John (2016) '"Sent out" and Stepping Back In: Stories from young people "placed at risk"'. *Ethnography and Education*, 11(2): 222–36.

Rodgers, Carol (2018) 'Descriptive feedback: Student voice in K-5 classrooms'. *The Australian Educational Researcher*, 45(1): 87–102.

Rose, Nikolas (1991) 'Governing by numbers: Figuring out democracy'. *Accounting, Organizations and Society*, 16(7): 673–92.

Rousell, David and Cutter-Mackenzie-Knowles, Amy (2020) 'A systematic review of climate change education: Giving children and young people a "voice" and a "hand" in redressing climate change'. *Children's Geographies*, 18(2): 191–208. DOI: 10.1080/14733285.2019.1614532.

Rousell, David, Wijesinghe, Thilinika, Cutter-Mackenzie-Knowles, Amy and Osborn, Maia (2021) 'Digital media, political affect, and a youth to come: Rethinking climate change education through Deleuzian dramatisation'. *Educational Review*, DOI: 10.1080/00131911.2021.1965959.

Rowe, Emma (2017) *Middle-Class School Choice in Urban Spaces: The Economics of Public Schooling and Globalized Education Reform*. Abingdon: Routledge.

Rowles, Georgia (2020) 'Why calling for a "climate emergency" is not climate justice'. Blog post for Australian Youth Climate Coalition, 2 June. Available at: https://www.aycc.org.au/climatejustice_not_climateemergency (accessed 6 August 2021).

Roy, Kaustuv (2003) *Teachers in Nomadic Spaces: Deleuze and Curriculum*. New York: Peter Lang.

Rubin, Beth C., Ayala, Jennifer and Zaal, Mayida (2017) 'Authenticity, aims and authority: Navigating youth participatory action research in the classroom., *Curriculum Inquiry*, 47(2): 175–94.

Rudduck, Jean (1999) 'Teacher practice and the student voice', in Manfred Lang, John Olsen, H. Hansen and W. Blunder (eds), *Changing Schools/*

*Changing Practices: Perspectives on Educational Reform and Teacher Professionalism*. Louvain: Graant.

Rudduck, Jean and Flutter, Julia (2000) 'Pupil participation and pupil perspective: "Carving a new order of experience"'. *Cambridge Journal of Education*, 30(1): 75–89.

Rudduck, Jean and Flutter, Julia (2004) *How to Improve Your School*. London: Continuum.

Rudolph, Sophie (2018) *Unsettling the Gap: Race, Politics and Indigenous Education*. New York: Peter Lang.

Ryder, Andrew (2018) 'Foreword', in David R. Cole and Joff P. N. Bradley (eds), *Principles of Transversality in Globalisation and Education*. Dordrecht: Springer, pp. v–viii.

Safi, Michael (2015) 'Anti-radicalisation kit never meant for use in schools, says key author'. *The Guardian*, 25 September.

Said, Edward W. (1989) 'Representing the colonized: Anthropology's interlocutors'. *Critical Inquiry*, 15(2): 205–25.

Saldanha, Arun (2007) *Psychadelic White: Goa Trance and the Viscosity of Race*. Minneapolis: University of Minnesota Press.

Saussure, Ferdinand de (1959) *Course in General Linguistics*, trans. Wade Baskin. New York: McGraw-Hill.

Schulten, Katherine (2020) 'Introduction', in Katherine Schulten (ed.), *Student Voice: 100 Argument Essays by Teens on Issues That Matter to Them*. New York: W. W. Norton, pp. xi–xiii.

Scott, Joan W. (1992) 'Experience', in Judith Butler and Joan W. Scott (eds), *Feminists Theorize the Political*. New York: Routledge, pp. 22–40.

Sebba, J. and Robinson, Carol (2010) *Evaluation of UNICEF UK's Rights Respecting Schools' Award*. Available at: https://www.unicef.org.uk/rights-respecting-schools/wp-content/uploads/sites/4/2014/12/RRSA_Evaluation_Report.pdf (accessed 26 August 2022).

Sedgwick, Eve Kosofsky (2003) *Touching Feeling: Affect, Pedagogy, Performativity*. Durham, NC: Duke University Press.

Sellar, Sam (2014) 'A feel for numbers: Affect, data and education policy'. *Critical Studies in Education*, 56(1): 131–46.

Semetsky, Inna (2003) 'Deleuze's new image of thought, or Dewey revisited'. *Educational Philosophy and Theory*, 35(1): 17–29.

Semetsky, Inna, ed. (2008) *Nomadic Education: Variations on a Theme by Deleuze and Guattari*. Rotterdam: Sense Publishers.

Semetsky, Inna and Masny, Diana, eds (2013) *Deleuze and Education*. Edinburgh: Edinburgh University Press.

Seuss, Dr. (1972/2012) *The Lorax*. London: HarperCollins.

Shanahan, Angela (2019) 'Kids caught up in climate panic'. *The Australian*, 27 September.

Sharpe, Christina (2016) *In the Wake: On Blackness and Being*. Durham, NC: Duke University Press.

## Bibliography

Shay, Marnee and Sarra, Grace (2021) 'Locating the voices of Indigenous young people on identity in Australia: An Indigenist analysis'. *Diaspora, Indigenous, and Minority Education*, 1–14. DOI: 10.1080/15595692.2021.1907330.

Shor, Ira (1980) *Critical Teaching and Everyday Life*. Boston, MA: South End Press.

Silva, Elena and Rubin, Beth C. (2003) 'Introduction: Missing voices: Listening to students' experiences with school reform', in Beth C. Rubin and Elena Silva (eds), *Critical Voices in School Reform: Students Living Through Change*. New York: RoutledgeFalmer, pp. 1–7.

Simmons, Kristen (2017) 'Settler atmospherics'. Blog post for Society for Cultural Anthropology. Available at: https://culanth.org/fieldsights/settler-atmospherics (accessed 26 August 2022).

Simons, Maarten (2015) 'Governing education without reform: The power of the example'. *Discourse: Studies in the Cultural Politics of Education*, 36(5): 712–31.

Simpson, Audra (2014) *Mohawk Interruptus: Political Life Across the Borders of Settler States*. Durham, NC: Duke University Press.

Skerritt, Craig, O'Hara, Joe, Brown, Martin, McNamara, Gerry and O'Brien, Shivaun (2021) 'Student voice and the school hierarchy: The disconnect between senior leaders and teachers'. *Oxford Review of Education*, 1–16. DOI: 10.1080/03054985.2021.2003189.

Smyth, John and Hattam, Robert (2001) '"Voiced" research as a sociology for understanding "dropping out" of school'. *British Journal of Sociology of Education*, 22(3): 401–15.

Smyth, John and McInerney, Peter (2012) *From Silent Witnesses to Active Agents: Student Voice in Re-engaging with Learning*. New York: Peter Lang.

Snaza, Nathan and Weaver, John A., eds (2015) *Posthumanism and Educational Research*. New York: Routledge.

Snaza, Nathan, Sonu, Debbie, Truman, Sarah E. and Zaliwska, Zofia, eds (2016) *Pedagogical Matters: New Materialisms and Curriculum Studies*. New York: Peter Lang.

Solvason, Carla (2005) 'Investigating specialist school ethos ... or do you mean culture?', *Educational Studies*, 31(1): 85–94.

SoundOut (2021) *Responsive Student Voices*. Available at: https://soundout.org/category/tools/teaching/ (accessed 4 August 2021).

Spalek, Basia and Imtoual, Alia (2007) 'Muslim communities and counter-terror responses: "Hard" approaches to community engagement in the UK and Australia'. *Journal of Muslim Minority Affairs*, 27(2): 185–202.

Spivak, Gayatri Chakravorty (1987) 'Can the subaltern speak?', in Cary Nelson and Lawrence Grossberg (eds), *Marxism and Interpretation of Culture*. Urbana: University of Illinois Press, pp. 271–313.

Spivak, Gayatri Chakravorty (1996) 'Subaltern studies: Deconstructing historiography', in Donna Landrey and Gerald Maclean (eds), *The Spivak Reader: Selected Words of Gayatri Chakravorty Spivak*. New York Routledge, pp. 203–35.

Springgay, Stephanie (2008) *Body Knowledge and Curriculum: Pedagogies of Touch in Youth and Visual Culture*. New York: Peter Lang.

Springgay, Stephanie and Rotas, Nikki (2015) 'How do you make a classroom operate like a work of art? Deleuzeguattarian methodologies of research-creation'. *International Journal of Qualitative Studies in Education*, 28(5): 552–72.

Spyrou, Spyros (2017) 'Time to decenter childhood?' *Childhood*, 24(4): 433–7.

Spyrou, Spyros (2018) *Disclosing Childhoods: Research and Knowledge Production for a Critical Childhood Studies*. London: Palgrave Macmillan.

SS4C (2021) *#FUNDOURFUTURENOTGAS PLEDGE*. Available at: https://www.schoolstrike4climate.com/pledge (accessed 26 August 2022).

St. Pierre, Elizabeth Adams (1997) 'Methodology in the fold and irruption of transgressive data'. *Qualitative Studies in Education*, 10(2): 175–89.

St. Pierre, Elizabeth A. (2011) 'Post qualitative research: The critique and the coming after', in Norman K. Denzin and Yvonna S. Lincoln (eds), *The Sage Handbook of Qualitative Research*, 4th edn. Thousand Oaks, CA: Sage, pp. 611–25.

St. Pierre, Elizabeth A. (2018) 'Post qualitative inquiry in an ontology of immanence'. *Qualitative Inquiry*, 25(1): 3–16.

St. Pierre, Elizabeth Adams (2019) 'Post qualitative inquiry, the refusal of method, and the risk of the new'. *Qualitative Inquiry*, 27(1): 3–9.

Stewart, Kathleen (2007) *Ordinary Affects*. Durham, NC: Duke University Press.

Strom, Kathryn J. (2018a) 'After postmodernism: Anti-fascist theories'. *Educational Philosophy and Theory*, 50(14): 1324–5.

Strom, Kathryn J. (2018b) '"That's not very Deleuzian'": Thoughts on interrupting the exclusionary nature of "high theory"'. *Educational Philosophy and Theory*, 50(1): 104–13.

Strom, Kathryn J. and Martin, Adrian D. (2017) *Becoming-Teacher: A Rhizomatic Look at First-Year Teaching*. Rotterdam: Sense Publishers.

Strom, Katie, Ringrose, Jessica, Osgood, Jayne and Renold, EJ (2019) 'PhEMaterialism: Response-able research & activism'. *Reconceptualizing Educational Research Methodology*, 10(2–3): 1–39.

Sundberg, J. (2014) 'Decolonizing posthumanist geographies'. *cultural geographies*, 21(1): 33–47.

Surin, Kenneth (2010) 'Partial objects', in Adrian Parr (ed.), *The Deleuze Dictionary*, rev. edn. Edinburgh: Edinburgh University Press, pp. 202–4.

Surin, Kenneth (2011) 'Force', in Charles Stivale (ed.), *Gilles Deleuze:*

*Key Concepts*, 2nd edn. Montreal: McGill-Queen's University Press, pp. 21–32.

Svirsky, Marcelo (2010) 'Defining activism'. *Deleuze Studies*, 4: 163–82.

Takacs, David (2021) 'We are the River'. *University of Illinois Law Review*. 2: 545–605.

Taylor, Affrica and Pacini-Ketchabaw, Veronica (2015) 'Learning with children, ants, and worms in the Anthropocene: Towards a common world pedagogy of multispecies vulnerability'. *Pedagogy, Culture & Society*, 23(4): 507–29.

Taylor, Carol A. and Ivinson, Gabrielle (2013) 'Material feminisms: New directions for education'. *Gender and Education*, 25(6): 665–70.

Taylor, Carol and Robinson, Carol (2009) 'Student voice: Theorising power and participation'. *Pedagogy, Culture and Society*, 17(2): 161–75.

Taylor, Emmeline (2017) '"This is not America": Cultural mythscapes, media representation and the anatomy of the Surveillance School in Australia'. *Journal of Sociology*, 53(2): 413–29.

Taylor, Emmeline (2018) 'Curating risk, selling safety: Fear of crime, responsibilitisation, and the surveillance school economy', in Murray Lee and Gabe Mythen (eds), *The Routledge International Handbook on Fear of Crime*. Abingdon: Routledge, pp. 312–21.

Taylor, Matthew, Watts, Jonathan and Bartlett, John (2019) 'Climate crisis: 6 million people join latest wave of global protests'. *The Guardian*, 28 September.

Tee, Kenneth (2019) 'In Malaysia, hundreds march for climate change as part of global strike'. *Malay Mail*, 21 September.

Teece-Johnson, Danny and Burton-Bradley, Robert (2017) 'People are still being mistreated, says Dylan Voller after royal commission final report'. *NITV*, 17 November.

Tegg, Jack (2018) 'Two students holding placards at climate action rally, Hobart'. *ABC News*, 29 November.

The Guardian ParlView (2018) 'Scott Morrison tells kids going on climate strike to get back to school – video'. *The Guardian*, 27 November. Available at: https://www.theguardian.com/global/video/2018/nov/27/scott-morrison-tells-kids-going-on-climate-strike-to-get-back-to-school-video (accessed 26 August 2022).

The Uluru Statement (2021) *Voice. Treaty. Truth. Uluru Statement from the Heart*. Available at: https://ulurustatement.org/ (accessed 26 August 2022).

Thiele, Kathlin (2016) 'Quantum physics and/as philosophy: Immanence, diffraction, and the ethics of mattering'. *Rhizomes: Cultural Studies in Emerging Knowledge*, 30: 1–6.

Thoburn, Nicholas (2003) *Deleuze, Marx and Politics*. London: Routledge.

Thompson, Greg and Cook, Ian (2012a) 'Manipulating the data: Teaching and NAPLAN in the control society'. *Discourse: Studies in the Cultural Politics of Education*, 35(1): 129–42.

Thompson, Greg and Cook, Ian (2012b) 'Spinning in the NAPLAN ether: "Postscript on the Control Societies" and the seduction of education in Australia'. *Deleuze Studies*, 6(4): 564–84.

Thompson, Greg and Cook, Ian (2013) 'The logics of good teaching in an audit culture: A Deleuzian analysis'. *Educational Philosophy and Theory*, 45(3): 243–58.

Thompson, Greg and Sellar, Sam (2018) 'Datafication, testing events and the outside of thought'. *Learning, Media and Technology*, 43(2): 139–51.

Thomson, Pat (2011) 'Coming to terms with "voice"', in Gerry Czerniawski and Warren Kidd (eds), *The Student Voice Handbook: Bridging the Academic/Practitioner Divide*, Bingley: Emerald Publishing, pp. 19–30.

Threadgold, Steven and Gerrard, Jessica, eds (2022) *Class in Australia*. Clayton, VIC: Monash University Press.

Todd, Zoe (2016) 'An Indigenous feminist's take on the ontological turn: "Ontology" is just another word for colonialism'. *Journal of Historical Sociology*, 29(1): 4–22. DOI: 10.1111/johs.12124.

Tormey, Simon (2005) '"Not in my name": Deleuze, Zaptismo and the critique of representation'. *Parliamentary Affairs*, 59(1): 138–54.

Truman, Sarah E. (2022) *Feminist Speculations and the Practice of Research-Creation*. New York: Routledge.

Tuck, Eve (2009) 'Suspending damage: A letter to communities'. *Harvard Educational Review*, 79(3): 409–28.

Tuck, Eve (2010) 'Breaking up with Deleuze: Desire and valuing the irreconcilable'. *International Journal of Qualitative Studies in Education*, 23(5): 635–50.

Tuck, Eve (2012) *Urban Youth and School Pushout: Gateways, Get-aways, and the GED*. New York: Routledge.

Tuck, Eve and Yang, K. Wayne (2014a) 'Introduction to *Youth Resistance Research and Theories of Change*', in Eve Tuck and K.Wayne Yang (eds), *Youth Resistance Research and Theories of Change*. New York: Routledge, pp. 1–23.

Tuck, Eve and Yang, K. Wayne (2014b) 'Unbecoming claims: Pedagogies of refusal in qualitative research'. *Qualitative Inquiry*, 20(6): 811–18.

Tyack, David and Tobin, William (1994) 'The "grammar" of schooling: Why has it been so hard to change?' *American Educational Research Journal*, 31(3): 453–79.

Tynan, Lauren (2021) 'What is relationality? Indigenous knowledges, practices and responsibilities with kin'. *cultural geographies*, 28(4): 597–610.

Ulmer, Jasmine B. (2017) 'Posthumanism as research methodology: Inquiry in the Anthropocene' *International Journal of Qualitative Studies in Education*, 30(9): 832–48.

## Bibliography

UNICEF (2021) *Convention on the Rights of the Child*. Available at: https://www.unicef.org/child-rights-convention (accessed 26 August 2022).

Unigwe, Chika (2019) 'It's not just Greta Thunberg: Why are we ignoring the developing world's inspiring activists?' *The Guardian*, 5 October.

United Nations (1989) Convention on the rights of the child, 20th November 1989, Treaty Series, vol. 1577. Geneva: United Nations General Assembly, 3.

Valencia, Richard (1997) 'Conceptualising the notion of deficit thinking', in Richard Valencia (ed.), *The Evolution of Deficit Thinking: Educational Thought and Practice*. London: Falmer.

Valencia, Richard (2010) *Dismantling Contemporary Deficit Thinking: Educational Thought and Practice*. New York: Routledge.

Variyan, George, Longmuir, Fiona and Gobby, Brad (2021) 'Student climate movement strike: In a crisis, what are the limits of "student voice"'? Monash University, 21 May. Available at: https://lens.monash.edu/@education/2021/05/21/1383255/student-climate-movement-strike-in-a-crisis-what-are-the-limits-of-student-voice (accessed 26 August 2022).

Verlie, Blanche (2022a) 'Climate justice in more-than-human worlds'. *Environmental Politics*, 31(2): 297–319.

Verlie, Blanche (2022b) *Learning to Live with Climate Change: From Anxiety to Transformation*. Abingdon: Routledge.

Verlie, Blanche and Blom, Simone Miranda (2021) 'Education in a changing climate: Reconceptualising school and classroom climate through the fiery atmos-fears of Australia's Black summer'. *Children's Geographies*, 1–15. DOI: 10.1080/14733285.2021.1948504.

Verlie, Blanche and Flynn, Alicia (2022) 'School Strike for Climate: A reckoning for education'. *Australian Journal of Environmental Education*, 38. DOI: 10.1017/aee.2022.5.

VicDET (2020) 'Priority: Positive climate for learning'. Available at: https://www.education.vic.gov.au/school/teachers/management/improvement/Pages/priority3positiveclimate.aspx (accessed 26 August 2022).

VicSRC (2021) *Victorian Student Representative Council*. Available at: https://www.vicsrc.org.au/ (accessed 26 August 2022).

VicSRC: Student Voice Hub (n.d.) *Students on School Council*. Available at: https://studentvoicehub.org.au/resource-hub/students-on-school-council/ (accessed 26 August 2022).

Vincent, Eve and Neale, Timothy, eds (2016) *Unstable Relations: Indigenous People and Environmentalism in Contemporary Australia*. Perth, WA: University of Western Australia Press.

Voight, Adam, Hanson, Thomas, O'Malley, Meagan and Adekanye, Latifah (2015) 'The racial school climate gap: Within-school disparities in students' experiences of safety, support, and connectedness'. *American Journal of Community Psychology*, 56(3): 252–67.

Wahlström, Mattias, Kocyba, Piotr, De Vydt, Michiel and de Moor, Joost

(2019) *Protest for a Future: Composition, Mobilization and Motives of the Participants in Fridays For Future Climate Protests on 15 March, 2019 in 13 European Cities*. Available at: http://cosmos.sns.it/wp-content/uploads/2019/07/20190709_Protest20for20a20future_GCS20Descriptive20Report.pdf (accessed 26 August 2022).

Walker, Catherine (2020) 'Uneven solidarity: The school strikes for climate in global and intergenerational perspective'. *Sustainable Earth*, 3(1): 5–17.

Walkerdine, Valerie (2013) 'Using the work of Félix Guattari to understand space, place, social justice, and education'. *Qualitative Inquiry*, 19(10): 756–64.

Wall, Kate (2012) '"It wasn't too easy, which is good if you want to learn": An exploration of pupil participation and Learning to Learn'. *Curriculum Journal*, 23(3): 283–305.

Wallin, Jason J. (2012) 'Bon mots for bad thoughts'. *Discourse: Studies in the Cultural Politics of Education*, 33(1): 147–62.

Wallin, Jason (2013) 'Get out from behind the lectern: Counter-cartographies of the transversal institution', in Diana Masny (ed.), *Cartographies of Becoming in Education: A Deleuze-Guattari Perspective*. Rotterdam: Springer, pp. 34–52.

Washick, Bonnie, Wingrove, Elizabeth, Ferguson, Kathy E. and Bennett, Jane (2015) 'Politics that matter: Thinking about power and justice with the new materialists'. *Contemporary Political Theory*, 14(1): 63–89.

Watkins, Meghan (2010) 'Desiring recognition, accumulating affect', in Melissa Gregg and Gregory J. Seigworth (eds), *The Affect Theory Reader*. London: Duke University Press, pp. 269–85.

Watson, Janell (2018) 'The transversal campus: Open black box?', in David R. Cole and Joff P.N. Bradley (eds), *Principles of Transversality in Globalization and Education*. Dordrecht: Springer, pp. 19–30.

Weaver, John A. and Snaza, Nathan (2017) 'Against methodocentrism in educational research'. *Educational Philosophy and Theory*, 49(11): 1055–65.

Webb, P. Taylor (2009) *Teacher Assemblages*. Rotterdam: Sense Publishers.

Weheliye, Alexander G. (2014) *Habeas Viscus: Racializing Assemblages, Biopolitics, and Black Feminist Theories of the Human*. London: Duke University Press.

Welton, Anjalé D. and Harris, Tiffany Octavia (2022) 'Youth of color social movements for racial justice: The politics of interrogating the school-to-prison pipeline'. *Educational Policy*, 36(1): 57–99.

Welton, Anjalé D., Harris, Tiffany O., Altamirano, Karla and Williams, Tierra (2017) 'The politics of student voice: Conceptualizing a model for critical analysis', in Michelle D. Young and Sarah Diem (eds), *Critical Approaches to Education Policy Analysis: Moving Beyond Tradition*. Cham: Springer, pp. 83–109.

## Bibliography

Welton, Anjalé D., Mansfield, Katherine Cumings and Salisbury, Jason D. (2022) 'The politics of student voice: The power and potential of students as policy actors'. *Educational Policy*, 36(1): 3–18.

Whitty, Geoff and Wisby, Emma (2007) 'Whose voice? An exploration of the current policy interest in pupil involvement in school decision-making'. *International Studies in Sociology of Education*, 17(3): 303–19.

Whyte, Kyle (2020) 'Against crisis epistemology', in Brendan Hokowhitu, Aileen Moreton-Robinson, Linda Tuhiwai-Smith, Chris Andersen and Steve Larkin (eds), *Routledge Handbook of Critical Indigenous Studies*. London: Routledge, pp. 52–64.

Wiame, Aline (2016) 'Deleuze's "puppetry" and the ethics of non-human compositions'. *Maska*, 31(179–180): 64–7.

Wilkins, Andrew (2016) *Modernising School Governance: Corporate Planning and Expert Handling in State Education*. London: Routledge.

Williams, Raymond (1983) *Keywords: A Vocabulary of Culture and Society*. London: Fontana.

Willis, Paul (1977) *Learning to Labor: How Working Class Kids Get Working Class Jobs*. Farnborough: Saxon House.

Wolfe, Melissa J. (2021) *Affect and the Making of the Schoolgirl: A New Materialist Perspective on Gender Inequity in Schools*. London: Routledge.

World Wildlife Fund (2020) *Australia's 2019–2020 bushfires: The wildlife toll – Interim report*. Available at: https://www.wwf.org.au/what-we-do/bushfire-recovery/in-depth/resources/australia-s-2019-2020-bushfires-the-wildlife-toll#gs.4lc0zi (accessed 26 August 2022).

Wu, Jinting, Eaton, Paul William, Robinson-Morris, David W., Wallace, Maria F. G. and Han, Shaofei (2018) 'Perturbing possibilities in the post-qualitative turn: Lessons from Taoism (道) and Ubuntu'. *International Journal of Qualitative Studies in Education*, 31(6): 504–19.

Wynter, Sylvia (1984) 'The ceremony must be found: After humanism'. *boundary 2*, 12/13(3/1): 19–70.

Wynter, Sylvia (2003) 'Unsettling the coloniality of being/power/truth/freedom: Towards the human, after Man, its overrepresentation – An argument'. *CR: The New Centennial Review*, 3(3): 257–337.

Wynter, Sylvia and McKittrick, Katherine (2015) 'Unparalleled catastrophe for our species? Or, to give humanness a different future: Conversations', in Katherine McKittrick (ed.), *On Being Human as Praxis*. Durham, NC: Duke University Press, pp. 9–89.

Yeung, Alexander Seeshing, Barker, Katrina, Tracey, Danielle and Mooney, Mary (2013) 'School-wide positive behavior for learning: Effects of dual focus on boys' and girls' behavior and motivation for learning'. *International Journal of Educational Research*, 62: 1–10.

Youdell, Deborah (2006) *Impossible Bodies, Impossible Selves: Exclusions and Student Subjectivities*. Dordrecht: Springer.

Youdell, Deborah (2011) *School Trouble: Identity, Power and Politics in Education*. Abingdon: Routledge.

Young, Helen (2017) 'Busy yet passive: (Non-)decision-making in school governing bodies'. *British Journal of Sociology of Education*, 38(6): 812–26.

Youth Forum at Garma (2019) *The Imagination Declaration*. Available at: https://www.sbs.com.au/nitv/nitv-news/article/2019/08/05/imagination-declaration-youth-forum-read-garma-2019 (accessed 26 August 2022).

Yusoff, Kathryn (2018) *A Billion Black Anthropocenes or None*. Minneapolis: University of Minnesota Press.

Zarabadi, Shiva (2020) 'Post-threat pedagogies: A micro-materialist phantomatic feeling within classrooms in post-terrorist times', in Bessie P. Dernikos, Nancy Lesko, Stephanie D. McCall and Alyssa D. Niccolini (eds), *Mapping the Affective Turn in Education: Theory, Research, and Pedagogies*. New York: Routledge, pp. 69–83.

Zembylas, Michalinos (2007a) *Five Pedagogies, a Thousand Possibilities: Struggles for Hope and Transformation in Education*. Rotterdam: Sense Publishers.

Zembylas, Michalinos (2007b) 'Risks and pleasures: A Deleuzo-Guattarian pedagogy of desire in education'. *British Educational Research Journal*, 33(3): 331–47.

Zembylas, Michalinos (2021) 'Affect, biopower, and "the fascist inside you": The (un)making of microfascism in schools and classrooms'. *Journal of Curriculum Studies*, 53(1): 1–15.

# Index

*A Thousand Plateaus* (Deleuze and Guattari), 30–1, 33–4, 56, 63, 67–8, 75–81, 93, 95n7, 103, 105, 113, 131, 148, 161, 190
Abdel-Fattah, R., 89, 123, 124, 135–6, 137, 140, 141, 144–5
ability, 85–7
ableism, 54, 60, 67, 190
Aboriginal and Torres Strait Islander Voice to Parliament, 10, 98, 118n1
accountability, 24, 92, 94n2, 144, 148, 151, 155, 168
activism *see* climate strikes; protest; social movements
adolescence, 84
affect, 30–2
    of climate change, 176, 191, 196
    and climate strikes, 185
    and fear, 124, 134, 145n2
    and language, 142
    and partial objects, 194
    and radical relationality, 52
    and RESP tokens, 162, 166
    in school council meetings, 111
    and school reform evaluations, 168–9, 170–1
    of speech on bodies, 80
affective aliens (Ahmed), 132
affective atmosphere, 132
affective intensities, 75, 109
affective needs, 151
affective sensorium, 117, 126, 114
affirmation, 13, 27, 32, 114, 145, 162, 169, 170
after, 39, 45n11
age, 79, 82–5
*Age, The*, 103
agencements, 32–4, 76
    collective agencements of enunciation, 32–3, 51, 76, 79, 134, 143, 200
    data-agencements, 90–2
    desiring-agencements, 35, 93, 161–3, 167–9, 169–71
agency, 16, 25, 32, 35, 50, 51–2, 171, 180, 190, 194, 197
Ahmed, S., 32, 57, 88, 89, 132, 202n4
Alcoff, L., 15, 18, 51, 59, 103, 130, 181, 200
Amazon, 30
Anderson, B., 32, 132
Anthropocene, 186–7
anthropological fieldwork, 59
*Anti-Oedipus* (Deleuze and Guattari), 63, 66, 75, 93, 94n2, 134, 141, 161–2, 167
Appadurai, A., 59–60
Apple (company), 30
Art Magic, 4, 172–3n6; *see also* Tango, H.
assemblage theory, 64
assemblages *see* agencements; teacher assemblages
'at risk' students, 80, 81, 87, 118, 123, 135, 137, 144, 145
atmos-fear, 122–3, 133, 134–7, 140
Australia
    Black Summer bushfires, 174
    climate strikes, 176, 177, 179, 182–3, 187, 188–9
    political representation, 97–8
    radicalisation and violent extremism, 135–6, 137–9
    teaching workforce, 98
    *Terra Nullius*, 2–3
    Uluru Statement from the Heart, 10, 201n1

## INDEX

Australia (*cont.*)
  Western Australia Department of Education, 107
  *see also* First Nations peoples
Australian Institute for Teaching and School Leadership, 98
Australian Youth Climate Coalition, 177
authorial voice, 1–2, 11–14

Ball, S., 11, 90, 124, 148, 172
banking mode of education, 19, 54
Barad, K., 47–8, 51, 52, 170, 177, 199
Barthes, R., 2
*Bartleby, the Scrivener* (Melville), 125, 141–2
Beckett, S., 126
becoming-imperceptible, 144
becoming-Indian, critique of (Byrd) 58
becoming-open, 198–9
behaviour management, 77, 82, 88–9, 154, 160
behaviour support *see* Positive Behaviour Interventions and Supports (PBIS)
behavioural tokens *see* RESP tokens
Berlant, L., 134, 200
Bhattacharya, K., 50, 58, 61
Bignall, S., 38, 57, 65, 116, 188
Birch, T., 176, 182, 184
Black Lives Matter, 2, 7n2, 175, 201n2
Black, R., 20, 25, 153
Black Studies, 7n2, 41, 47, 61
Black Summer bushfires, 174
bodies, 30, 75, 78–9, 80, 84
Bowlby, J., 84
Bowman, B., 179, 184, 185
Bragg, S., 9, 14, 16, 20, 24, 25, 27, 72, 124, 132
breathing, 1, 2, 174–5, 178
breathing together, 43–4, 196–8, 199, 200
bushfires, 174
Butler, J., 54
Byrd, J., 58

"Can the Subaltern Speak" (Spivak), 59, 116, 181

capacity to act, 35, 43, 54, 110, 150, 168–9, 170, 171; *see also* affect
capitalism, 118, 122, 123, 175, 179, 187
catalytic validity (Lather), 54
change, theory of (Tuck and Yang), 48, 50, 111–12, 123, 153, 167–8
children, 15–16, 84, 85–6, 94n2, 137
child's voice
  historicising voice in research, 49–51
  mis/uses in research, 41–2, 46–8, 53–7
  reconceptualising voice, 51–2
  *see also* student voice
Chomsky, N., 49, 84
Choy, T., 2, 43, 175, 178, 195, 197, 198
class, 18, 32, 33, 44–5n4, 66, 67, 84, 85, 86, 87, 88, 94n2, 97, 98, 106–9, 111, 117, 130, 155, 161, 184, 189, 190
classification, 34, 73, 78, 87, 88, 104
climate justice, 178–9, 184, 201n1, 202n6
climate strikes, 43, 174–80
  con-spiracies (Choy), 195–201
  school responses, 190–5
  speaking for others, 181–90:
  speaking for climate strikers, 181–5; speaking for trees, 178, 185–90
co-authorship with students, 13
codes, 75–6, 79, 85, 88, 92, 93
cognitive capacities, 85, 86
Colebrook, C., 35, 64, 76, 162, 187
colonial capitalism, 73, 187
colonial dialogical encounter, 109, 129–30
colonial gaze, 2–3
colonial knowledge practices, 62–3, 123
colonial language, 116, 117
colonial structures of schooling, 3, 122
colonial suppression, 86, 94n2, 116
colonialism, 58, 175, 176, 179
  philosophical, 57
  settler, 3, 45n4, 187–8
common sense, 73–4, 76, 82, 94n2, 104–5, 182

# Index

Common Worlds Research Collective, 180, 197
communication, 75, 87, 109
connection, 22, 26, 34, 58, 131, 133, 137, 145, 146–7n4, 171, 188–9, 194, 199
consensus, 17, 106, 118, 156, 198, 200
conspiracies, 2, 9
con-spiracies (Choy), 43–4, 178, 195–201
Cook-Sather, A., 9, 13, 14, 21, 27
Countering Violent Extremism (CVE), 136, 137, 138–9
Country, 2, 40, 187–90
COVID-19 pandemic, 175, 195, 197
critical pedagogy, 19, 27
cruel optimism (Berlant), 200

data, 25, 41, 46, 50, 52, 62, 82, 133, 145, 148, 151–3, 168, 169, 199
data-agencements, 90–2
decolonial refusal, 182
decolonial struggles, 103
decolonising thought (Wynter), 74
deficit discourses, 151, 155
deficit gaze, 2, 15
deficit logics, 35, 85; *see also* lack
deficit thinking, 87
Deleuze, G.
  educational reform after, 28–38
  mis/use of, 63–5
  thinking with and after, 38–40
  *see also* A Thousand Plateaus (Deleuze and Guattari); *Dialogues II*; *Difference and Repetition* (Deleuze); "Intellectuals and Power"; *Logic of Sense, The;* "Postscript on the Societies of Control" (Deleuze); *What is Philosophy* (Deleuze and Guattari)
Delhi, 174–5
democracy, 18, 36, 37–8
Derrida, J., 51
desire, 34–6, 64, 66, 93, 150, 169
  and power, 32, 35, 76, 116, 129, 161–2
deterritorialisation, 65, 142, 195
Dewey, J., 21

dialogical encounters, 42, 109, 120–1, 146–7n4
  atmos-fear, 122–3, 133, 134–7, 140
  puppet scenarios, 121–5, 141: im/possibilities of dialogue, 129–32; right to opacity, 141–4; transcript, 127–8
  school climate, 132–3
dialogical understanding, 16–18, 120–1
dialogue, 40, 88
  and countering violent extremism, 137–41
*Dialogues II* (Deleuze), 33–4, 40, 56, 79, 120, 130–1, 133, 143
difference
  recognition of, 104–8
  speaking to one's, 114–17
*Difference and Repetition* (Deleuze), 73, 82, 94, 104–5, 108, 113, 114–15, 117
digitisation, 9
disciplinary societies, 26–7
discourse, 95n5
disruptive speech, 71–2, 87
dividual material (Deleuze), 91, 151–2
Djab Wurrung people, 187–8
doctoral research study, 53–7
dogmatic image of thought, 73, 126, 172
Don Dale, 175
Dungay Jr, D., 175

education
  banking mode of, 19, 54
  problem-posing mode of, 19
  radical, 44n2
educational reform *see* school reform
Ellsworth, E., 21, 27, 121
emotionality, 80, 81, 82, 88
emotions, 31–2, 87–92
empowerment, 8, 18–21, 27, 88, 101, 121, 137, 145, 149, 152, 191, 199
enactment, 11
ethics, 52
ethnography, 122
evaluation, 43, 149–50, 197
  majoritarian evaluations, 151–4, 160, 167

## INDEX

evaluation (*cont.*)
  minoritarian evaluation, 43, 150, 160, 161, 167–72
  student voice initiative evaluation, 154–8: RESP tokens, 160–7; RESP values, 158–60
expert witnesses, 14

fascism *see* microfascisms
fear, 124, 128, 129, 131, 132, 140, 141
  figuration of, 123
  pedagogy of, 137
  *see also* atmos-fear
feminist new materialism, 57
feminist poststructuralism, 27
feminist scholarship, 88
feminist standpoint theories, 15–16
Fielding, M., 8–9, 14, 16, 17, 18, 24, 29, 44n2, 92, 149, 167, 181
figuration of fear, 123
Finneran, R., 23, 24, 45n7, 153
First Nations children, 85–6, 94n2; *see also* Indigenous students
First Nations peoples, 58, 175, 187–9; *see also* Indigenous people
Floyd, G., 2, 175
Foucault, M., 26–7, 32, 65, 66–7, 95n5, 114–15, 116, 135, 161–2, 165
Frazier, D., 175
Freire, P., 19, 29, 54, 72
Freud, S., 49, 84
Fridays for Future, 177; *see also* School Strike for Climate

Garma Festival, 10
Garner, E., 175
gender, 11, 18, 86, 88, 96n10, 97, 107, 111, 146n3, 202n6
gender-based violence, 97
Gerrard, J., 58–9, 62–63, 106–7
Gillies, V., 88, 89
*Giving an Account of Oneself* (Butler), 54
Glissant, É., 18, 86, 120, 122, 143
Gómez-Barris, M., 186–7
Google, 30
governance *see* school governance councils

grammar of schooling, 20, 93
grammar (Wynter), 78, 197
grasp, 40, 120, 122, 123, 133, 143, 145, 161, 179, 185, 194, 195, 199
Groupe d'Information sur les Prisons, 115
Guattari, F.
  educational reform after, 28–38
  mis/use of, 63–5
  thinking with and after, 38–40
  *see also* *A Thousand Plateaus* (Deleuze and Guattari); microfascism; "Institutional Schizo-analysis"; transversality; *Schizoanalytic Cartographies* (Guattari); *What is Philosophy* (Deleuze and Guattari)

Habermas, J., 17, 106, 120, 129
Habtom, S., 197
Hall, G.S., 84
Haraway, D., 11, 42, 200
Hartsock, N., 15
Harvey, D., 26
Hazelhurst Art Gallery, 3–4, 172–3n6
  "Hiromi Hotel: Moon Jellies" exhibition, *164*
Hemming, S., 188, 189
heteronormativity, 54, 61
Higgins, B., 97, 98
"Hiromi Hotel: Moon Jellies" exhibition, *164*
history, mis/use of, 58–9
Hogarth, M., 86
homonationalism, 64
human rights, 36–7; *see also* United Nations Convention on the Rights of the Child (UNCRC)
humanism *see* liberal humanism; posthumanism
Hume, D., 73

ideal speech situation, 17, 129
Imagination Declaration, 10
immanent normativity, 154
imperialism, 58, 74
incorporeal transformations, 79–80, 81
India, 174–5
Indigenous knowledge systems, 64, 187

## Index

Indigenous people, 58, 61, 123, 175, 184, 197; *see also* First Nations peoples
Indigenous relational ontologies, 180, 187
Indigenous sovereignty, 176, 188, 201n1
Indigenous students, 10, 94n2, 192; *see also* First Nations children
indirect discourse, 77–8
"Institutional Schizo-analysis" (Guattari), 33
intellectuals, 116
"Intellectuals and Power" (Deleuze and Foucault), 114–15, 119n6
Intelligence Quotient tests, 85, 86
intergenerational injustice, 176
international student voice initiatives, 13
*interpretosis*, 49, 172n5
intersectionality, 45n6, 64
Irigaray, L., 198
Islamophobia, 137, 138, 145, 155

Jackson, A.Y., 12, 33, 38, 51, 54
Jackson, Z.I., 61
joy, 65, 150, 169
judgement, 49, 79, 86, 88, 90, 108, 113, 130, 143, 148, 149, 154, 197
"Junior Council of the Year" sign, 24
jurisprudence, 36–7, 202n9

Kafka, F., 125–6, 131–2, 142, 195
Keeling, K., 18, 65, 126, 144, 145
Kia Aroha College, 19–20
King, T.L., 58, 61, 63, 66, 74
Klein, M., 161, 194
knowledge
  colonial practices, 62–3
  Indigenous, 64–5
  students, 14–16
Kuala Lumpur, 174

La Borde clinic, 28–9
lack, 3, 34, 35, 58, 85, 87, 88, 162
language, 17, 76, 77, 78, 80, 85–6, 142; *see also* speech
Lasczik, A., 187
laughter, 166, 167, 171, 195

Laville, S., 174–5
Lawrence, D.H., 37
Leboiron, M., 6n1
Lévi-Strauss, C., 95n6
liberal humanism, 39, 47, 73, 97, 105–6, 111, 175; *see also* Man (Wynter)
line of rigid segmentarity, 33–4, 78, 168
lines of flight, 33, 34, 37, 58
linguistic capacities, 85, 86
linguistic voice, 85–7
linguistics, 76
listening, 21, 22, 43, 109, 117, 118, 121, 134, 144, 171, 180, 197
Little Hans, 49
*Living Safe Together* (Commonwealth of Australia), 136, 137, 147n5
*Logic of Sense, The* (Deleuze), 56
López López, L., 85, 93
*Lorax, The* (Dr Seuss), 178, 187, 194, 201–2n3
Lovett-Ahern, C., 188
Low, R., 138
Lugones, M., 18
Luiz, M., 74, 197

Maher, K., 188
Mager, U., 22
major figure, 105, 111; *see also* Man (Wynter)
major language, 126
majoritarian evaluations, 149, 151–4, 160, 167, 169
Man (Wynter), 73–4, 94–5n3, 97, 149, 187
Malaysia, 174
Manning, E., 31, 32, 143
marionettes *see* puppet scenarios
Marx, K., 19, 124
Marxism, relationship to Deleuze and Guattari, 26, 29, 33, 34, 37, 38, 167
Marxist critique of new materialism, 41, 61
Massumi, B., 31, 78, 120, 122, 123, 124, 133, 134
Mazzei, L., 12, 33, 51, 52, 77, 131
Mbembe, A., 175

media representation, 183
Melbourne's March 4 Justice, 97
Melville, H., 125, 126, 141–2
Members of Parliament (MPs), Australia, 97–8
Messiou, K., 22
*Metamorphosis* (Kafka), 125, 131–2
micro-aggressions, 20
microfascisms, 65–9, 190
Microsoft, 30
minor literature, 125–6, 132, 142–3, 195
minoritarian evaluation, 43, 150, 160, 161, 167–72
mis/use of Deleuze and Guattari, 63–5
mis/use of history, 58–9
mis/uses of voices, 41–2, 46–51, 53–7
Mitra, D., 13, 21, 159
Mockler, N., 138
Mohammed, I., 135
molar lines, 48, 131
molecular line, 33, 34, 67, 190
Moreton-Robinson, A., 3, 6–7n1
Morrison, S., 98, 181, 194, 202n7
Moten, F., 80, 93
multiplicity, 56, 73, 85, 105, 106; *see also* difference
murmurs, 73, 77
Muslim communities, 135–6
Muslim young people, 137, 140, 141, 145
Myers, N., 178, 198

Nakata, S., 81
Nakate, V., 183
neoliberalism, 26
nervousness, 123–4, 132; *see also* fear; atmos-fear
neurotypicality, 63
new materialisms, 57
'new' ontologies, 61–3
New Sociology of Childhood, 15, 49
new, violence of the, 57–60
newspapers
  *The Age*, 103
  *Sydney Morning Herald*, 192
Ngarrindjeri people, 187, 188–9
Noelle-Neumann, E., 140
nonsense, 144, 195

O'Donnell, A., 136
Oedipal complex, 35, 49, 125, 161, 194; *see also* interpretosis
ontological turn, 47, 51–2
  critical and creative engagements with(in), 57–63: responses to critique, 63–5
  and microfascisms, 67–8
  opacity, towards the right to, 118, 123, 126, 141–4
opinions, 37
order words, 42, 77–82, 156, 161
  ability, 85–7
  age, 79, 82–5
  emotions, 87–92
  *see also* pass words
ordering-agencements, 90–2
Oury, F., 29
Oury, J., 28
outcomes, 148, 154–5

Pacific Climate Warriors, 176, 177
parent representatives, 107, 108, 111
Parnet, C., 40; *see also Dialogues II* (Deleuze and Parnet)
partial objects, 161
  partial narratives of, 163–6
Participatory Action Research, 19
partnership, 106
pass words, 82, 93, 165; *see also* order words
patriarchy, 15, 61
Patton, P., 38
pedagogical relations, 16, 21, 28, 30, 45n9, 90, 92, 144, 167, 198, 199
pedagogy of fear, 137
Per Capita, 97
performativity, 90, 124
Petersen, E.B., 62
Phelan, P., 17, 130
Phillips, J., 2–3
philosophical colonialism, 57
Piaget, J., 49, 84
policy enactment, 11
political immediacy, 132
political representation, 97–8
political struggles, 103
politics, 185

of feeling, 121, 134
radical, 44n2
of student voice, 23–6
positionality, 6–7n1, 11, 54, 61
Positive Behaviour Interventions and Supports (PBIS), 89, 150, 156–8, 160–1; *see also* RESP tokens
postcolonial critiques of voice, 17, 59, 116, 129; *see also* Said, E.; Spivak, G.C.
post-qualitative research, 58–9, 69–70n1
posthumanism, 57–8, 61, 69–70n1
poststructural critiques of voice, 27, 51, 59; *see also* Ellsworth, E.; Jackson, A.Y.
"Postscript on the Societies of Control" (Deleuze), 36, 91, 151, 168, 171–2
*potentia*, 35
power, 17, 20, 27, 29, 35, 105, 109, 130, 152, 154, 162, 169; *see also* capacity to act; empowerment; microfascisms
power relations, 16, 17, 18, 30, 31, 78
pragmatic linguistics, 76, 95n5
praxis, 18–19, 29
"Prevent" programme, 136, 137
*Preventing Violent Extremism and Radicalisation in Australia (PVERA)*, 136, 137
Prison Information Group, 115
privilege, 7n1, 18, 44n3, 45n5, 51, 54, 59, 61n1, 91, 98, 99, 107, 108, 184, 192
problem-posing mode of education (Freire), 19
protests, 2, 9, 97–8, 115, 116, 118, 174–6, 178–9, 191–2
psychoanalysis, 84, 125, 130
psychology, 15, 84, 87–9, 124, 132, 136
Puar, J., 64, 135
public opinion, 37
puppet scenarios, 46, 47, 69
  dialogical encounters, 121–5, 141: im/possibilities of dialogue, 129–32; right to opacity, 141–4; transcript, 71, 83, 127–8

mis/use of voice, 53–7, 59–60
ordering voices, 71–3, 79, 81: ability, 87; age, 82–3; data-agencements, 92; emotions, 87, 89
understanding, 118
pure difference, 114; *see also* difference-in-itself

qualitative data, 152–3
queer temporality (Keeling), 65, 123

racism, 19–20, 54, 61, 88, 91, 137, 145, 155, 176, 202n6
radical collegiality (Fielding), 8, 18, 44n2
radical education, 44n2
radical empiricism, 73–4
radical politics, 44n2
radicalisation, 135–6, 137, 138–9; *see also* violent extremism
rationality, 88
recapitulation theory, 84
recognition, 73, 81, 86, 94, 102, 103, 104–6, 108, 113, 114, 117, 144, 145, 154, 160–1, 165, 166, 185, 200
reform, 36–8, 115, 143; *see also* school reform
refusal, 65, 125, 126, 143, 144, 167, 172, 181, 182, 199, 200
Reich, W., 66
Relation (Glissant), 122
representation, 97–9, 114
  democratic, 97, 98, 107
  stakeholder model of, 103–4
  *see also* media representation; student representation
repression, 35–6, 115, 141, 144; *see also* desire; self-censorship
research projects, 12–13
resistance, 167, 171
RESP tokens, 149, *150*, 157, 160–7, 169, 170
RESP values, 156–7, 158–60
respair, 6, 178, 201
respect, 8, 132, 137, 149, 155–6, 159, 165, 189, 198
respiratory violence, 175
response-ability, 52, 170, 187, 199

responsibility, 85, 89, 139, 170
re-turning (Barad), 47–8, 177–8, 194
revolutionary action, 115–16
rhizomatic interconnectedness, 58
rhizovocality (Jackson), 51
rights, 8, 36–8, 81–2; *see also* United Nations Convention on the Rights of the Child (UNCRC)
Rights Watch UK, 137
Rigney, D., 64–5, 188, 189
Ringrose, J., 29, 34, 35, 176

Said, E., 17, 18, 109, 129–30
St Pierre, E., 38, 70n1
Saldanha, A., 99, 108, 119n5, 183
*Schizoanalytic Cartographies* (Guattari), 32–3
school choice, 91
school climate, 22, 122, 132–3, 190–1
*School Communities Working Together* (NSW Government), 137
School Effectiveness and School Improvement (SESI), 132–3
school ethos, 22, 132
school governance councils, 42, 100–4
 and difference, 104–8
 as representing others, 108–14
 seating plan, 110
 and speaking to one's difference, 114–17
school improvement, 21–2, 132–3
school reform, 21–3, 36, 115, 148–9, 153, 200
 limits of, 171–2
 majoritarian evaluations, 151–4
 and politics of student voice, 23–6
 student voice initiative evaluation, 154–8: RESP tokens, 160–7; RESP values, 158–60
 towards minoritarian evaluation, 167–72
School Strikes for Climate, 177, 189, 191–5
school values, 156–7; *see also* RESP values
schooling
 colonial structures of, 122
 order of, 82–92: ability, 85–7; age, 82–5; data-agencements, 90–2; emotions, 87–92
Schools Security Programme, 139
Schulten, K., 10
*Security, Territory, Population* (Foucault), 27
Sedgwick, E., 28
Seed, 176, 177
segregation, 82, 86–7, 91, 94n2
self-censorship, 23, 111, 140–1; *see also* repression
sense perceptions, 73
Serriere, S., 13
settler colonialism; *see* colonialism
Sharma, A., 175
silence
 and fear, 140, 141
 puppet scenarios, 129, 132, 142, 143, 144
 "Religion, Radicalisation and Critical Education", 139
 in school reform evaluations, 153
 and voice, 1, 34, 78, 121
Simmons, K., 197, 198
Simons, M., 90, 152, 154
singularity, 94, 117, 121, 143; *see also* difference
Snaza, N., 52
social movements, 10; *see also* youth climate justice movement
soft data, 152–3
SoundOut, 8
space, 78, 99, 130
speaking for others, 15–16, 23
 intellectuals, 115–16
 speaking as Country, 40, 187–90
 speaking for climate strikers, 181–5
 speaking for trees, 178, 185–90
 student representatives, 112, 113
speaking to one's difference, 114–17
speech, 80, 142
 disruptive, 71–2, 87
 ordering of, 85, 86–7
 school council meetings, 109
 social function in schooling, 76, 78
 *see also* ideal speech situation; language
Spelman, E., 18
Spinoza, B., 30, 31, 35, 169

## Index

Spivak, G., 59, 103, 109, 116, 117, 121, 181
standpoint epistemologies, 14–16, 45n6
stakeholders, 103, 105
statements, 76–7, 79–81, 95n5
Steering Committee, 12, 72, 149–50, 155–7, 166; *see also* students as researchers (SaRs)
strategic essentialism (Spivak), 103
student activism *see* social movements; youth climate justice movement
student representation
　school governance councils, 42, 100–4: being recognised as representing others, 108–14; recognising difference, 104–8; seating plan, *110*; speaking to one's difference, 114–17
　Student Representative Councils (SRCs), 98–9
student-teacher dialogues *see* dialogical encounters; dialogical understanding; pedagogical relations
student voice, 8–11
　and authorial voice, 11–14
　climate strikes, 190–5
　and countering violent extremism, 137, 138
　definition, 8
　and dialogical encounters, 120–1
　as disruptive, 71–2, 87
　and enactment, 11
　historical rationales, 14–23: critical pedagogical rationale, 18–21; institutional reform rationale, 21–3; liberal humanist rationale, 16–18; standpoint epistemological rationale, 14–16
　inconsistencies, contradictions and critique, 26–8
　mis/uses in research, 46–8, 53–7
　ordering of, 42, 72, 75–82: ability, 85–7; age, 82–5; data-agencements, 90–2; emotions, 87–92
　politics of, 23–6
　re-thinking/re-working, 28–38: affect, 30–2; agencements, 32–4; desire, 34–6; reform and rights, 36–8; transversality, 28–30
　as reform, 200
　as school marketing, 9, 24–5, 36, 193
　as soft data, 25, 152–3
　thinking with and after Deleuze and Guattari, 38–40
　*see also* child's voice
student voice initiative evaluation, 154–8
　RESP tokens, 160–7
　RESP values, 158–60
students
　empowerment, 18–21, 27
　knowledge, 14–16
students as mediators, 112, 113
students as researchers (SaRs), 12, 72, 149–50, 155, 156, 157; *see also* Steering Committee
students as theorists, 46, 53–4
subjectification, 80, 95n5, 130, 146n3
subjectivities, 78
Sundberg, J., 57, 58
surveillance, 25, 124, 135, 139–40
surveys, 9, 25, 30, 91–2, 101–2, 133, 179
suspect communities, 135
suspension rates, 148
Svirsky, M., 185
*Sydney Morning Herald*, 192

Tango, H., 3–4
　Art Magic, 4, 172–3n6
　"Hiromi Hotel: Moon Jellies" exhibition, *164*
Taylor, E., 139, 140
Teach the Teacher programme, 13, 153
teacher anxiety, 123–4
teacher assemblages, 91
teacher-student dialogues *see* dialogical encounters; dialogical understanding; pedagogical relations
teaching workforce, 98
*Terra Nullius*, 2–3
terrorism studies, 135
theory of change (Tuck and Yang), 48, 50, 111–12, 123, 153, 167–8

# INDEX

"thinking with" (Jackson & Mazzei), 38, 54
Thompson, G., 91–2, 148, 151
Thunberg, G., 176, 179, 184
Todd, Z., 58
Tosquelles, F., 29
totalitarianism, 66
transversality, 28–30, 45n8
trees, speaking for, 178, 185–90
trust, 3, 8, 22, 26, 102, 140, 141, 144
Truman, S., 48, 59, 74
Tuck, E., 3, 39, 50, 58, 59, 62, 63–4, 66, 88, 111, 123, 153, 199
Tynan, L., 187, 202n8

Uluru Statement from the Heart, 10
understanding, 8, 120–1, 122, 125, 130, 139, 142, 143, 144; *see also* grasp
United Nations Convention on the Rights of the Child (UNCRC), 8, 19, 81, 85, 95–6n9
University of Cambridge Student Voice seminars, 13

Valencia, R., 87
values, 156–7; *see also* RESP values
ventriloquism, 55–6, 58, 59–60
Verlie, B., 174, 180, 190–1, 199
Victorian Student Representative Council (VicSRC), 13, 101, 102–3
  students on school councils policy advocacy, 101, 103
  *Teach the Teacher* program, 13, 153
violence
  gender-based, 97
  of the new, 57–60
  respiratory, 2, 175
violent extremism, 135–6, 137–41
viscosity, 99, 108, 117, 119n5
voice, 1–2, 9–10, 10–11, 49–52
  *see also* Aboriginal and Torres Strait Islander Voice to Parliament; authorial voice; breathing; child's voice; student voice
voicing Rivers, 202n9
Voight, A., 133
Voller, D., 2, 175

Von Kleist, H., 56
vulnerability, 136, 137, 141, 176

war on terror, 64, 126, 134
Warrior-Researchers, 19–20
Washick, B., 61
Watson, J., 30
Weaver, J., 52
Weheliye, A., 61, 64, 70n6
well-being, 9, 21, 124, 189
Western ethnography, 122
*What is Philosophy* (Deleuze and Guattari), 37–8, 75–6, 135
White supremacy, 7n2, 59, 66, 74, 84, 91, 200
Whiteness, 2, 6–7n1, 106, 107, 183
Wiame, A., 56
Wilkins, A., 100, 107
willfulness, 57
Willis, P., 165, 167
Wolfe, M.J., 31, 32
Wu, J., 59
Wynter, S., 73–4, 78, 93, 94–5n3, 97, 187, 197

XR Youth, 177

Yang, K.W., 50, 62, 111, 123, 153, 199
Yannarumi, 188, 189
Youdell, D., 12, 44n2, 88, 91
Young, H., 111
young voice, 82–5; *see also* child's voice; student voice
youth climate justice movement, 43, 174–80
  con-spiracies, 195–201
  school responses, 190–5
  speaking for others, 181–90: speaking for climate strikers, 181–5; speaking for trees, 178, 185–90
youth detention centre, 175
Youth Participatory Action Research (YPAR), 19, 20
Yusoff, K., 186, 187

Zarabadi, S., 123, 134–5, 137, 140, 141

EU representative:
Easy Access System Europe
Mustamäe tee 50, 10621 Tallinn, Estonia
Gpsr.requests@easproject.com

www.ingramcontent.com/pod-product-compliance
Lightning Source LLC
Chambersburg PA
CBHW070816250426
**43671CB00037B/2338**